12 PRINCIPLES
OF HIGHLY SUCCESSFUL LANDLORDS AND PROPERTY MANAGERS

ALL STATES

BEING A LANDLORD/PROPERTY MANAGER
MADE CLEAR

HOW TO – STEP BY STEP – PRINCIPLE BY PRINCIPLE

TABLE OF CONTENTS

FORWARD

CHAPTERS

d. Sexual Orientation

e. Familial Status

f. Religion/Creed

g. Gender

h. Age

i. Disabilities/Handicaps

    i. What is a disability/handicap?

    ii. Dangerous Persons with a Disability/Handicap.

    iii. Equal Opportunity to Use and Enjoy the Dwelling.

    iv. Landlord/Property Manager Must Allow Reasonable Accommodation.

      1. Landlord/Property Manager must permit reasonable and necessary modifications of policy and accommodations to help the disabled.

      2. Where on the property is the Landlord/Property Manager required to allow a reasonable accommodation?

      3. Who pays for the accommodation/modification?

      4. What happens with the modifications made for the accommodations at the end of the Residency?

      5. The Landlord/Property Manager can make reasonable inquiry regarding the disability and the need for an accommodation.

        a. Non-animal reasonable accommodation:

          i. Medical verification for reasonable accommodation

        b. Animal (service or assistive) reasonable accommodation:

          i. Medical verification for reasonable accommodation

j. Military Service

4. Principle #4 - The Property Tour

a. Require a Government Issued ID

b. If you Feel Afraid for Your Safety

c. Have a Phone with You

5. Principle #5 - The Application

a. More is Better

b. Purpose of the Application

c. Sample Application and General Questionnaire

d. Authorizations

e. Know Your Jurisdiction

f. Red Flags - Protection

6. Principle #6 - The Rental Criteria

a. Criminal History

    i. HUD Guidelines Article

b. Crime Free Addendum

c. Insurance

d. Income to Rent Ratio

e. Financial Score

f. Rental History

g. Other Credit Issues

h. Foreclosures

i. Repossessions

j. Occupancy Standards

k. Bankruptcy

l. Smoking

m. Pets

n. Verifiable Current and Prior Employment

o. Verifiable Income

p. Verifiable Bank Information

q. Personal References

7. Principle #7 – Adequate and Proper Resident Screening

a. Why is Proper Resident Screening Critical and What is It?

b. Instant Background Check or Background Investigation

c. Background Investigations Should Not be a Profit Center

d. Too Many Companies Provide Bad Information

8. Principle #8 - The Lease

a. General Landlord/Property Manager Obligations

b. General Resident Obligations

9. Principle #9 - MOVE-IN

a. Move-In Walk-through Inspection Sheet

10. Principle #10 - HOW TO HANDLE Issues that arise while the Resident lives in the property.

a. Notices and Service of Notice to a Resident
  1. Always Use Written Communication
  2. What is a Notice?
  3. Delivery of Notice to Resident – How to do it
  4. Examples

b. Common types of Notices for Residents
  1. Material Falsification or Misleading Information
     i. Curable
     ii. Non-curable
  2. Material Non-Compliance of the Lease Agreement
  3. Health and Safety Breach
  4. Material Non-Compliance – Same or Similar
  5. Material and Irreparable Breach
  6. Resident's Failure to Pay Rent
  7. Bounced or NSF Rent Check
  8. Unauthorized Occupant
  9. Access of the Unit by Landlord/Property Manager
  10. Mutual Termination Agreement

11. Principle #11 – Move-Out

a. Move Out Inspection Notice

12. Principle #10 - Court

a. Do's and Don'ts

BONUS PRINCIPLE: Premises Liability & Negligence – Know the Law and Keep the Property in Compliance – How to Avoid Getting Sue

What is Premises Liability and Negligence and why is it vitally important for Owners, Landlords and Property Managers to understand. It's about keeping your profit.

FORWARD

By: Gerald Romine
(Real Estate Expert and Highly Successful Entrepreneur)

Talk about cutting through all the nonsense and telling an Owner, Landlord and Property Manager how to be successful and profitable by someone who knows and has been there – this book should be your landlord-tenant Bible. There are lots of ways I could say this, but I am going to say it in the easiest and most straight forward way possible. If you want to ensure you have fewer problems with Residents and are successfully profitable, then let me make it really simple for you – **FOLLOW WHAT DENNY SAYS TO DO IN THIS BOOK!** It does not matter if you are an experienced Owner, Landlord or even Professional Property Manager, or new to the business of being a Landlord/ Property Manager, to avoid problems with Residents and make money - do what Denny says.

Being an Owner, Owner Landlord, Landlord or Property Manager is a business fraught with expensive pitfalls and perils that you absolutely must avoid and that you only learn through experiences – either your own experiences or other people's experiences. These experiences are costly to someone. You just don't want that someone being you. Being a successful and profitable Owner, Landlord or Property Manager is about protecting your investments and Denny walks you literally step-by-step through all of the phases of being a landlord or property manager and shows you what to do to be successful in various situations that will arise. You can't argue with the amazing success that Denny and his clients have had over the last 40 years. Some of the ideas and counsel Denny gives you will be familiar to you. Some of the information will shake you to your foundations and open your understanding with new vision, and avenues for how to tackle the situation staring you in the face. You know what they say, *"you can make all the mistakes yourself and learn the hard way"*, or you can follow Denny's guidance and avoid costly mistakes along the way.

I have been an Owner Landlord for many years, I have taught hundreds of classes and seminars of property ownership and even I could not stop reading this book. It presented me with new perspectives, new vision, greater understandings and a huge bag of priceless gems to implement. I see how I can save time and money in ways I never thought of before. Denny's experiences are mind opening. It is amazing that such little things, consistently performed, can change a property so dramatically for the better. I met Denny when he was teaching a Crime Free Housing class sponsored by the Phoenix Police Department. He taught a lot more than just Crime Free Principles. He taught about tenant notices, premises liability, what to do in court, how to avoid discrimination, how to screen tenants and much more. His teaching methods where raw and visual. He is not an ivory tower attorney. He has been in the trenches – where none of you want to ever be. That is what makes this book so appropriate and useful for you.

As you implement Denny's proven formulas and lessons to make your properties run smoother, you will be more profitable, have less management headaches, and both you and your Residents will be happier. You don't have to have a lot of education to be successful managing properties. You just have to follow each point in this book. I implore you to become thoroughly entrenched in this book. You will be amazed by its simplicity and wisdom and in your own ability to do it.

Gerald (Jerry) Romine, M.B.A

ABOUT THE AUTHOR

J. Denton (Denny) Dobbins, Jr.

Denny is a former partner in the law firm of Koglmeier, Dobbins & Smith, P.L.C., where he was a trial and transactional attorney practicing in a variety of the legal areas, including, Emphasis in Landlord Law, Fair Housing Law, Real Estate, Business Organization and Formation, Contracts, Business Consulting, Premises Liability, Negligence and Negligent Hiring and Retention, Asset Protection, Personal Injury, Emphasis in Criminal Law, Credit Correcting, and Collections. He received his B.S. degree from Arizona State University in Business and his Doctorate in Law from the University of Arizona.

After prosecuting criminal cases, Denny became a Criminal Defense attorney handling major Felony and Misdemeanor cases, including, but not limited to, murder, attempted murder, manslaughter, aggravated assault, violent crimes of all types, sex crimes, theft, fraud and most other types of crimes. Denny has tried almost every type of criminal charge. Denny has tried 26 jury trials and hundreds of bench trials in his career.

Denny was the co-founder of a very unique non-profit company called, "The International Crime Free Association". Denny was its General Legal Counsel and the Assistant Executive Director for 18 years. The program became known as "CRIME FREE" which touted the "CRIME FREE LEASE ADDENDUM" that Denny wrote wherein residents agreed to engage in a crime free lifestyle during the lease term. The Organization taught Police Departments, Police Officers, Owners, Landlords, Property Managers and Residents how to detect and deter criminal activity in Multi-Family, Single Family, Condos, Homeowner Associations, Mobile Home Parks, Mini-Storages, Hotels and Motels, Retail, Commercial, Industrial and Professional properties. Denny is a certified National Crime Free Trainer and has taught Crime Free principles to Officers, Owners, Landlords and Property Managers from all over the world.

Denny is a former HUD commissioner and a former member of the FBI Joint (Anti) Terrorism Task Force. Denny is also a lifetime member and Instructor for the Arizona Crime Prevention Association. Denny is also a member of ASIS and licensed private investigator.

Denny is General Legal Counsel and the Executive Vice President for CrimShield, Inc. and Rent Perfect, Inc. CrimShield helps companies ensure that their customers, facilities, construction sites and information are safe when using employees or contractors to perform sales, demonstrations, installations or service for those customers. Most of CrimShield's employees are licensed private investigators that perform identity investigations, criminal and other background investigations for purposes of employment, security, volunteering, or for any reason for which a person may need a security clearance. Rent Perfect is a company that helps landlords avoid FCRA issues and helps ease the pain of lease agreements and other Landlord/Tenant issues.

Denny is a former Board Member and member of the Arizona Multi-Housing Association (AMA). He participated with the AMA as an instructor teaching Landlord/ Tenant Law, Fair Housing Law, Premises Liability Law, Negligence Law and Criminal Law, and where he was a member of the Government Affairs Committee for a number of years. Denny has written legislation and codes/ordinances for a number of States, Counties and Cities.

Denny was a member of and instructor for the Independent Real Estate Owners Association (IROC), was an associate member and instructor for the Institute of Real Estate Management (IREM) and a member of the National Apartment Association (NAA). Denny is a Lifetime member of and instructor for The Arizona Real Estate Investors Association (AZREIA) and former member of the Southeast Valley Regional Association of Real Estate Investors Association (SEVRAR).

Denny taught for years at the Arizona School of Real Estate and wrote a quarterly article for the Arizona Business and Real Estate Journal. Denny has also been a Landlord himself and understands the complexities than can exist.

Denny has been featured on Hard Copy, multiple news stations and in many periodicals for his trial work. He also has been featured numerous times in the Arizona Republic Real Estate Section. Denny wrote a monthly article for the Arizona Multi-housing Association Apartment News magazine and the Arizona Real Estate Investors Association's monthly publication, The AZREIA Advantage, on landlord law and real estate/landlord-tenant issues and has been published in multiple magazines and publications throughout the Nation. Denny is a former attorney of the month in Arizona.

The Idaho State Bar Association Journal called the Advocate published Denny's article on the 2016 HUD Guidelines to help attorneys navigate the Landlord minefields related to criminal history and background investigations regarding residential tenants. Denny also co-authored amendments to the Idaho Landlord and Tenant forms for the Idaho Bar.

Denny was recently interviewed by RHJ – Rental Housing Journal in the article, "No Guns In My Apartments: Can A Landlord Say That And Put It In A Lease?"

Denny published a book called "Stop Eating You Big Fat Pig" about his personal journey. He has a new book going to print in 2022 called "Twelve Principles of Highly Successful Landlords."

He is an energetic and accomplished nationally acclaimed speaker regarding Crime Free Principles, Landlord Law, Premises Liability Law, Criminal Background Investigations, and Discrimination/Fair Housing Law. Denny was a featured speaker at the ASIS annual conference on the tragedy of the Naval Yard shooting and how to prevent such terrorist attacks in the future.

Denny started in law enforcement in 1978 as a police radio dispatcher. He started his first private investigation company in 1980 which he sold in 1985. He then became the Executive Director of the International Podiatric Biomechanical Foundation before attending law school. Denny has started and been involved in many business ventures and has a wide array of business experience.

Denny played High School and College Basketball. He coached youth, Jr. High and High School basketball. Denny founded the Wham Jam Slam youth basketball league in Mesa, Arizona and had over 1,500 enthusiastic kids in the league. He also coached an AAU basketball team winning the State Championship and who competed in the National AAU tournament. He coached all of his own boys and now loves to coach his grand kids.

⌣

PRINCIPLE #1

PHILOSOPHIES OF SUCCESSFUL LANDLORDS AND PROPERTY MANAGERS

Key Elements to Incorporate into Every Landlord and Resident Relationship

The best way to read this book, especially when you are in a crisis, is to just go to the table of contents and find the area that you need RIGHT NOW as the book is put together chronologically for easy use.

I know that reading legal writing is painful. Therefore, this book is written in easy to read, everyday English by a person who has lived what you are living.

What you will find in this book is how to be a successful, profitable Owner, Owner/Landlord or Professional Property Manger according to me, Denny Dobbins, a Landlord/Tenant attorney and who has been involved on the Owner/Landlord/Property Manager side in one way or another in well over 250,000 evictions. I have handled hundreds of discrimination allegations and complaints, drafted hundreds of leases, tried numerous cases in court before a judge and a jury, dealt with countless vendors and employee issues, and have handled all types of rental related disputes. I have taught thousands of owners, landlords, property managers and police officers. I have presented over 400 programs on Landlord and Professional Property Manager matters including all areas of landlord law applications, premises liability, and discrimination; and have protected over 150,000 homes/apartments/and other types of rental units over the years. Simply put, all of my experience on landlord law, judges, Landlords, Property Managers and Residents are in this book for your use.

In my time as a private investigator since 1980; a Landlord attorney since 1991; a Landlord since 1987; legislative bill writer; long-time educator of police, attorneys, property managers, Landlords, and owners since 1992, I have watched hundreds and hundreds of Landlords make great decisions and make terrible decisions. Just when I think I have seen every situation that a Landlord/Property Manager can get into, there is always a new crazy situation popping up. However, regardless of the fact pattern, the Principles to remedy those situations remain constant. I have been on the cutting edge of Landlord law across the Country, and it never ceases to amaze me how government tries to fix Landlord and Resident problems and instead just make a worse mess of things in the process. That is one of the reasons I wrote this book; to help Landlords and Professional Property Managers understand what they need to do and how to do it to free themselves from all of the challenges that arise with Residents and the law.

Therefore, this book provides Landlords and Property Managers with: my 40 years of unique landlord/tenant experiences; experiences from 100's of years of legal experience derived from my partners and attorneys in my law firms and other law firms; experiences with offices of attorneys general in various States; experiences with offices of various State Real Estate Departments; my dealings with real estate investment groups; my dealings with real estate and property management companies; my experiences teaching at Real Estate Schools; my experiences from the halls of legislators and city councils; my experiences working in the back rooms of State Capital buildings writing legislative bills with all types of stakeholders; my experiences with perhaps over 100 judges and how they look at facts, law and human dispositions; my experiences from opinions and facts of hundreds of actual cases; and from my mistakes and the mistakes and successes of thousands of Owners, Landlords and Property Managers in the trenches. All of this is condensed into a step-by-step, chronological, how-to guide for being a successful and profitable Landlord/Property Manager and for how to handle most Landlord-Tenant related issues that arise - and to do it from a practical and legal perspective.

You can shorten the time and reduce the pain of dealing with Landlord/Tenant problems (I am now switching to the word "Resident" in place of "Tenant" as I believe it is more respectful) by finding the issue of concern and its remedies as set forward in this book, developing a plan to remedy your particular situation, running your solutions and plans by your local attorney and other Landlords, Property Managers and/or consultants you have close to you, and getting to the core of the issue without wasting time and money.

The first couple of chapters may sound a bit preachy. They may even sound somewhat elementary, or as if I am talking down to you. That is not the intent. Well, maybe preachy. This book is for new and seasoned Owners, Landlords and Professional Property Managers. You may say, "I already know that". Great. I am hoping every reader knows a good deal of what is contained in this book. However, I will guarantee you that you will find information that can help you in this book. I guarantee you that you will find some golden nuggets that you may not have thought about before to help you to be more successful and avoid some of the learning curve pitfalls. My job is to make you look like a hero and avoid costly challenges.

It is important to know the general nuances of the law and how the laws and the facts work together in Landlord/Resident situations generally; and to know how a judge will think about your situation. Each jurisdiction is a bit different and has nuances that I am not familiar with. You will need to be familiar with your particular jurisdiction.

My job is to save you money and headaches based on my years of experience and all the experiences of others that are captured in this work. But remember, and this is critically important, every case is a bit different in facts and law. Applying your local laws to the facts takes skill and knowledge. So, once you determine what to do in a situation regarding using the concepts and information in this book, if you are not sure about the remedy in your jurisdiction you need to run it by your local attorney and/or other professionals that you trust to ensure you are making the right decision based on the totality of the circumstances, facts of the case, the law in your jurisdiction and how your judges apply to the law to the facts.

At times my information may feel like a parent to a child conversation or attorney to client conversation – that is exactly what it is. You may be an Owner, Landlord or Professional Property Manager beginner or a seasoned vet. I just want you to be safe and profitable. I tell my clients, you can either do what I am telling you or I will see you soon and you can pay me a whole bunch of money to fix what you did because you did not listen to me. They usually chuckle. Most listen and some like to give me money to fix the problems.

THE WHOLE MOTIVATION FOR THIS BOOK IS TO HELP OWNER LANDLORDS AND PROFESSIONAL PROPERTY MANAGERS NOT TO ACT IN A REACTIONARY WAY BECAUSE THEY HAVE ALREADY ACTED PROACTIVELY AND THEY ARE PREPARED FOR WHATEVER COMES THEIR WAY. YOU ARE REASONABLE WITH AND TREAT EVERY RESIDENT WITH RESPECT AND FAIRNESS. YOU COMMUNICATE WITH YOUR RESIDENTS SO CLEARLY THAT THEY CANNOT MISUNDERSTAND. YOU ENSURE YOUR RESIDENTS UNDERSTAND YOUR EXPECTATIONS. YOU FOLLOW THE LAW, AND YOU FOLLOW THROUGH.

You always want to be ahead of the game, ahead of your Residents, ahead of the judges and in harmony with the law.

As you will see in later chapters, for over 30 years I have added helpful provisions into my lease agreement; provisions that take care of numerous issues that arise that simply cannot be set forth with specificity in the law. The law cannot, and does not, specifically mention or list every situation that arises. So, you have to set forth as many situations that may arise during the residency in the lease agreement itself and how the parties will address those issues. You need to clearly take away a judge's ability to make decisions about your property because you and the Resident have already decided the matter.

Most leases do not cover enough situations that arise, leaving your property in the hands of a judge to decide your future and the future of your asset. Generally, leases are horrendous and woefully deficient. You want to set forth every possible and practical situation in your lease that you can and how each situation will be handled so that the Resident knows what to do and so a judge knows how to rule. A short or poorly written lease leaves the Landlord and Resident with no pre-determined way to handle matters and dooms them to court. Not having a situation covered in a lease is a recipe that could spell disaster for the Owner, Landlord, Professional Property Manager and the Resident. So, you want your lease to be inclusive of as many situations as possible in order that the lease can have a built-in solution. That requires a longer, rather than shorter, and carefully drafted agreement. Many Landlords/Property Managers laugh at a long lease and say they cannot use such a long lease as Residents won't sign a long lease. However, Property Managers are generally familiar with long leases to some degree. It is the Owner/Landlord that is generally not familiar with a longer lease.

It is the Landlord's/Property Manager's financial funeral if the Landlord/Property Manager uses a short lease; and that is exactly what I have seen in court. The Landlord/Property Manager can either take my advice based on years and years of experience, or just risk it with a sloppy attempt at a lease. I will specifically cover lease clauses later in the book that will help any Landlord/Property Manager clarify handling possible Resident situations.

I compare this book to a set of road signs or a road map to help you avoid the pitfalls of the rental business as you move along your leasing journey. Why are there road signs all along the road? Of course, to reduce risk to the driver and to reduce risk at the same time to other drivers. This book contains a plethora of Landlord/Property Management road signs, if you will. Landlords/Property managers have a choice whether or not to abide by the road signs or just hope for the best and ignore the road signs. If you want to get to your destination which usually is to make money, doing what is mapped out in this book is the most sure way to reach your destination.

It is also important to note that most Residents do not read the whole lease no matter how long it may be. They should, but they don't. Although it is the Resident's responsibility to read the lease and know what is contained in the lease, whether the lease is one, two or twenty pages, it is still generally not read by the Resident. But the Landlord/Property Manager is not required to read the lease to the Resident. Residents will often try and say in court that they never read the lease, that it was too long to read or that they did not understand the lease. That usually does not go well for them. Residents usually don't start reading the lease until an issue arises when in search of defenses.

If an issue does arise the Landlord/Property Manager better be able to point to the exact section in the lease that applies to the situation so the judge can analyze the facts and the law the way the Landlord/Property Manager had hoped for. The lease better unmistakably explain how the Landlord/Property Manager and the Resident agreed the matter is to be handled/remedied.

For purposes of the remainder of this book, "Owner", "Landlord" and "Property Manager" are treated as one and the same and are interchangeable as terms for who it is that is responsible for managing/operating/running the property. The words "Tenant" or "Resident" are also treated as one in the same and are interchangeable. For purpose of adding dignity and respect to the residential Landlord and Tenant relationship, I refer to a Residential Tenant as a "Resident" and a Tenant of a Non-Residential dwelling as "Tenant".

Furthermore, an Owner, Owner/Landlord, Landlord, and Property Manager are generally referred to as the same entity under most State laws, unless very specific language is used by the parties in the lease regarding the property management agreement where the property manager is acting only as an agent for the Owner. Therefore, Owner, Owner/Landlord, Landlord and Property Manager will be referred to as Landlord/Property Manager throughout the remainder of this book.

There should not be different motivations between the Owner, Landlord and the Professional Property Management Company for owning/managing a property, but sometimes it can happen. It is human nature that a property manager at times may be more interested in their own monetary interests than in the owner's monetary interests. I have found that not to be the general case with professional management companies, mainly because the better the property is managed the more money both the management company and the owner will make. Regardless, everyone must be interested and motivated in providing a reasonably safe and habitable place for a Resident to live at a market price. In fact, it is the Landlord's and Property Management Company's duty to provide a reasonably safe and habitable place to live. If both the Owner, Landlord and Property Manager does not have at least that basic interest, then they should not be in the business of "Land-lording" or rental property ownership/management. "Land-lording" is a word I created to describe the processes and performing of the acts that all Owners, Landlords and Property Managers must accomplish. I use the word "Land-lording" as a verb to incorporate actions that must be taken by Landlords/Property Managers.

So now let's discuss some practical basics for being successful.

BUYING THE PROPERTY RIGHT FOR YOUR GOALS

I have made one critical assumption for any reader of this book. That assumption is that the property was bought correctly for your purposes and that now you want to manage the property correctly, according to the law, in an effort to make a profit with as few headaches and expenditure of time as possible. There are many books on how to buy a property right. This book is NOT about how to properly buy a property. Obviously, money is most easily made when you get a good price on the property at purchase time. The higher the CAP rate, generally the better the purchase. For purposes of this book, I am assuming that your property will cash flow when you factor in all of the costs associated with being a Landlord/Property Manager, including, but not limited to, debt payment; regulation compliance; Resident acquisition costs; hiring, training and retaining staff; management issues; association fees; insurance; vacancy rates; taxes; weather; pandemics; riots and war; inflation: escalation of interest rates; management fees; maintenance costs; deferred maintenance; occupancy rates; evictions; attorney fees; accountancy fees, and etc.

People have different goals when investing in real estate. Some people invest in turn-key properties that are well maintained so maintenance is not a big issue. Sure, you pay more for great properties, but management is generally easier from the start.

Some people invest in distressed or low-end properties and that is great if you are going to be in the rehab and babysitting businesses and can deal with all the running around that is required to bring the property up to speed while you clean out all the dead wood.

Some investors flip and some hold.

The principles in this book will help all of these kinds of properties to make good profit.

I have a client in Phoenix that finds distressed, low-end multi-family properties. He seeks them out to show the owner(s) how to manage their properties with the principles set forth in this book. He does very well at turning nasty, money losing properties into a beautiful, money making properties. He is a master at finding those kinds of properties and then implementing crime free and CPTED (crime prevention through environmental design) principles (we will cover these topics later) and turning those properties into cash cows with happy Residents and happy owners; and doing so remarkably fast.

If you are investing for retirement, then I assume you are investing in properties that are in good condition with the intention for Residents paying off the property over time so you will have a cash producing property for years to come.

Whatever the reason for purchasing your properties, once purchased, now comes the Land-lording part of the process in what should be an effort to increase the value of the property and make income by profitable management and by appreciation – that is real Land-lording.

Regardless of what kind of property you have purchased, successful Land-lording is the same if you are holding the property or going to sell the property in one fashion or another. If a Landlord/Property Manager really wants to limit struggles, difficulties, and complexities in Land-lording, the principles in this book are essential to long-term simplicity for being a Landlord/Property Manager, whether by hiring a professional management company or doing it yourself, the processes and procedures are identical. The difference in the type of property purchased determines the amount of Land-lording you will have to do. Assuming that you have purchased a property in a way that will allow the property to appreciate in value, have great cash flow, or both, now you need to get to the business of getting your property filled up with the right Residents that are going to pay you timely each month and not cause you problems that will cost you money in the future.

It does not matter if you are going to manage the property or if you are going to have it managed by some other entity; the very same things must be done to, and for, the property to make it a profitable venture - meaning that when you sell the property it will be worth a lot more than you paid for it, and/or it will produce income for you prior to selling.

Like any investment, it will behove you to watch your investment and your property manager very closely to ensure that management is doing the things not only in the way you want them to be done, but in the way that things must be done if you are going to make money and avoid the multiple and various headaches that can happen with any rental property. If you hire a management company, watch that company very closely as you are ultimately responsible for their actions to a great extent.

GET FAMILIAR WITH YOUR STATE AND LOCAL RULES FOR LANDLORDS/ PROPERTY MANAGERS AND RESIDENTS

Your State likely has a variety of laws that govern rental properties and Landlord and Resident relationships. If your state has a Landlord and Tenant act, get familiar with it, even if you have your own attorney. Many states have different governing documents for general landlord/tenants, manufactured housing, hotel/motel, mini-storage, Homeowner Associations, retail/commercial/industrial, etc. If your State does not have a Landlord and Resident act your state will surely have various statutes and/or local laws/ordinances that apply to Landlord and Resident relations. There are also many Federal rules that govern rental properties, including, but not limited to all kinds of discrimination prescriptions, the fair credit reporting act, the fair collections practices act, the equal employment opportunity commission regulations and HUD Guidelines, to name a few, that you must be familiar with or at least parts thereof. Don't be discouraged. It is all manageable.

This book is intended as a practical guide for all Owners/Landlords/Property Managers to use on an everyday basis to handle challenges as they present themselves.

We will go on a chronological Landlord/Property Manager journey including how a Landlord/Property Manager should think about being a Landlord/Property Manager, how a Landlord/Property Manager should act towards a Resident, how to show the property to a applicant and how to comply with fair housing rules throughout the entire Land-lording process, what is important for an application for residency, how to screen the applicant and who should do it so you don't get stuck with a lemon, what you should include in a good lease, what violations of the lease or statutes commonly arise, how to assert your rights as a Landlord/Property Manager when the Resident does not fulfill the Resident's end of the agreement, key components of the court process, and how to take back possession of your property or unit.

I have seen a lot of Landlord/Property Manager management books over the years. They are generally written by attorneys for attorneys. Most such books are hard to read and not very practical to use for Landlords/Property Managers. This book is both easy to read and practical for everyday use. This book was written by a Landlord attorney who knows the ins and outs of being a Landlord and who also knows the ins and outs of the legal obligations of both Landlords/Property Managers and Residents. It is intended as an easy guide where the reader can quickly find answers to the circumstances that are occurring at the moment.

So, let's discuss a few housekeeping principles for being a successful and profitable Landlord/Property Manager.

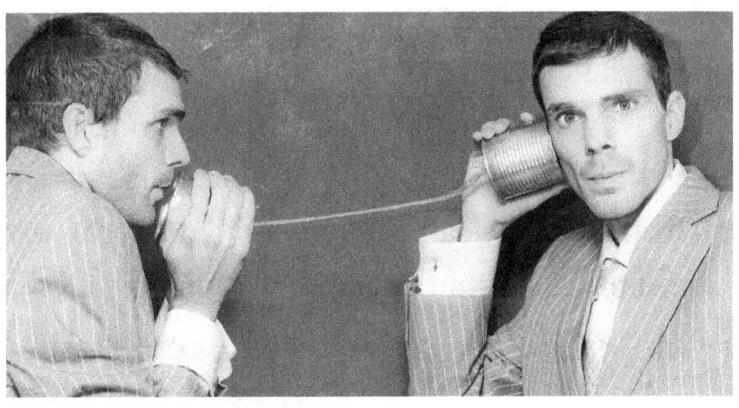

EFFECTIVE COMMUNICATION

It is best to be brutally honest and straight forward with your Residents. That does not mean the communication is adversarial or combative. It means it is EFFECTIVE - open, honest and to the point. You want the Resident to like you. It is always easier to have a good relationship when the parties like each other. People usually like you because they like your personality. They like how you treat them. They like how you interact with them. They trust you. So, when you are cheerful, happy, approachable and easy to talk, you have a much better chance of successfully dealing with the Resident, even in difficult circumstances.

However, you are about to entrust a person with an expensive asset; a person that you likely do not know, except for the limited research you have performed, so you need to protect your investment. The applicant needs to understand and agree to the rules that will govern the relationship. They need to know that you will enforce the agreement you make with them and that you will absolutely follow through with your obligations as well. You need to make sure that they know and understand how everything will work and the consequences of failing to abide by the rules. And all of this needs to be done in a kind and caring, but firm way.

If you have ever had a teenager learning to drive a car you know what I am talking about. You are not going to let your teenager drive your car alone anywhere until you are comfortable that they understand the rules about driving, that they can and will control the car, and that they understand that the car can kill people, including themselves. You, of course, want to teach them as much as possible to protect them, your car and others. You know there has to be clear communication about your strict criteria regarding who can be in the car, when they have to be home, how they drive the car, that no cell phone can be used while driving, where they can go, and so forth. Communication must be clear and resounding. I think in Landlord law, we as Landlords/ Property Managers, take way too much for granted. We think Residents know how we want them to act and how they are required to use our home/unit. Too often we think Residents will automatically act the same way we would act if we were in possession of someone else's home/unit. Don't kid yourself. Communication must be just as clear with your Residents as it is with little Susie about driving your car.

You need to provide anyone who wants to move past the showing/tour stage with a set of your rental criteria, including financial, criminal history (be careful here as there are some jurisdictions that limit if and when you can discuss, obtain or use criminal history as a criteria), occupancy, rent to income ratio, crime free policies, animals, smoking, when rent is due, what happens if rent is not paid timely, and other applicable policies.

In this way you can help save time for yourself and the applicant. If the applicant does not want to abide by the written criteria that you present to them, or if they realize they will not qualify for residency under your rental criteria, then it is likely that you will not hear from that person again. Written criteria are a definite and distinct deterrent factor for avoiding bad tenants. Bad guys, people who have nefarious ideas in mind while living in your property, and perhaps other folks that that do not qualify pursuant to your criteria, do not want to have anyone paying attention to them at the property, especially not you as the Landlord/Property manager. With these written policies and criteria in place, and in our Resident's hands early in the screening process, they get the idea very quickly that lack of attention will not be the norm with your property.

GOOD FAITH, FAIR DEALING AND THE GOLDEN RULE

There are all types of individual owners and property management philosophies about how a rental property should be operated. Through the years it has become clear that professional management companies generally do a very good job managing property – at least generally much better than smaller owners or owners that own just one or a few units. This is the case mainly because professional management companies are highly involved in training their employees. That professionalism and knowledge comes at a high cost paid by the professional management companies in time and money. Professional management companies generally stay up on the law, have an attorney at hand, and don't fall into the deep pits that smaller or new owners can easily fall into. There are a lot of dynamics to juggle while learning how to manage property. Smaller owners generally don't have the time, money or the training to do what needs to be done – especially new mom and pop owners. Effective and efficient management of real property requires education and time. However, there are some great smaller, and mom and pop owners that do an excellent job; those who have spent the time and money to learn what they need to do.

One of the things this book is about is how to take whatever property you purchased and sell it for a lot more money than you bought it for. Or, if you want to hold the property for an income stream, how to get the most out of your property over time. For Example, if you purchased a property for say $60,000.00 a door, following the principles in this book will show you how to turn that property into $140,000.00+ per door – quite quickly. It is the implementation of principles that will make your property soar in value and keep your Residents happy.

You may fit into a number of owner/manager categories; seasoned, beginner or somewhere in between. You may be a large professional management company, a small management company or an individual owner/manager of a single-family home, small multifamily units, large multifamily units, commercial property, hotel-motel units, mini-storage, condos, planned community homes, mini-storage or manufactured homes; it does not matter what kind of property. The principles outlined in this book will work for every type of rental property. I have represented every type of Landlord/Property Manager with every type of management philosophy.

Sometimes Owners/Landlords get too emotional about their property. I have found by sad experience that decisions made based on emotions, greed, laziness, lack of knowledge, disdain for Residents, nickel and diming a Resident, refusing to keep the property in good repair, etc., are usually bad business decisions and systemic of deeper personal issues or character flaws not suited for property management. On the other hand, decisions made based on trying to do the right thing considering the particular circumstances and the funds needed/available, and upon sound people and business practices, generally turn out pretty good. When you are in the Landlord/Property Manager business, you are in the people business.

A simple Example for good Land-lording in a multi-family community is to walk the property every single day or night to see the state and condition of the property, including, but not limited to, damages; trash area; buildings; laundries; parking issues; pool/spa; gates issues; trees, parking lots, dangerous situations – sidewalks, stairs, ice, snow; people just hanging around, and etc. The goal of a good Landlord/Property Manager, whether owner or management, regardless of the type of property or type of Resident, should be to provide the Resident a reasonably safe and habitable premise to live in for a reasonable, market-based price. Remember that the Resident actually lives there and has to deal with whatever is going on. Everyone wants a good place to live and by following the principles of this book, everyone gets what they want.

TAKE CARE OF THE BASICS AND EVERYTHING ELSE FALLS IN PLACE

So, what is basic for a Landlord/Property Manager? Pretty much everything; every step is basic for a Landlord/Property Manager. I know that sounds crazy. But good management is a line upon line, precept upon precept and a progressionary process. No part of the recipe can be left out. It includes chronological steps that are important and necessary. Every step along the way is basic; from finding the right property, to showing the property properly, to finding the right Resident, to the right lease application, to the right lease, to the proper walk-through move-in, to continued proper management of the property, to proper move-out and so on. Not paying attention or not following the principles of any of the steps along the way could be calamitous. Basic principles have to take place each step of the way. It is no different than being a doctor, banker, electrician or any other profession. Do each step right and you are successful and profitable.

It goes without saying that to be a successful Landlord/Property Manager that the Landlord/Property Manager keeps the premises in habitable and safe condition. Taking care of the property is a basic essential. This means that all of the essential services are in good working order - the premises are up to code. The plumbing, electrical, HVAC all work properly. The carpet, tile, wood, counters, tubs, showers, doors, remotes, yard, frig, toilets, sinks, wall, etc. are in good working condition. The outside of the unit/home is likewise in good, clean and attractive condition with proper lighting. Many Landlords/Property Managers do not keep their property in attractive condition. That is a huge mistake which we will go into in more detail later. Failing to keep the outside pristine is a great way to draw the criminal element right into your property. Many Landlords/Property Managers are just too stupid, and/or too cheap and don't want to spend the time or money to make the place look great, or at least presentably nice. Again, big, big mistake. I will cover this principle in the CRIME FREE chapter.

Suffice it so say, if the Landlord/Property Manager does not stay on top of the basics – step-by-step, it will be impossible for the Landlord/Property Manager to be successful or profitable. Some Landlords/Property Managers have bragged that all they want is their money from the Resident and the property condition is not important to them. Well, they are in it for the wrong reason – and not only will they constantly have bad Residents they will always be allusively chasing money and their property appreciation will never realize much. Plus, they will have the fun of dealing with all the issues, headache and time loss brought on by their bad decisions.

The smart, successful Landlords/Property Managers buy the property right, follow the law, do the right things for the property and the Residents, follow proven principles to improve the property value and then make a good money when they sell, and/or enjoy the money stream in the meantime.

If you want to make money, you treat the Residents right. Remember your property is their home. They deserve your care. Really, you will make more money if you treat Resident with respect and provide a nice place to live. You don't have to rent to bad Residents, unless you do not follow the principles outlined in this book. If you do not follow the principles in this book, then you will only be able rent to bad Residents, and you will constantly be fighting an uphill battle.

When you run your properties the way successful Landlords/Property Managers run their properties, then your good Residents will tell their friends, and their friends will also want to live at your property. Then, your problems just vanish as you create a happy, friendly Landlord-Resident eco system and culture. It works the same way for bad Residents.

If you are going to be a Landlord/Property Manager, even if you do not abide by all of the principles contained in this book, you must follow this principle. If you are going to be in the business of providing housing, you must put a product on the market that meets at least the minimum acceptable standards of habitability, safety and aesthetics, along with adhering to basic management functions you must perform. It is not a one-time endeavor. It requires a consistent, vigilant effort. Otherwise, there is no reason to be in the business. Afterall, being a landlord or property manager, like any business, requires dedication and focus. If you fail to do so, upset Residents and the law will financially feast upon your arrogance, stubbornness, ignorance and stupidity. Remember, besides one's family, one's home is their most precious of possessions. This is where they live. If you do not provide the basics, you are just asking for trouble.

If you fail to adequately provide decent housing, any profits you thought you would make will soon become your worst financial nightmare dealing with the Resident's attorneys, the city and possibly the office of the attorney general or other government and quasi-government agencies. You will fast be looking for a way out, but it will be too late.

LANDLORD'S/PROPERTY MANAGER'S DUTY TO REASONABLY PROTECT THE PROPERTY AND RESIDENTS

The photos above are similar properties, in a similar area of the same town, at a similar price point. One is well maintained at a low cost and the other is obviously not maintained. Which do you think will attract a Resident looking for a place first?

We will discuss this issue in greater detail in the last section of this book under the chapter entitled "Premises Liability and Negligence," but a good Landlord/Property Manager has a duty to protect the property and the Residents, and to operate the property in such a way that the property is not the source of damage to Residents or others. It does not matter if the property is an A, B, C or D property. There is no way to avoid the obligations and duties that a Landlord/Property Manager has to its Residents and its Residents' invitees to ensure the property is in a good, safe and habitable condition. You cannot write away those obligations in a lease. The law trumps the lease. There are no shortcuts to managing and maintaining rental property. But there are proven ways to do it right and still make money.

There are many of Federal and State laws that govern housing. Hereinafter all statutes, regulations, guidelines and ordinances regarding housing will be referred to as "the law."

Simply put, regardless of your religious affiliation or political persuasions, the principles for the greatest success as a Landlord/Property Manager is to treat Residents the way you want to be treated based on the particulars of the lease, the law and the totality of circumstances regarding the property. Judges look at every case this way. Judges are people and not easily fooled. They don't like it when they see Residents being mistreated or not respected or being or not being treated with justice. Landlords/Property Managers usually are on the right side of the law and generally do things right. But when a Landlord/Property Manager fails at its obligations or treats a Resident badly – watch out Landlord/Property Manager!! Be fair, cordial, and reasonable, at all times. The idea of good faith is the prevailing theme for a Landlord/Property Manager and Resident relationships; especially when you find yourself in front of a judge or a jury. Keep your cool with your Residents - no matter what. When you keep your cool you often disarm and diffuse the situation, even when the Resident may be behaving outrageously. More importantly you stay in control of your thoughts and your actions. If the Resident does something stupid, you have plenty of remedies. Watch, listen and think, and you will win the day when things get tense or hostile. There is never a good enough reason to sink to foul language, nastiness or irrational behavior as a Landlord/Property Manager. There are also cameras and recording devices everywhere in today's world. Always assume you are being video-taped or tape recorded and that will help you get through those tough moments with honor. If you follow the other principals contained in this book, you will never want to stoop to lowlife behavior, and you won't feel you have to.

Over many years of practice, my law firms saw a variety of ownership/management philosophies that are not necessarily in harmony with those stated above. Sure, Landlords/Property Managers need to make a profit either through rental income or through appreciation, but not while doing a disservice to the quality of living for a Resident. There are good Landlords/Property Managers and bad Landlords/Property Managers – mostly good. Typically, good Landlords/Property Managers take very good care of their property and treat Residents with dignity. In so doing such Landlords/Property Managers are better able to attract the quality of Residents that are consistent with the smooth operation of the property.

On the other hand, bad Landlords/Property Managers who do not care about how the property looks and sometimes see Residents as a necessary evil, will draw that very type of Resident to their property; and more bad Residents will come. When this happens, the very thing that the Landlord/Property Manager sought – profits and/appreciation, will allude the Landlord/Property Manager because the first principle was not followed. Land-lording will just turn into a series of ugly challenges.

Unfortunately, when the property was not bought properly, sometimes the Landlord/Property Manager turns to ugly Land-lording tactics because there is not enough money to properly manage the property. However, that is still a big mistake because if the principles set forth herein are followed, even if you poorly purchased property you can accelerate the success of the property through the principles in this book.

CLEAR EXPECTATIONS

Clear expectations go hand in hand with your ability and responsibility to communicate well with your applicants and your Residents. You may feel like talking plainly and clearly to someone is difficult or intimidating. Get over it. You are in the Land-lording business and it is critical to be clear and completely understood. Which lady will your Resident see, the old lady or the young lady? Your job is to ensure that your Resident interprets things the way you do and see the lady you want your Resident to see, and nothing else. It may take extra discussions and time to both be on the same page. Don't allow any issues to be miscommunication.

Just like with our children, we want to be fair and deal with Residents in good faith and kindness. Communicating clear expectations is vital to avoiding conflict with children. Children want clear boundaries and fairness as much as they say they don't. So it is with Residents, we must start with the end in mind. We must be clear and to the point; so clear, that there can be no misunderstanding or miscommunication. The rental criteria, the application and lease are the documents you must create to provide that clear understanding.

If you have ever had a child, or for that matter, babysat a child, you soon learn that children will take as much advantage of you as you will let them. If standards are not simple, clear, well communicated and followed through upon, there is usually chaos.

I am only comparing Residents to children to drive home a point. Once the rules are agreed upon, you do not change the rules, unless there is an overwhelming and over-riding reason to do so, such as an incompatibility with another statute, rule, regulation, guideline, ordinance or law.

The lease agreement and the law controls the relationship between Landlord/Property Manager and Resident. Once a lease agreement is entered into, both the Landlord/Property Manager and Resident need to abide by it. If the rent is due on the first day of the month, then that is when it is due; not on the third day or the eighth day. If the Landlord/Property Manager is supposed to do something on a specific date, then the Landlord/Property Manager needs to get it done.

EXAMPLE Take the single mother who works and takes care of the home, or the mother who stays at home with the kids and has all of the housework to do on top of her duties in nurturing the kids and managing the household – sometimes moms just get so inundated that they do not follow through on their rules or what they instructed the children to do. The kids know if she will follow through or not and will take her to her limits. That is just what many kids do. That's what happened to my mother. We learned what we could get away with.

But not was doing, and she would catch me screwing up or getting into mischief. I could not pull her chain. I could not get away with a fib or half-truth. She just knew. After a while it was pointless for me to even try to get away with anything. She always knew everything. I never knew how she did it. She was always there around the corner to keep me in line. There were basic and reasonable rules that I was supposed to follow. I knew what the rules were. They were well explained. There were clear expectations, and they were to be followed or there would be immediate consequences. I knew it and she knew I knew it.

My mom on the other hand was always very busy, with the other kids, the house, her friends and working at her job. There was no follow through on the basic house rules or her instructions to the kids. I knew it and took advantage of it. I did pretty much whatever I wanted to do and whenever I wanted to do it. I would make up stories to deal with my failures to follow the rules. There were rules mind you. However, I just did not think that I would ever see any consequences for breaking them. And, for the most part there were no negative consequences to my breaking the rules. She even made excuses for my inexplicable behavior – strange as that was. I would break rules, as many as I could and for as long as I could. I would take her to her limits and get out the way when she was at the end of her rope.

Not so with my grandmother. It never got that far because she always followed through, no matter what. I knew she would follow through and she knew I knew she would follow through if I failed to abide by the rules or did not perform as instructed. So, what was the point? I was caught before I got started. I just stopped trying to break the rules and complied. Besides, if I did screw up too much, she could always send me home and she knew I liked being with her and my grandfather more than being home. She was always nice to me. However, she was also firm and steadfast with the rules. Not only what the rules were, but maybe more importantly, why they existed at all. Our relationship was a good one because she set forth the expectations in a way that I could not misunderstand, and then she followed through promptly and completely.

Obviously, owners who manage their own properties, and professional managers alike, have multiple job responsibilities that take a great amount of time to accomplish. My Landlord attorney partners, and I, found that managers and owners that are nice, but firm, and followed through on the rules, had much less problems than those managers and owners who are either not nice and/or did not follow through on the rules. Nice, but firm, always seemed to work the best.

My partners and I have been involved in hundreds of thousands of evictions and hundreds of trials. Over the years, each of my partners has been a Landlord and have learned that being NICE BUT FIRM with Residents, is a huge key for success. Being nice does not mean that you are naive. It means both parties understand that there are specific written standards that will be enforced. The expectations are clear and resounding. There is no room for misunderstandings. When dealing with a Resident, as Ronald Reagan said, "Trust, but verify". Even if a Resident does not like what you say, if you say it in a pleasant enough way, even in a difficult situation, both Resident and Landlord/ Property Manager can walk away with an understanding of how things will play out and avoid further or heightened confrontation over the matter.

DON'T BEND THE RULES

Once the lease terms, rules and regulations are agreed upon, if you bend them for a Resident's particular circumstances, experience has shown that that is when you get burned. Not that you should not be kind in your relations with your Residents, but rather, lowing standards, changing standards or lowering expectations is what will hurt you. Now, you have to bend or change the rules in some select cases where the government has control, but we will discuss that later.

If rent is due on the 1st day on the month no later than 5:00 pm and it is not paid by that time, then follow the lease and when rent has not been paid by 5:01 pm, provide a written notice to the Resident for failure to pay rent. Do not use a drop box – ever. A Drop box just causes problems. In this way you immediately let the Resident know that you are aware that the rule was not kept and that you have followed through. Not only do you turn on the clock for possible eviction since the rent has not paid timely, you have sent a message that every month if the rent is not paid as agreed you will be there with a notice for failure to pay rent timely. In multi-family communities the word spreads very quickly that 5:00 pm means 5:00 pm. No one takes advantage of the other in the relationship. How to handle the situation was agreed to in the lease agreement and you have followed through. Both have obligations to honor. You wind up sending a clear message that you will follow through or there will be immediate consequences. You also wind up getting payment on time in the future.

We have often heard it said by Landlords/Property Managers that they want to, "work with their Residents". That is a great thing to do, when it is appropriate. However, you must be careful when doing so. The notion of "working with a Resident" sometimes can raise fair housing concerns, for what you do for one Resident you must do for all Residents. Remember, you have already "worked" with the Resident when you negotiated the lease agreement. In general, to continue to re-negotiate terms of the lease when a lease is already in place not only sends the wrong message to a Resident, but it can drive a Landlord/Property Manager batty. Whatever it is you want in the lease agreement, negotiate it, put it the lease, and then stick to it and follow through.

Sure, you want to be nice about how you enforce the lease and the law, but that does not mean that you lower your standards or expectations. One way that helps is not to have the property in your name. I think in today's legal environment most investors have their properties in LLC or some kind of corporate structure. If the property is legally deeded to a limited liability company, a trust, partnership or corporation, that instrument can help you diffuse many uncomfortable situations regarding enforcement. When a difficult situation arises where the Resident wants you to "work with them" in a way that does not make sense or is just inappropriate, it provides you a way to avoid confrontation by giving you a legal and honest way to indicate to the Resident that the ownership of the property will not allow their request for a deviation of the lease terms. Or just say it straight out that you just cannot do what they are requesting if in fact you cannot oblige.

As a Landlord/Property Manager you must enforce the lease and the law equally, timely and consistently. It is simply much easier when you do not have to say you are the owner. It is often very hard to enforce the lease and the rules, just as it is with our children, because you have a heart.

EXAMPLE Have you have ever had a fifteen-year-old child ask to stay out an hour or two past curfew when no special event was happening? You love your child and want your child to be happy and you don't want conflict that brings a bad feeling into the home. You also want to protect your child. There is a tendency just to say, "ok" and make it easy. However, because you really want to show your love for them you know nothing good can take place outside of your home after the curfew hour, or you would have never set that curfew time in the first place. You have to follow through, absent extraordinary circumstances. Otherwise, you are setting up a destructive and self-defeating precedent for you child. Otherwise, you are setting up a destructive and self-defeating precedent for you child.

FOLLOW THROUGH

It was Zig Ziegler that said, "It was character that got us out of bed, commitment that moved us into action discipline that enabled us to follow through". Brian Tracy said, "Follow up and follow through, until the task is complete, the prize is won". Follow through in Land-lording will save you lots of money and headaches.

 When trying to quit smoking or drinking, if you had to decide every time you had the urge to smoke or drink whether or not you would smoke or drink at that moment, you would likely never be able to quit. You make the decision once, then you stick to. If you need help you get it – you follow through. It is that simple. So it is with lease provisions and the law. The decisions are already made. You do not keep analyzing and changing your rules over and over again. The decisions are over. That is why you have a lease. That is also why you need a good lease instead of one you pick up from a copy center, drug store or your friend. You can't allow yourself to fall into the habit of second guessing yourself. Get it right to start with and be done with it. You will find that being a Landlord/Property Manager is much easier if you will stick to what was agreed upon and only deviate if it is absolutely necessary or when you are correcting a provision of your lease to ensure compliance with the law.

FINDING GREAT RESIDENTS

Every Landlord/Property Manager wants good Residents that will pay rent on time and not damage the property or cause problems. Bottom line, the better your property looks, regardless of the area it is in, the better chance of attracting the best potential Residential candidates in that market.

You should be familiar with the concept known as Crime Prevention Through Environment Design referred to in the industry at "CPTED". There are lots of study materials on this subject. Suffice it to say for this book that it means that your entire property is in an orderly and safe condition, that will not hurt anyone, or cause anyone to think you are not a conscientious Landlord/Property Manager.

1. The lighting is good (parking, walkways, common grounds).
2. The property is well painted and maintained.
3. There are no tree roots making concrete walks uneven.
4. Laundry rooms are secure.
5. Playgrounds are safe.
6. No holes or uneven places in the grassy areas.
7. Electric boxes/panels are all locked.
8. Storage areas are secure.
9. Managers are not left alone in the office with surveillance.
10. If there are video cameras on the property they work and are recording.

CPTED concerns not only help prevent lawsuits regarding premises liability issues, many of the CPTED factors create the first impression for your property. That first good impression is key to landing the right kind of Resident. If you do not have your property in pristine physical appearance (regardless of its age), then you will attract bad Resident risks. Bad Resident risks are looking for a property where it looks like the Landlord/Property Manager does not care much about the property in the hope that if the

Landlord/Property Manager does not care much about how the property looks then the Resident can get away with doing anything the Resident wants to do.

These CPTED factors may seem overkill or silly, but I guarantee you that they matter and will definitely help you eliminate future problems. The following is a list of CPTED factors to help protect your property against criminal elements and bad risks. You should also give this list to your Residents to help them be more responsible and safer and let you know if a problem occurs with one of the elements in the list. Landlord/Property Manager does not care much about how the property looks then the Resident can get away with doing anything the Resident wants to do.

These CPTED factors may seem overkill or silly, but I guarantee you that they matter and will definitely help you eliminate future problems. The following is a list of CPTED factors to help protect your property against criminal elements and bad risks. You should also give this list to your Residents to help them be more responsible and safer and let you know if a problem occurs with one of the elements in the list.

HERE IS THE KEY: IF THE LANDLORD/PROPERTY MANAGER FAILS TO DO THESE THINGS, YOU COULD BE LIABLE SHOULD AN ISSUE ARISE REGARDING THE SAFETY OF YOUR RESIDENT.

RESIDENTIAL SAFETY CHECK LIST FOR A HOME OR APARTMENT AND MULTI-FAMILY SAFETY CHECK LIST CPTED Inspection Report

Exterior Doors:	Yes	No	N/A
All doors are locked at night and every time you leave the house - even if it's just for a few minutes			
Doors and frames are solid hardwood or metal.			
Doors feature wide-angle peepholes at heights everyone can use.			
If there are glass panels in or near doors, they are reinforced in some way so they cannot be shattered.			
All entryways have a working, keyed entry lock and sturdy deadbolt lock installed into the frame of the door (1" throw, 3" screws for the plate).			
Spare keys are kept in a trusted, secure place.			
The locks were changed before anyone moves in.			
Entry points can be seen from public areas.			
Garage and Sliding Door:	Yes	No	N/A
The door and frame leading into the home from the garage is solid wood or metal and protected with a quality keyed door lock and deadbolt.			
The overhead garage door has a lock so that reliance is not solely on the automatic garage door opener to provide security.			
Garage doors all lock.			
The sliding glass door has a strong, working key lock.			
A dowel or a pin to secure the sliding glass door has been installed to prevent the door from being shoved aside or lifted off the track.			
The sliding glass door is locked every night and each time we leave the house.			
Protecting Windows:	Yes	No	N/A
Every window in the home has a working lock.			
Windows are always locked, even when they are opened a few inches for ventilation.			
Outdoor Security:	Yes	No	N/A
Shrubs / bushes are trimmed so there is no place for someone to hide (3' down and 7' up).			
There are no dark areas around the house, garage, or yard at night that would hide prowlers.			
Use inhospitable plants (cactus) or landscaping material (thorny) to discourage prowlers.			
Every outside door has a bright, working light to illuminate visitors.			
Floodlights are used appropriately to ensure effective illumination.			
Outdoor lights are on in the evening whether someone is home or not or a photocell and motion-sensitive lighting system has been installed.			
The house/apt number is clearly displayed so police and other emergency vehicles can find the house quickly.			
The property is clean and clear of debris.			

Security When Away From Home/Apt:	Yes	No	N/A
At least two light timers are set to turn the lights, t.v. or radio on and off in a logical sequence when away from the home/apt.			
The motion detector or other alarm system (if there is one) is activated when leaving the home.			
Mail and newspaper deliveries are stopped or arrangements for a neighbor/friend to pick them up are made when gone for a period of time.			
A trusted neighbor is asked to watch the home when away.			
Outdoor Valuables and Personal Property:	Yes	No	N/A
Gate latches, garage doors, and shed doors are all locked with high-security, laminated padlocks after every use.			
Grills, lawn mowers, bicycles and other valuables are stored in a locked garage or shed, or if left out in the open, are hidden from view and securely locked to a stationary point.			
Firearms are stored unloaded, locked away and secured with trigger guard locks.			
Serial numbers of valuable items, such as television, stereos, guns and computers have recorded.			
A home inventory is up-to-date and includes pictures of items that don't have serial numbers. A complete copy is kept somewhere securely out of the house			

EXTERIOR	Yes	No
1. Community address numbers posted and visible.		
2. Building and unit numbers posted and visible.		
3. Community locator map or directory.		
4. Trash receptacle areas are clean and safe.		
5. Stairways secure/free of debris.		
6. Property clean and free of debris.		
7. Building numbers painted on roof.		
LIGHTING:	Yes	No
1. Main entry/exit to property.		
2. Address/sign.		
3. Pathways and common areas.		
4. Covered parking.		
5. On-site parking.		
6. Adjacent parking areas.		
7. Mail pickup/delivery sites.		
8. Units (front/rear).		
9. Stairways.		
10. Office and commercial areas.		
11. Common use areas.		
12. Swimming pool.		
13. Child recreation areas.		

LAUNDRY ROOMS	Yes	No
1. Exterior doors equipped with deadbolt locks.		
2. Self closing and locking doors.		
3. Windows equipped with anti-lifts/slide.		
4. Visibility inside before entering.		
DOOR SYSTEMS:	Yes	No
1. Exterior doors solid core construction.		
2. Door frames in good condition.		
3. Exterior doors fit securely in door frame.		
4. Pins on exterior hinges.		
5. 180-degree eye-viewers.		
6. Single cylinder deadbolt locks.		
7. Deadbolt locks have minimum 1" throw.		
8. Strike-plates fastened with minimum 3" screws.		
9. Deadbolt extends minimum 1" into frame.		
10. Locks re-mastered for new residents.		
11. Sliding doors with anti-slide/lift modifications.		
WINDOW SYSTEMS:	Yes	No
1. Sliding windows with anti-lift/slide modifications and track properly.		
2. Anti-lift/slide modifications while systems open.		
3. Double hung systems modified for security.		
LANDSCAPING:	Yes	No
1. Shruberry trimmed down for natural surveillance.		
2. Trees trimmed up for natural surveillance.		
3. Area clean of landscaping debris.		
4. Landscaping interferes with lighting patterns.		
SWIMMING POOL:	Yes	No
1. Security fencing as required by code.		
2. Entry/exit gates self-closing and locking.		
3. Lifesaving equipment present and in working order.		
4. Warnings, rules, and regulations posted.		
5. Area clean and free of debris.		
6. Telephone.		
FIRE SAFETY:	Yes	No
1. Operational smoke detectors on each level.		
2. Smoke detectors in bedroom.		
3. Fire extinguisher within 75 feet of apartment.		
4. Clearly marked fire lines.		
5. Current confidence test in fire alarms/sprinkler system.		
6. Recommended extinguisher 2A10BC(5lb).		

Now that you are ready to protect yourself and your Residents, let's give you even more protection with Crime Free principles.

CRIME FREE ADDENDUM

You should always use the crime free addendum. I have the crime free language in my lease and in a separate addendum with the same language because the issues are so important to me and my clients being successful and profitable landlords. You may ask, what in the world is a crime-free addendum?

The addendum is an addition, a separate document, to the lease agreement where the Resident agrees to live a crime free lifestyle while residing at the property and while being off of the property – and the Resident agrees to ensure that the Resident's occupants, guests and invitees will do the same. This is a critical part of screening and a critical part of the lease agreement signing. The Resident agrees that if there is a violation of the Crime Free Addendum that the Resident may be immediately evicted. It is also a deterrent to attracting bad Residents. See a copy of the crime free addendum in this Chapter set forth below.

This Agreement is truly an amazing and significant principle for successful and profitable Landlords/Property Managers. Public Housing uses a form of the same agreement. I was a Co-Founder, Assistant Executive Director and the General Legal Counsel of the International Crime Free Association. I held those offices for eighteen (18) years. Officer Tim Zehring of the Mesa, Arizona, Police Department, was the executive director and spearhead of The International Crime Free Association from its inception in 1992. He brought me into the organization to help keep the program up to date on the legal side and to teach Crime Free principles. I am a "Certified Trainer". I watched the Crime Free Programs grow from a small local program to a National and International powerhouse.

All good Landlords/Property Managers should be trained in Crime Free Principles. The training is free through many local police departments. The programs have been taught in over 2800 communities. Be sure to have your Resident sign the Crime Free Addendum even if you do not get Crime Free training.

Over the last 30 years this agreement has been a great asset for Landlords/Property Managers. It is imperative to go over the Addendum with your Resident prior to signing the lease, (or even at the tour) as it is a significant deterrent to winding up with bad Residents. I know it takes time to go over the lease and the Crime Free Addendum with the

Resident, but you are trying to make sure you are both in the same ballpark and that your asset is protected; that expectations are set. Having the Resident understand the Crime Free Addendum goes a long way to having the Resident understand that no criminal shenanigans will be permitted.

Now that you have a applicant in front of you that may qualify; having verified their application, to complete the screening you must have your applicant sign the Crime Free Addendum. The Resident is simply promising to live a Crime Free lifestyle during their residency. I wrote the Crime Free Addendum years ago for the private housing market for the International Crime Free Association. The concept was taken from the Public Housing Crime Free Addendum created in 1988 by Jack Kemp, the then Director of Housing and Development under the Reagan Administration.

See the private housing version of the Crime Free Addendum below the following Crime Free Logos.

CRIME FREE ADDENDUM

This addendum agreement is made part of the lease between the parties and incorporated in the lease agreement. Using the Crime Free Addendum does not mean the property will be free of crime, but it is a deterrent to criminal activity.

Resident understands that crime can and does occur in every segment of life as well as in every rental community and neighborhood, regardless of the location. No property can or should be considered totally safe and free from crime regardless of the measures taken to the contrary. Hence, Owner/Landlord/Property Manager does not, and cannot, in any way warrant or guarantee Resident, Resident's occupants, Resident's guests, or Resident's invitees safety or security at, on, near or off of the property. Resident understands that the safety of Resident and Resident's household is Resident's responsibility and not the responsibility of the Owner/Landlord/Property Manager.

Therefore, as part of the consideration for the execution of the lease agreement or renewal or extension thereof, Resident agrees as follows:

1. Resident shall not engage in any criminal activity, while on, near or off the leased premises.

2. Resident shall ensure that Resident's guests, Resident's occupants and Resident's invitees shall not engage in any criminal activity, while on, near or off the leased premises.

3. Resident shall ensure that Resident's occupant's, guests and invitees shall not engage in any criminal activity, while on, near or off the leased premises.

4. Resident, Resident's occupants, guests and a invitees shall not engage in any act that is intended to or actually facilitates any criminal activity, on, near or off of the leased premises.

5. Resident shall not permit the dwelling unit, leased premises or common ground to be used for any criminal activity.

6. Resident, all occupants, all guests and all invitees shall not engage in any act of violence or threat of violence, including, but not limited to, the display or unlawful discharge of a firearm, a racial slur, a hate crime, or any property damage on or to the leased premises.

7. Resident understands that management cooperates with law enforcement agencies by allowing management to release any information contained in management's file regarding Resident and Resident's occupants to any law enforcement agency upon request. Resident agrees that Owner/Landlord/Property

1

Manager may use any police generated report as direct evidence, without objection by Resident or its occupants, in any court action, including, but not limited to eviction.

8. **<u>VIOLATION OF ANY OF THE ABOVE PROVISIONS IS A MATERIAL AND IRREPARABLE VIOLATION OF THE LEASE AND GOOD CAUSE FOR IMMEDIATE TERMINATION OF TENANCY</u>**. *A single violation of any of the provisions of this addendum shall be deemed a serious, material and irreparable violation and noncompliance of the lease, regardless of whether or not Resident has any knowledge of the violation by an occupant, guest or invitee and regardless of whether on or off the property*. It is understood and agreed that a **<u>single</u>** violation shall be good cause for immediate termination of the lease. Proof of the violation <u>shall not require criminal conviction,</u> but rather, shall require only a preponderance of the evidence.

9. In case of conflict between the provisions of this addendum and any other provisions of the lease, the provisions of the addendum shall govern. This Lease Addendum is incorporated into the lease or renewal thereof, executed or renewed at any time between Owner/Landlord/Property Manager and Resident/Lessee.

Property Name and Address:

_____
_____
_____

_____   Date: _____
Resident Signature -- Lessee

_____   Date: _____
Resident Signature -- Lessee

_____   Date: _____
Owner/Landlord/Property Manager
Signature – Lessor

DOCUMENTATION IN GENERAL

Written documentation is critical in every phase of Land-lording. Get used to documenting everything you do. Really! Everything!! Write down or record everything: Who you see, who you talk to, what they do, what they say, where you go, who was with you, who was with them, what you did, when you did it, how you did it, what witnesses were present, and etc. Is it a pain? Yes. Is it necessary? Yes.

The more documentation you have the better protected you are from false claims, misunderstood information or events, or misremembered information or events. Remember that the files about the Residents and the property belong to you and not to your Residents. Be careful never to record anything derogatory in your files such as your personal opinions, ethnic comments, the way the Resident may look, the way the Resident may talk, or jokes or innuendos about anyone. Remember to keep your writings and records about pure facts and reasonable suspicions so that if your writings or recordings ever come into evidence in a court setting or by subpoena, your records show professionalism and respect regarding your Residents. That will build credibility for you.

Know your particular State laws to see if you can legally tape record a conversation between you and another person when only you know that the recording is being made. If your State allows recordings of conversations when only one party (you) to the conversation knows about the recording, record everything with an easy retrieval system in case you need the conversation later.

Here is a list for easy review to see where your State stands on the issue:

States that Only Require One-Party Consent to Taping a Conversation:

- Alabama
- Alaska
- Arizona
- Arkansas
- Colorado
- District of Columbia
- Georgia
- Hawaii
- Idaho
- Indiana
- Iowa
- Kansas
- Kentucky
- Louisiana
- Maine
- Minnesota
- Mississippi
- Missouri
- Wyoming
- Nebraska
- New Jersey
- New Mexico
- New York
- North Carolina
- North Dakota
- Ohio
- Oklahoma
- Rhode Island
- South Carolina
- South Dakota
- Tennessee
- Texas
- Utah
- Virginia
- West Virginia
- Wisconsin

States That Require All-Party Consents To Taping Of A Conversation:
These states clearly or potentially require consent from all parties under some or all circumstances:

- California
- Connecticut
- Delaware
- Florida
- Illinois
- Maryland
- Massachusetts
- Michigan
- Montana
- Nevada
- New Hampshire
- Oregon
- Pennsylvania
- Vermont
- Washington

Therefore, right now only fifteen (15) States have a law that requires the consent of everyone involved in a conversation or phone call before the conversation may be legally recorded. The rest of the States and the District of Columbia only require one party to know about the recording – YOU. However, be aware that these rules can change by a stoke of legislative/executive office pen.

PRINCIPLE # 2

WRITTEN POLICIES AND PROCEDURES

You need to assemble a policy and procedure manual (a three ring or binder of some type – or now in the digital world, have a simple digital filing system) setting forth all of your policies and procedures, what you do, how you do them, from beginning to end, for the management of each property. That is right – if you have multiple properties that are not managed in the same way, you need a separate policy and procedure manual for each property. This is not just a good thing to do. This is a must. This type of manual is critically and essentially helpful if you ever have a discrimination complaint, have a lawsuit brought against you, or are ever in court, provided you follow your own policies and procedures. If your policies are clear and legally sound, and your team follows them, then you are generally in good shape.

If your team does not follow your own policies, your own policies will damn you. Don't think by this comment that it will be better not to have written policies. If you have no written policies, you will be completely crippled in an investigation. You must train your staff in all of your policies and procedures. Make a record of every training session, including what was taught, who taught it, who attended and the date of the training event.

 Here is some of the information you need to cover in your policies and procedures to create your policy manual.

1. ADVERTISING: You may think that how you advertise your property is not a big issue. It is. You must keep a copy of all advertisements. Make sure your attorney reviews every ad before it is placed in any advertising medium. It is way too easy to violate the law when it comes to advertising. Even the best of intentions, and sometimes because of your best intent, the law can be violated unintentionally. Discrimination in advertising is easy to do by accident. This area of the law can be brutal on a Landlord/Property Manager and the Landlord/Property Manager may not even realize it. Advertising can get you into trouble before you even get a Resident into the unit. Simply put, all Landlords/Property Managers would like to have quiet Residents that are not going to cause problems, not cause damage to the property, not cause problems for the property, and that will pay their rent on time. This desired rental scenario is sometimes difficult to find and advertising for that type of Resident can be tricky. Now you can advertise just that:

"Home for rent for quiet Residents who won't cause problems, won't damage the property and that will pay their rent on time." However, I have never seen that ad. It is actually a good ad with specific, legally acceptable, desired content, but no pizzazz or appeal whatsoever.

The following is an actual advertisement posted by a mom-and-pop owner that is probably exactly what they wanted to say. **Do you see any problems?**

"Looking for quiet, retired, married couple, non-smokers with no children and preferably over 60, to rent a 1,200 square foot house in a lovely European themed neighborhood near a Methodist Church right around the corner."

It looks like a pretty good ad, right? It sets forth clear desires on the Landlord's/ Property Manager's part. It explains the neighborhood and even that there is a church nearby. Sounds like a lovely place to live. The Landlord/Property Manager may feel very good about it and may mean no disrespect, harm, or discrimination to anyone while thinking they have done a wonderful job looking for the Residents of their dreams, having placed their perfectly articulated ad. Well, as wonderful as the Landlords/Property Managers may think this ad might be, it violates all kinds of guidelines/laws. The ad is full of what is called "steering" and other highly discriminatory language.

Steering is a term used to allege that the Landlord/Property Manager is trying to secure a particular kind of Resident while at the same time trying to dissuade other types of Residents from the property by means of words or actions that negatively impact, as in this particular advertisement, race, national origin, religion, familial status, and age. You may be saying, "You have to be kidding. What are you talking about?" Let me explain.

From a fair housing evaluation a Landlord/Property Manager must avoid verbiage in an ad that mentions or alludes to protected classes such as race (all races), color (all colors), religion (all religions), familial status (any family make-ups), age (except if an actual over 55 community exists), Americans with disabilities (any disability), gender (any gender), sexual orientation (any sexual orientation – although not yet a Federal protected class, many states, counties and local jurisdictions have prohibitions in place), military service, and national origin (any national origin).

Therefore, a Landlord/Property Manager cannot mention churches even though the mention of a church may not seem unimportant on its face, especially if those churches are actually on the "corner". There is the possible backhanded or under toned taint that the ad is actually or even unintentionally saying to readers that only Methodists need apply and others are not welcome.

The phrase "married couple" could be looked at by other applicants as a slap to familial status and that the Landlord/Property Manager may want only one kind of family as residents "married", which is prohibited in housing law.

The same goes for "no children". Unless this particular home is actually located in a designated and qualifying 55 or 62 and older community it is a violation of the protected class of familial status and age.

The word "quite" is fine under the law for the ad. The phrase "non-smoker" is fine under the law as smoking is not a protected class.

The phrase "European themed" will not fly as it has the taint of telling non-Europeans that they are not, or may not be, welcome, even if the area is actually a European-themed community. It smacks of National Origin discrimination and possible race discrimination.

Perhaps a better way to advertise this home, if it not in an over 55 or over 62 community, the ad might read something like this:

> ***"Looking for quiet, non-smokers to rent a 1,200 square foot home in quiet, historically themed neighborhood with unique, historical architecture within a short walking distance."***

If the home is in an over 55 or 62 community perhaps it might read like:

> ***"Looking for quiet, non-smokers over 55 (or 62 if it applies) years of age to rent a 1,200 square foot home in quiet, 55 (or 62 if it applies) and older community in a historically themed neighborhood with unique, historical architecture within walking distance."***

We will deal with discrimination issues in more detail in Chapter 3. Suffice it to say, any ad you place in of any kind of media, you should first run the ad by your attorney as even an ad appearing to be very simple may harbor unintended discriminatory language that you must avoid. Attorneys that deal in this area of the law can quickly recognize and remedy the ad for you.

Discrimination does not have to be intentional to be actionable. It can just be ignorant or negligent, and you wind up paying an ugly settlement to get out of a court battle that you would likely lose.
and remedy the ad for you.

 For another EXAMPLE, if you include people in your ad copy that let's say has only white people pictured, but your ad is for a property in an area that has an equal or relatively large population of Hispanics, Asians, African Americans or other group, you could be hit with a discrimination claim even if you did not even think about it, were oblivious to the issue or did not mean anything derogatory with the ad.

You also get placed on the "watch list" where you could get micro-managed and even "shopped" by government or quasi-government agencies that may attempt to catch you violating the law. Shopping the watch list can also means that a government or government funded agency sends out real or fake applicant(s) to your properties to see if you are violating your settlement agreement promises, regulations and/or laws. You must be prepared for such a situation by ensuring that you understand the law and treat everyone accordingly.

Non-Discrimination Statement: Ensure you have this statement in your policy documents that reads:

"We _____, do not discriminate based on race, color, national origin, familial status, religion/creed, gender, age, disabilities/handicap, sexual orientation or military service." Then make sure your whole staff understands the law and enforces it. You are in the Land-lording business and are now controlled by the government to a great degree. Therefore, you must comply or face severe and even draconian consequences.

1. **Rental Criteria: (This is the Big One!)**

   A. Criminal History Requirements:

This whole issue of a Landlord/Property Manager knowing about criminal history of an applicant has become a political hot potato. It can be a terrible trap for Landlords/Property Managers trying to properly and thoroughly vet prospective Residents. How you go about vetting an applicant's criminal history is fraught with snares and nonsensical and counter-intuitive rules. In my opinion, over the last several years there has been a political push to protect people with criminal histories by placing the burden of putting those with dangerous backgrounds on society by dumping them so on the Landlord/Property Manager.

Some State, county and local jurisdictions require Landlords/Property Managers to provide the applicant with all requirements regarding the lease criteria including how the Landlord/Property Manager evaluates criminal history criteria, BEFORE the applicant is even given an application to sign. That is perfect for a good Landlord/Property Manager. But some rules go too far by not allowing Landlords/Property Managers to mention or discuss criminal history until after the financial analysis is completed and approved, which financial analysis includes the Landlord/Property Manager having completed the credit report, employment verifications, banking verifications and other financial information. Pretty much a waste of time if the applicant has a criminal history that is disqualifying. In such jurisdictions, only after all of that work is completed may the Landlord/Property Manager order a criminal background investigation, background check or consumer report. Some jurisdictions do not allow criminal history of a Resident to be used at all for analysis by the Landlord/Property Manager for leasing purposes which rules completely handcuff the Landlord/Property Manager and puts their asset at risk of harm.

You have to know your local jurisdiction. We will cover this issue in more detail later in the book under criminal background checks/criminal background investigations. It is vital that you read that section and completely understand how this criminal history issue works in your local area.

Require a government issued ID and a social security card as these documents may be needed for ensuring that the applicant is the person who they say they are for identity verification purposes.

Provide your applicant a copy of the Crime Free Addendum and explain it to the applicant as soon as your jurisdiction will allow.

B. Financial Requirements:

a. FICO or Other Financial Scores – Decide on a minimum score that is acceptable to you for your particular property. Obviously, the higher the score the more limited the pool of applicants will be available to you, but also the lower the risk of possible damage to your property and possibility of receiving rent untimely or not at all. This is just a harsh reality, and in general, it is just the truth. It may sound peculiar, but my experience proves it out. Even in a jurisdiction that limits or does not allow criminal history as part of the application evaluation, it is a fact that the higher the financial score requirement or rent to income ratio, lower is the chance that the applicant has criminal history or income issues. Again, this may sound peculiar, but there is no way to get around the fact of what it is.

b. Set a rent to income ratio requirement.

c. Perform employment verifications.

d. Perform an identity verification.

e. Perform banking verifications.

f. Set forth the day and time the rent is due.

g. Set forth late fee amounts and when late fees begin to accrue.

h. Provide the Resident a copy of the rental application.

i. Explain animal policies.

j. Explain smoking policies.

k. Provide any State, county or local verbiage required.

Show these policies to your perspective Resident. In this way you can help save time for yourself and the applicant. If the applicant does not want to abide by, or does not like the rules, then it is likely that you will not hear from that person again.

AVOIDING DISCRIMINATION CLAIMS

EQUAL HOUSING OPPORTUNITY

Discrimination issues are found at this point in this book because all Landlords/ Property Managers must have some working knowledge of the basics about discrimination responsibilities <u>before</u> performing all the other functions of getting a good Resident renting the property. Discrimination issues, knowledge and application start before you ever have contact with an applicant. A Landlord/Property Manager can step into harm's way here without even knowing it happened. The discussions below are by no means a complete rendition of what a Landlord/Property Manager must know and do, but the ideas discussed do provide Landlords/Property Managers with critical and practical understandings of the issues, what to watch out for, what to be sensitive to, what should give reason for high alert and what to do.

In general, the Fair Housing rules regarding discrimination apply to the following individuals in the housing context:

- The renter;
- Any person living with the renter;
- Any person associated with the renter;
- Terms, conditions or privileges of the premises including services and facilities connected therewith;

In general, the following are prohibited actions by a Landlord/Property Manager:

- Refuse to rent housing for a reason in violation of the law;
- Refuse to negotiate for housing;
- Refuse to communicate with a perspective renter;
- Make housing unavailable (like making up reasons that do not actually exist or that do not really apply to Residents);
- Lying or presenting misinformation or misrepresentations to the renter about housing;
- Set different terms, conditions or privileges rental of a dwelling;
- Provide a person different housing services or facilities;
- Falsely deny that housing is available for inspection or rental;
- Make, print or publish any notice, statement or advertisement with respect to the rental of a dwelling that indicates any preference, limitation or discrimination;
- Impose different rental charges for the rental of a dwelling;
- Use different qualification criteria or applications, or rental standards or procedures, such as income standards, application requirements, application fees, credit analyses, or rental approval procedures or other requirements;
- Evict a Resident or a Resident's guest in violation of the law;
- Harass a person;
- Fail or delay performance of maintenance or repairs;

- Limit privileges, services or facilities of a dwelling;
- Discourage the rental of a dwelling;
- Assign a person to a particular building or neighborhood or section of a building or neighborhood;
- For profit, persuade, or try to persuade, a renter to move by suggesting that people of a particular protected characteristic are about to move into the neighborhood (blockbusting);
- Refuse to provide or discriminate in the terms or conditions because of the race, color, national origin, familial status, religion/creed, gender, disability, sexual orientation, age and military of the owner and/or occupants of a dwelling;

Understand that there are also State and local laws and ordinances regarding discriminatory classes to watch out for.

Now we will discuss each protected class separately. Most of the following information set forth below is the law on the subjects and are not just my opinions:

1. Race

Race discrimination means treating an applicant unfavorably because of their race. The legal definition of race discrimination includes mistreatment based on characteristics associated with race and discrimination because of an applicant's spouse. Creating a hostile environment because of racial harassment also qualifies as race discrimination. Race discrimination violates the law and victims can sue for damages.

The following is a sad but funny lesson (not at the time though) from my own experience:

I was teaching a fair housing class in a large room filled with about 300 Owners Landlords and Professional Property Managers in attendance. When I teach a fair housing class, it is very animated and full of real-life examples. I don't try to hide the real words and actions used by stupid/uninformed Owners, Landlords and Professional Property Managers, because it is imperative that the students understand exactly what happened so they will not make the same mistakes. I give real life cases and

44

use the discriminatory words that were actually said in the cases I present in class. My classes are very pointed and very colorful. I give a disclaimer at the beginning of each presentation so as not to be tainted with the discrimination or that somehow, I condone what Landlords in my examples have done or said. It is sometimes hard for me say the actual words and tell the actual stories that have happened for example purposes, and I have been told on a number of occasions that some of what I say is also difficult to listen to. However, the stories are gripping and I hope they get the point across in vivid ways.

While I was teaching a particular discrimination principle, I was discussing a case I had where a Landlord client of mine had decided not to rent to a particular race of people because he said he "hated" them. He called this particular group of people all kinds of names. I tried to help him understand that this mentality would get him in hot water. He did not care. This Hispanic Landlord Owner indicated that he had had serious run-ins and disputes with former Residents who were from the Philippines. He hated them and was not afraid to let the world know about his disdain until the Attorney General got hold of him and filed a complaint for his alleged discriminatory actions. He had to learn the hard way about discrimination for not taking my advice over the years.

As I explained the case to the class, about a third of the way back in the large room was an older couple that kept raising and vigorously waving their hands and arms to get my attention. They clearly either had a very pressing question or at least wanted to be immediately heard on the subject. Therefore, I stopped talking and called on the gentleman. This is what he said. I will try and spell what he said as he said it. Remember, he is from Alabama and he has a deep Southern accent. This does not happen only in Alabama:

"No, no, no Mr. Dobbins. You goter all wrong thar' boy. It ain't them damn Philipeners that cause all of the trouble and problems on our property. It's the dang darkies. The blackies. The dang niggers - the coons. That's who you gota bein a watchen out fer. Them folksel be stealin ya a blind. They be dirty and leaven your place in a tarnashion of a mess, they will. I tell ya I seen it a hundurd times. That thars the dang problem. Ya gota be real careful who ya guna be a renten ta, iffen ya knowin what ima sayen."

Well, in a room of 300 plus people you could have heard the preverbal pin drop. I could hardly contain my laughter bursting out because the couple seemed like cartoon characters. I soon learned that they were dead serious. I had seen this ideology many times before, as sad as that is. So, instead of shutting him down I just let him keep digging the hole until he finally figured out that he was a racist idiot. He shut up and dropped down in his chair, as if he could hide. I saw some steam coming out of a lot of ears that day. It was a great teaching moment.

Interestingly, and sadly, directly behind the old racist couple was a middle-aged African American couple. I just watched their faces as the old racist went on and on. I saw the shock set in as the words that came out of the man's mouth were so direct and crazy. I talked to the couple after the meeting, and they said they had never really seen blatant and direct racism like they just heard, having grown up in California. They said that the racism they were used to was much more subtle. They indicated that they were surprised by the old Alabama couple and it seemed like it was right out of a movie. We both agreed racism is out there, and more importantly, it is usually hidden and does indeed come out in more subtle ways in today's society. We also agreed that race relations are getting better as time goes by, and that these types of antics are on the decline.

Another experience I had regarding racial discrimination was in my own family. Back in the early 90's I was in Alabama (Alabama seems to be getting a bad rap in this book) at the hospital when my Grandpa was having some medical issues. He was raised in the deep South and born in the 1919. This was the first time I had ever seen direct, deep and ingrained racism where the actor did not really even realize that the actions constituted racism. I don't blame my grandfather for his racist thoughts and actions as that stuff was taught by father to son for many generations, especially in the South, and it took a guy like my dad to break the cycle. Fortunate for me.

Anyway, I walk into the hospital room and my dad is sitting in a chair watching the doctor trying to get an IV needle into my grandpa's arm. After the seventh try the nurse walked into the room and took over. She got the needle in the right place on the first try. In response to the doctor's many tries and the nurse's single successful attempt, my Grandpa said, "Boy, how long you been a doctorin?" In a heavy East Indian accent, the doctor said he had been a doctor for 22 years. Grandpa said,

"You mean to tell me you been a doctorin for 22 years and you caint even get a needle in an old man's arm in seven tries, but that little nigger lady can do it on one try? Why don't that take the cake."

My dad, who does not have a prejudice bone in his body was trying to slither away out of his chair to exit the room. Surprisingly, the nurse took it in all stride as if she had heard this kind of crazy talk many times.

Those teachings are hard to break. If those thoughts are in a Landlord/Property Manager, they will have a habit of coming out in various ways. Our jobs as good Landlords and Property Managers are to never, for any reason, stoop to labeling any people with any negative label and discussions. My dad once told me that I should trust a person until that person gives me a good reason not to trust them. And that is how it must be as a housing provider. Leave your prejudices in the confessional, in the car, or better yet figure out a way to educated yourself to get rid of them. You are a housing provider now and there is no room for that mindset in this industry. It will cost you a lot of money and

46

it will hurt a lot of people if those prejudices are not weeded out.

2. Color

Color discrimination is highly tied to race discrimination and it means treating a person poorly because of the color of their skin. It can include discrimination based on lightness or darkness of the person's skin or another color characteristic of the skin. Refusing to rent to an applicant because of the color of their skin is to engage in color discrimination. Discrimination laws prohibit color discrimination against everyone, including Caucasians.

Color discrimination is often subtle—so subtle that victims may be completely unaware that they were rejected or treated differently because of their race or color. Race and color may overlap, but they are not the same thing. Race refers to socially defined categories based on their background, while color refers to skin tone. Discriminating against employees because of their race or color also violates federal, state, and local laws.

3. Ethnic or National Origin

Under the Fair Housing Act "FHA", it is unlawful for a Landlord, property manager, real estate agent, or property owner to treat someone differently because of their national origin. National origin includes birthplace, ethnicity, ancestry, culture, and language. National origin discrimination involves treating people unfavorably because they are from a particular country or part of the world, because of ethnicity or accent, or because they appear to be of a certain ethnic background (even if they are not).

I remember right after 911 an incensed and clearly mentally unstable, nutjob shot and killed a 7/11 owner because he thought the owner was a Muslim here in America to commit Jihad on Americans. It was not in Alabama this time. It was in Arizona. The owner was in fact an East Indian Sikh. Don't make assumptions. No need to do so. Just treat everyone the same. They are Residents or applying to be Residents. You chose this industry.

National origin includes a region within a country or a region that spans multiple countries. The FHA may be violated even if a Landlord/Property Manager does not know a person's particular national origin or is mistaken about a person's national origin.

If a Landlord/Property Manager treats someone differently because he or she speaks with an accent or speaks a language other than English, it may constitute national origin discrimination. Similarly, selectively enforcing language-related housing policies (such as only prohibiting some languages or only telling certain applicants about those policies) may also violate the FHA.

National origin discrimination also can involve treating people unfavorably because they are married to (or associated with) a person of a certain national origin.

Interestingly, discrimination can also occur when the victim and the person who inflicted the discrimination are of the same national origin.

 This story is a combination of race, color and national origin with a touch of familial status tossed in. Familial status is more fully covered below.

I had a client who owned a single-family home. He rented the home to a Hispanic couple with two teenage boys. He chose to not extend the lease and gave the family a 30-day notice to the family to vacate. The family asked him why my client wanted them to move. He told the parents that since the lease term was ending that he no longer wanted to contract with them for a lease extension. They again asked why he did not want to contract with them and extend the lease for another year. My client had some very specific reasons, but he did not want to explain the specifics as he did not want a confrontation. That should have been the end of it right? Nope! The family filed a discrimination claim against my client claiming race, color and national origin discrimination. The Resident's (of the attorney for the AG) rationale was that because he would

48

not give a reason for not renewing their lease that the only possible reason had to be the fact that the Residents were Mexican and dark-skinned while my client was white.

We filed a response to the complaint and the litigation was on. My client insisted that he did not care what race the tenants were and that their race had no bearing on his decision to no longer rent to them. He said he just wanted to find a different renter because they had caused problems for him on the property. I asked what kind of problems they caused, but for reasons unknown, he did not want to go into those reasons. I told him that his reasons would come out if this case continued to deposition or trial. I told him that I really could not properly represent him without know his exact rationale. He said he would let everyone know when he thought the timing was right. I told him that the time was right now, and that I needed to know to properly represent him. Still, he refused. I was tempted to tell him to get another attorney. I told him he was paying me a lot of money for representation, and that if I did not know what I was walking into it would be impossible to prepare his defense. He said he had his reasons.

We wound up in a deposition of my client where he explained for the first time that he did not discriminate and refused to renew the lease because the Residents were Mexican or because they had darker skin than him being white. He explained that his wife was Mexican and that he loved her and all of her extended family in Mexico. I was hoping that was all that was needed to kill the case. However, he just kept talking even when no question was before him and after I told him to ONLY answer the specific questions asked of him and then to SHUT UP. Well, he could not contain himself and his emotions got the best of him in the moment. Things started to go VERY, VERY sideways. I was kicking him under the table to try to get him to shut up. I requested a recess, but he said he wanted to continue. The deputy attorney general looked at me like, "this guy is quite a cowboy, that I had lost him, and that he was about to hang himself." I looked at her with the expression that, "I know and am hanging on for dear life here". I even said that I would like a moment to confer with my client – but he blurted out on the record, "No – I have something to say, and I am going to say it all. I am not putting up with this nonsense any longer."

Then this case really started to take a dive. My client continued and said,

"I'll tell you exactly why I did not want to give them a new lease. I was trying to spare them embarrassment and heartache. I did not want to tell them the real reasons. I felt bad for them. I did not want to hurt them. I knew they were struggling. I thought if I did not say the reasons why that they would just move. But now they have me in here on trumped up charges that are just silly. I don't even think they are responsible for this complaint. I do not think they would do this to me on their own. They are forcing me to have to lay it on them. I did not think they were this stupid. I sincerely thought, at least deep down they knew the reasons why I would not lease to them any longer. It has to be the attorneys leading them down this path of insanity."

49

Everyone in the room was on the edge of their seats, even the court reporter was waiting to hear his reasons. The room was still and silent. He proceeded.

"If you must know, I hate your kids."

I thought, "Oh no – familiar discrimination! Please just stop talking!!!"

In my mind I raced to the amended complaint that would surely be coming down and thought, how am I going to put a muzzle on this guy and get him to tell me everything before he is complete toast. I am seeing the dollar signs start to roll for damages he is going to have to pay.

Then, suddenly as he continued the whole thing took a complete 180 degree turn for my client. He continued and said:

"I don't hate kids in general. I just hate your kids. Their behavior while living at my house has been just terrible. How many times were the police called to the property because of their behaviors? How many times was the fire department called to the property for an emergency where I had to get to the property in the middle of the night? I don't want to do that anymore. I don't want my house damaged anymore. I know you can't afford to make the repairs, and I am going to get stuck with all the bills just like in the past. Remember when your boys stuffed material down the gas exhaust pipe on the roof and almost killed you all and emergency services had to go out and evacuate you all? Remember when the boys nailed tires on the roof and were hitting golf balls up there and breaking windows of neighbors in the process? Remember when the boys were hitting golf balls off the roof over to the reception center across the street when they were having a wedding? Remember when they were throwing oranges from the alley at cars traveling 45 miles an hour down the road causing cars to run off the road? Remember when the cops had to come out because the boys kept spitting on the neighbor's wife when she would get out of her car when she came home from work? Remember when the boys beat every one of my trees at the house to mere stumps with 2 x 4s? Well, I am sick of it. That is why I did not renew your lease. I was sure you knew the reasons. I did not want to have an argument. I tried to be kind to you even more than I would normally, because I knew you were struggling with your jobs and with monitoring and disciplining your boys. But look, enough is enough. I am not their parent, and I am not your bank. And that is all I have to say. If the government thinks I needed to try harder than I did, then I will just sell the house and not be a Landlord anymore. I just don't care anymore, and I do need this SH$%."

You should have seen the face of the AG's attorney. It told the whole story. Surprise and dismay. The sincerity of my client was stunning. Not a shake of the head or an utterance from the renters. Needless to say, the case was dismissed. My client sold the house.

So, what is the lesson from this? When there is a violation of the lease – **FOLLOW THROUGH** and give the appropriate notices for the particular violations. Do not let this stuff linger or continue. No good can come from any of it.

4. Religion/Creed

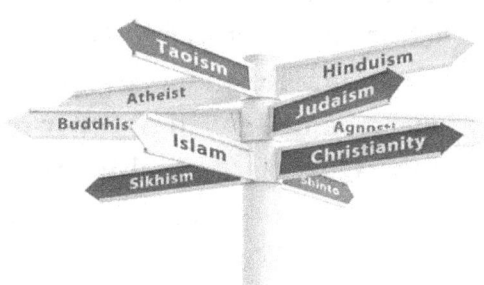

The Fair Housing Act prohibits housing providers from treating renters differently because of their religion, because they wear religious clothing, or because they engage in religious practices and/or rituals. Religious discrimination also means being treated differently by any person with the authority to rent or deal with applicants or Residents for a housing accommodation.

Discrimination based on religion may come from the housing provider, the housing provider's employees or other Residents. This means you have a high responsibility to put a stop to such discrimination. The following are some examples:

- A housing provider tells a Resident that they he needs to know a Resident's religion before the housing provider will rent to an applicant;
- A housing provider refuses to rent to a prospective woman Resident because the woman wears a hijab;
- A housing provider tells a prospective Resident that they won't like the neighborhood because there isn't a church, mosque or synagogue nearby;
- A housing provider, its employee or other Resident says rude things about a Resident's religious practices or dress;
- A housing provider, its employee or other Resident says Muslims are terrorists and not welcome;
- A housing provider ignores a Resident's complaints that its employee or another Resident is harassing them based on their religion, such as by using offensive names or painting swastikas or other symbols of religious hatred;
- A housing provider tells a Resident that they he needs to know a Resident's

religion before the housing provider will rent to an applicant;

- A housing provider refuses to rent to a prospective woman Resident because the woman wears a hijab;
- A housing provider tells a prospective Resident that they won't like the neighborhood because there isn't a church, mosque or synagogue nearby;
- A housing provider, its employee or other Resident says rude things about a Resident's religious practices or dress;
- A housing provider, its employee or other Resident says Muslims are terrorists and not welcome;
- A housing provider ignores a Resident's complaints that its employee or another Resident is harassing them based on their religion, such as by using offensive names or painting swastikas or other symbols of religious hatred;
- A housing provider allows some Residents to display Muslim images, but won't allow you to display Christian or Jewish or other religiously significant items;
- A housing provider allows Christian, Muslim, Jewish or etc., Residents to use community rooms for religious purposes but does not give other non-Christian, non-Muslim or non-Jewish, etc., Residents the same opportunity.

Be careful not to use religious language or symbols in your advertising and marketing materials unless the symbol is part of a registered trademark or logo. Although there is some instances of the word "chapel" and "kosher" that are permitted it is better to avoid the words.

Do not ask any questions that refer to an applicant's religion, whether he/she belongs to a church, or a religious organization. Be careful how you respond if you are asked about your religion. It is better to either change the subject or simply state that the laws do not allow you to discuss that issue. Do not comment on religious clothing an applicant or Resident is wearing, such as a hijab or facial scarf. Be careful in regard to your own employees as well. They may be allowed to express their religious preference at work as long as it does not impose undue hardship on you or others.

Don't refer to particular religious holidays or religions; just celebrate the festivity of the season in general. I know it sounds crazy and maybe even sad or ridiculous, and you may even feel it kind of takes away from traditional U.S. holidays of years past, but in today's world anything to do with religion can be seen as discriminatory. Don't appear to give a preference to any religious anything. Sadly, for many, terms such as Seasons Greetings instead of Merry Christmas have to be the words used to avoid even the possibility of discrimination. Use neutral messages, colors, and themes in decorating. Invite all Residents to parties regardless of religion, but do not require attendance. Make sure greeting cards, emails, newsletters are neutral as well so as to avoid preference of one religion over another. Make sure you allow equal access to community rooms for all groups of faith, or none at all.

Discrimination based on creed includes the perception of those beliefs by others.

IMPORTANTLY: You do not need to support a belief to be discriminated against because of it. The negative perception of others may be based on your dress, jewelry, a book you carry, or a symbol on a tee shirt, tie or dress. So, be careful.

5. Familial Status

Under the FHA, familial status discrimination occurs when a Landlord/Property Manager, real estate agent, or property owner treats someone differently because they have a family with one or more individuals who are under 18 years of age. The Act provides an exemption from familial status discrimination for "housing for older persons," which includes certain senior housing facilities and communities. The Act also does not limit the applicability of reasonable local, state, or federal restrictions regarding the maximum number of occupants permitted to occupy a dwelling.

Below are some **EXAMPLES** of Familial Status Discrimination:

- Refusing to rent to families with children;
- Evicting families once a child joins the family through birth, adoption, custody, etc;
- Requiring families with children to live on specific floors or in specific buildings or areas;
- Imposing overly restrictive rules about children's use of the common areas (e.g., pools, hallways, open spaces).

To qualify as a "child", the person must be under 18 years old. Also, the FHA does not simply protect people who just happen to be living with their children. Protection requires that there be at least one person in a household under 18 years old.

 A husband and wife who are seeking to rent a home with an 18-year-old child is not protected under FHA. A husband and wife who seek renting a home with a 16-year-old child loses familial status protection on the child's 18th birthday.

Residents are protected if they are expecting a child to become part of their household. A housing provider cannot discriminate against a person because the applicant or Resident is pregnant or in the process of adopting a child. Housing providers cannot count the person for occupancy purposes until the person is born or adopted.

The FHA protects families with children even if the children aren't living with their biological parents. Children may live with a biological parent, step-parent, foster parent, grandparent, or any other adult who has legal custody of them. Furthermore, if a child is living with someone whom a parent or legal custodian has designated in writing, then that household is also protected.

The marital status of adult Resident is not relevant. It makes no difference if the adult members of the family are married, divorced, single, widowed, or separated.

EXAMPLE A single mother with one child is protected just as much as a married couple with three children is protected.

For communities with a pool and/or a hot tub, strictly barring children from the swimming pool or hot tub violates the FHA. However, a rule requiring adult supervision at all times for children while using the pool or hot tub should not cause fair housing concerns; but it can. There are arguments made that if there is an age prohibition for children over 15 years old it may be too burdensome, and therefore, it can be discriminatory. I have taken the approach that anyone not of majority age needs to have adult supervision when using a facility that can cause serious injury or death as the Landlord/Property Manager will not, and is not legally required to, accept liability for the same.

Actual Case **EXAMPLE** of Familial Discrimination:

EXAMPLE A husband and pregnant wife who was seven (7) months along in the pregnancy appear at a multi-family community with 5 kids under the age of 14 to tour a 2-bedroom apartment. They loved it and want to live there. The Property Manager refused to allow them to fill out an application because it was a waste of time since they would not qualify as the policy for occupancy was, "no more than two persons per bedroom".

This is an example that typifies familial discrimination. A property has a right to its occupancy standards if those standards meet state and local rules; and in this case, they did. You may say, how then could this be discriminatory behavior by the Property Manager? As a Landlord or Professional Property Manager you certainly don't want to jam 8 people in a 2-bedroom unit, right?

When the owner and management company got the complaint from the Attorney General's Office they are confused. They think, why would we let 8 people live in a 2-bedroom apartment? What have we done wrong? What should the Property Manager have done to avoid a discrimination complaint?

Let the prospective Resident fill out an application. If they don't qualify, then they don't qualify. Generally, unless you demonstrably feel threatened, let the prospect fill out the application.

Come to find out in this case the husband and wife were just babysitting four of the wife's sister's kids for the day that they took the tour. The applicants did not say anything about the children because they did not think their babysitting that day was an issue. The Property Manager did not say anything about all the kids at the time because the Property Manager was caught off guard and thought the very question may be discriminatory. Unfortunately, the Property Manager jumped to a wrong conclusion that all the kids belonged to the couple, with no facts. Unusual, but it happens. It is usually some anomaly that leads good Landlords/Property Managers to a discrimination claim. In any event, Familial Status discrimination occurred in this case. By the way, discrimination does not have to be intentional and in fact many times, if not in most times, it is not intentional, as in this case.

Allowing every applicant to fill out the application can avoid issues like this. Once the application is completed and submitted, only then should you analyze whether the applicant qualifies pursuant to your legal rental criteria.

If the applicant is disruptive, assaultive, boisterous, etc., just call the police and in such a case that applicant does not get the opportunity to fill out the application. Today, many applications are filled out online anyway. More and more housing units are completely entered into online without actually seeing the unit before the applicant takes possession. That trend is simply the norm today.

6. Gender

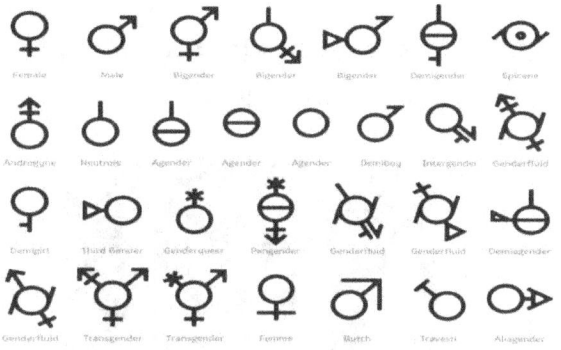

Sex discrimination involves treating someone unfavorably because of that person's gender. Gender discrimination stems from enduring traditions and long-standing legal distinctions in which representations of femininity and masculinity have had an impact on housing availability and conditions for women and men. For example, during the nineteenth and twentieth centuries, inhabitants were rarely thought of as being women, as though only men, whether single or as the head of a family, could purchase or rent their housing. These representations have not completely disappeared from public and private housing policies.

The law indicates that gender discrimination may encompass sexism and is discrimination toward people based on their gender identity. Gender discrimination is especially defined in terms of rental inequality. It may arise from social or cultural customs and norms as stated above.

It is also unlawful to harass a person because of that person's sex. Harassment can include "sexual harassment" or unwelcome sexual advances, requests for sexual favors, and other verbal or physical harassment of a sexual nature. Harassment does not have to be of a sexual nature; it can include offensive remarks about a person's sex.

 It is illegal to harass a woman by making offensive comments about women in general. Both the victim and the harasser can be either a woman or a man, and the victim and harasser can be the same sex.

Although the law does not prohibit simple teasing, offhand comments, or isolated incidents that are not very serious, harassment is illegal when it is so frequent or severe that it creates a hostile or offensive environment or when it results in an adverse decision.

Today, as in no other time, transgender and other non-traditional sexually oriented people are taking a voice and their rights are extending. More gender complaints are being filed against Landlords and Property Managers. This is an area where you need to take extra precautions regarding state and local jurisdictions to avoid expensive claims. This is also an area, like color and race discrimination, where the discriminator acts can be very subtle. Be sure to be clear in all your communications to exhibit non-discrimination.

7. Sexual Orientation (technically sexual orientation is not part of the Fair Housing Act, but treat it as it is to avoid issues and costly legal fees)

Gender is closely tied to Sexual orientation relating to housing discrimination. Lesbian, gay, bisexual, transgender, and queer known as "LGBTQ", and now an "A" has been added to the acronym making it LGBTQA. The "A" stands for "Asexual" or some say, "sexual atheism". LGBTQA individuals can face discrimination in access to housing, and there is no federal law against it. However, there may be some states and local laws against it. It can get very confusing for Landlords and Property Managers. Simply put, sex discrimination involves treating someone unfavorably because of that person's sexual orientation.

When I first started teaching discrimination law in 1993, I saw this area of discrimination coming towards housing. It is clearly here so Landlords and Property Managers need to be alert and vigilant to avoid claims of discrimination in this area. I see it becoming a federally protected class, so get used to it. Just treat everyone the same. The bottom line is the government is going to protect every person so that they have rights regarding being discriminated against when it comes to having a place to reside.

Similar to gender discrimination issues LGBTQA and other non-traditional sexually oriented people are filing more complaints against Landlords/Property Managers. These people need to also be treated equal to other people by Landlords/Property Managers. This is also an area where Landlords/Property Managers need to take extra precautions against state and local jurisdictions to avoid expensive claims as the law is not yet fully formed in this area. This is also an area, like color and race discrimination where the discriminator acts can be very subtle.

The arguments that have been made, are now being made, and that will continue to be made in Congress is that whether sexual orientation happens subtly or blatantly, such discrimination can hinder individual's access to safe and affordable housing and to the neighborhoods where they want to live. This kind of discrimination, like any type of discrimination, can diminish access to schools, transportation, and other resources that foster economic and social prosperity. I see sexual orientation being a federally protected class fairly soon. Over 20 States currently have statutes to protect sexual orientation discrimination.

8. Age (technically age is not part of the Fair Housing Act, but treat it as it is to avoid issues and costly legal fees)

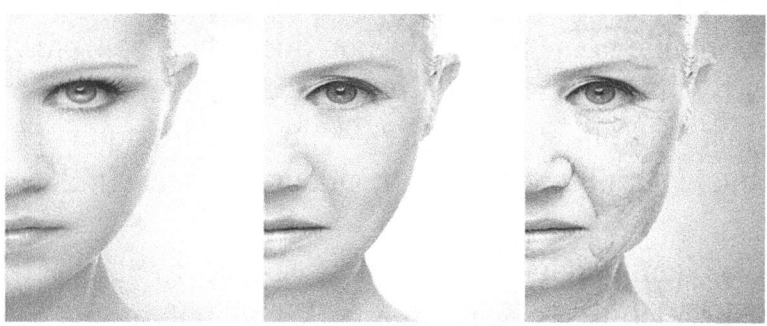

In my practice representing Owners/Landlords/Property Managers, age was never a huge issue for housing discrimination. In fact, Owners/Landlords/Property Managers love older Residents for obvious reasons. I have only seen a handful of cases in 30 years.

Age does come up in 55+ communities in a number of ways. The two most misunderstood rules about age protected communities are who can and cannot be a Resident and who can and cannot be an occupant.

To qualify as a 55+ community at least 80% of the Residents must be at least 55 years old. This shows an intent on the part of the Landlord/Property Manager to provide housing primarily to 55+ Residents. The most common reason why someone wants to live in an age protected community is because most of the people in the community are at the same place in life and it gives everyone the opportunity to mingle with older people and leave the world behind, including children and young people in general. Congress thought it was a good idea and therefore protected the notion. In such communities, the lowest age for a spouse or partner is 40 years old and the youngest age for a child is 18 years old.

There is also 62+ communities with their own rules where everyone who lives in the community must be at least 62 years of age.

In one case I had the Attorney General filed a complaint against my client for which my client was completely confused and upset about the complaint, as was I at the time – not having all of the pertinent information about the situation from my client. My client did not even know enough to explain the details because he did not understand what details were relevant. Sometimes your clients do not give you ALL of the information.

In any event, my client owned and managed a 55+ manufactured home park. A 43-year-old lady purchased a manufactured home in the park and moved in with her and her 16-year-old son. The owner gave the family a notice of eviction and demanded that they either sell the home and move out or move the home out of the park as the mother was not 55 and the son was not 18.

So why was the Attorney General involved? Here is the part that the client failed to mention. When the park was first built it was a family park open to all ages. When my client purchased the mobile home park, he wanted it to be a 55+ park. It is very hard to convert a family park into a 55+ community since you have no control over who moves in and you cannot just kick out all of the Residents that are under 55 years of age. It is hard and costly to move a mobile home. A resident is in a catch 22.

Well, when my client purchased the park he started, or at least tried to start, renting only to 55+ Residents. However, when the park was purchased, the park already had over 50% of the park Residents under 55 years of age. The fact is my client had no idea that that information was even important and did not recognize the situation as a possible legal issue. What was really happening was that he was in front of the Attorney General not just for age discrimination, but also for familial discrimination because he was trying to evict a family for no legitimate legal reason since the park never qualified as a 55+ park as the occupancy never made the threshold of 80% of the Residents being 55+.

Even after the case was settled, he still was not really understanding why he could not make the switch from what was clearly a family park to a 55+ park. The change can be made naturally, but in a family community my client had no practical way to convert to a 55+ occupancy and keep out those under 55 years old Residents at the same time. A 55+ park really needs to start off as a 55+ park. He was still bewildered by the whole thing. He felt like the government had tied his hands and would not let him do what he wanted to do with his own investment. That is true. And that is the law. Welcome to the business. So, you can see that age is often a factor that must be part of the equation.

When you are in the housing business and you have a majority partner (the Government) watching your every move; a partner who has a trump card, beware! Housing is ruled by the government and if you are going to play in the housing ballpark you also have to play by all of their rules.

9. Disabilities/Handicaps

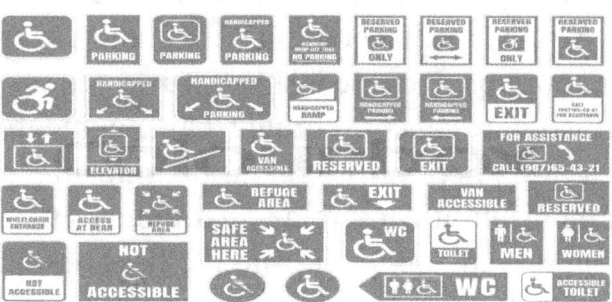

This is the discrimination area that has been most prevalent for Landlords/Property Managers over time. There is a lot to know about what disability discrimination consists of and how to navigate the minefields. This is an area where you need to rely on your experienced Landlord/Property Manager attorney to guide through the mazes, and sooner rather than later. Some things about disability discrimination are counter-intuitive. It is the kind of thing that if you don't know the law relating to a particular situation, many times you won't even know you missed the issue or made the wrong decision until it is too late. You may not understand the situation until it hits you in the head through a demand or a lawsuit. That is why it is so important to have an attorney you can trust close at hand from whom you can get quick advice regarding the situation before you. Attend discrimination classes and be thoroughly trained.

So, let's start some training now with the understanding that what is in this book is just the tip of the iceberg and will only get your toes, and maybe your legs, wet. We could do a whole book just on this issue. In fact, there ARE whole books on this issue. The following information will provide you first line protection and guidance to handle this are of the law, but remember you need constant training in this area as it changes all the time, and a competent attorney to bounce things off of when the situation arises – and they will arise.

**** *Never ask anyone if they have a disability/handicap. Whether or not a person is disabled is not part of your rental criteria. If they, or their agent, independently tell you that they have a disability at the time of the application process, at the lease signing or later in the residency, or if the disability is clearly obvious to you as it would be to any reasonable person, then you deal with the circumstances as outlined below.*

A. What is a Disability/Handicap?

A physical or mental impairment substantially limiting one or more of a person's "major life activities."

This includes emotional challenges; attention deficit disorder; recovering drug addicts or alcoholics in a rehabilitation program not otherwise convicted of a drug or alcohol related crime; AIDS; mental retardation; mental illness; people with infectious, contagious or communicable diseases; deafness; cancer; blindness; paralysis; tuberculosis and the list goes on with hundreds or other disabilities/handicaps. Some of the more common ones are lost limb, uses crutches, in a wheelchair, brain injury, autism, bipolar disorder, cancer, chronic pain, dementia, depression, diabetes, turrets, ALS, mental health, epilepsy, dyspraxia, hearing impairment, multiple sclerosis, mental health, learning disability, migraine, myotonic dystrophy, disability etiquette, visual impairment, blindness, schizophrenia, and the list goes on and on.

B. Dangerous Persons with a Disability/Handicap:

A dangerous person with a handicap is an exception to the rule on non-discrimination for handicaps. A Landlord/Property Manager does not have to rent to someone whether that are disabled or not. I will tell you this does not happen very often. A definition of a dangerous person with a handicap is:

A person whose tenancy would constitute a direct threat to the health or safety of other individuals or whose tenancy may result in substantial physical damage to the property.

Although this language is somewhat clear, learning of such a danger about someone with a handicap (or anyone else) at the screening stage is very difficult because the government has hampered your ability to make inquiry about the disability.

 Take a current drug user, or seller or manufacturer of drugs, how would you ever know if no conviction shows up in the background stage? Further, you can make no further or greater inquiry into the disabled person's background than you can into someone's background who has no disability. You cannot ask the person for privileged medical information regarding a possible handicap. So how do you tell if someone with a disability may be a danger? Usually, it is only when that person acts out and exhibits dangerous behavior during the lease term. Then, you follow through and take action.

C. Equal Opportunity To Use And Enjoy The Dwelling:

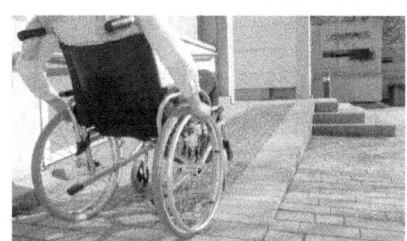

A handicapped person has a right to modifications of the rules, policies, practices and services necessary to enjoy the premises. *In such a case, the Landlord/ Property Manager must make a reasonable accommodation for the Resident. If a handicap later develops during the residency, the Landlord/Property Manager must also make reasonable accommodation for the Resident.*

D. How the Landlord/Property Manager Must Allow Reasonable Accommodation(s):

*** PRACTICAL POINT: THIS IS AN AREA WHERE LANDLORDS/PROPERTY MANAGERS MUST PAY SPECIAL ATTENTION AS A MATTER OF EVERYDAY PRACTICE

The Landlord/Property Manager Must Permit reasonable and necessary modifications of policy and accommodations to help the disabled:

The Landlord/Property Manager must permit reasonable and necessary modifications of rules, policies and services.

 If your policy or rule states no pets (or animals) allowed, but the Resident has a health care provider diagnose the Resident with a disability with a need for an accommodation for that disability, then the Landlord/Property Manager must allow the accommodation, if it is reasonable.

Accommodation means allowing a modification of the policy/rule/procedure to allow an animal - as in the case of a blind person who needs an assistive animal (not a pet, as an assistive animal is not considered a pet) or in the case of a person that has a physiological, psychosocial, or physiological impairment where the Resident needs a companion/support animal as an accommodation. In this case, if animals are allowed on the property, but there is **breed or size restrictions**, such restrictions would be **waived** for the disabled person. Further, any **pet fees** would **not apply** since the animal is not a pet. If you understand that for a disabled person the **animal is not considered a pet,** it is easier to mentally compartmentalize the issue. That does not mean that the disabled person does not have to clean up after their animal and keep the animal under control so as to not interfere with the peaceful and quiet enjoyment of other Residents. They do. The animal cannot scare or exhibit vicious behavior toward another Resident. The animal cannot cause damage to the property either.

If the disabled Resident's animal causes damage to the property, the disabled person is responsible for the cost of repair although the Landlord/Property Manager may not charge the disabled person a "pet fee" or "animal fee" or even a pet deposit. The disabled Resident is also subject to eviction for animal damages and for animals with vicious tendencies or that exhibit viciousness.

But an accommodation is not just for an animal. There are many types of accommodations that might be needed for a person's disability and there are many types of disabilities.

Remember, the Fair Housing rules are simply trying to help those who cannot otherwise help themselves in an effort to put them back on a level of living and enjoyment of life as if they did not have their particular disability. If you think of it in this way, it is easier to understand and not to look at it as if the disabled person is getting something that every other resident is not getting, even though they are.

Another way to think through the issue is to not do anything that would discourage a disabled person from renting from you, but rather to help them so that their particular life's major activities are not so substantially impairing. Having had a severely handicapped/disabled brother, I better understand why this law has evolved. Fair Housing rules are simply to help those who for so long were not only hampered by their own physical or mental limitations, but society, in general, did nothing to help ease their plight when they could do so much with little to no cost. People with disabilities typically don't want a handout. Rather, the disabled person just wants a helping hand from someone who has one to offer so they can help themselves.

Where on the property is the Landlord/Property Manager required to <u>allow</u> a reasonable accommodation?

A.   The dwelling unit – **EXAMPLES**:
 1. Handrails in the bathroom, halls or bedroom – anywhere needed.
 2. Lowering or changing door handles and water fixtures;
 3. Lowering peep-holes;
 4. Removing carpet to accommodate a wheelchair;
 5. Bathrooms, kitchens, hallways, bedrooms, doorways – anywhere in the unit.

B.   The common areas and exterior spaces - **EXAMPLES**:
 1. Pool;
 2. Spa;
 3. Recreational areas;
  a. Parking areas.
  b. Pathways;
  c. Clubhouse;
  d. Anywhere on the property.

Who is Responsible to Pay for the Modification:

Generally, the Resident is responsible to pay for the modification for a reasonable accommodation provided the accommodation requested is not a request that should have already been made based on the age of the structure. This is an area for which the Landlord/Property Manager needs to contact an attorney, if unsure.

Structures built or renovated after March of 1991 are subject to accessibility requirements, therefore, certain changes or modifications should already be made. If such accessibility requirements are not already made, then the Landlord/Property Manager would have to pay the cost of the accommodation, if the requested modification should have been in place. Also, be careful, if the modification desired has to do with any public area like the club house, walkways, lobby and etc., because it should already be accessible, and the Landlord/Property Manager would have to pay for the modification to make it accessible pursuant to the ADA as well.

What Happens with the Modifications Made for the Accommodations at the End of the Residency:

The Resident is required to restore the modification to the prior condition at the end of the residency before returning possession to the Landlord/Property Manager. However, if the Resident failed to restore the unit to its prior condition the Landlord/Property Manager now has a special unit that could be used for other similarly situated individuals with disabilities. Be careful though, if the prior disabled Resident had the modifications made, if the Landlord/Property Manager re-rents that dwelling unit with the modifications made by the prior Resident, the Landlord/Property Manager is responsible to ensure that the modification was properly made and is safe to use for the new Resident. The Landlord/Property Manager is also responsible to maintain the modification in a safe condition thereafter.

The Landlord/Property Manager can and should require the Resident to have a licensed, bonded and insured contractor make any modification and provide a signed lien waiver by the Resident's vendor before the modification(s) is/are made.

A Resident with a disability requested a reasonable accommodation for the bathtub to have handrails installed. The Property Management Company rightly agreed and notified the Resident that the request was approved. The Resident had the handrails installed. When the Resident gave notice to move, the Property Manager told the Resident they did not need to remove the handrails. The Property Manger then re-rented the unit to a new Resident that was also disabled. Everyone was very happy with the situation. Upon first use of the bathtub handrails the new Resident pulled the handrails right out of the wall while trying to get out of the tub. The Resident fell back into the tub, hitting their head on metal faucet, and cracking their skull in the process. The Property Manager made a number of mistakes. They did not:

A. Obtain the name of the company/person that installed the handrails;
B. Require the bond number from the installer;
C. Secure the insurance information from the installer;
D. Approve or even check the work performed when completed, and;
E. Ensure the safety of the handrail before re-renting the unit.

Come to find out, when the handrail was installed, the installer just used tiny plastic sleeves to anchor the handrails instead of securing the handrails with screws into studs. The results of the many errors were disastrous and costly.

The Landlord/Property Manager Can Make Reasonable Inquiry Regarding the Disability Regarding the need for an Accommodation:

Once a person notifies the Landlord/Property Manager of a Resident's disability and need for an accommodation, the Landlord/Property Manager can make reasonable inquiry as to whether the person actually has a disability and whether allowing a particular reasonable accommodation for that person is appropriate.

There are two basic types of forms to use for ascertaining whether the Resident has a disability and is in need of a particular accommodation.

One form is for a reasonable accommodation for general, non-animal related issues such as the Resident's need for a wheelchair ramp, a special door handle, a closer parking spot or whatever the need may be.

The other type of accommodation form is specifically if the reasonable accommodation is a request for an animal.

These two different forms have separate purposes and are to be completed by a health care provider, not by the Resident.

The following is a form for the Resident to provide to a health care provider for a non-animal request for a particular reasonable accommodation. The Resident can bring the form to the health care provider.

MEDICAL VERIFICATION FOR REASONABLE ACCOMMODATION

Doctor/Health Care Provider:_____
Address:_____
_____
Reference:_____
Patient's Name:_____
Patient's Date of Birth:_____
Patient's Address:_____
_____
Patient's Phone Number:_____

Request for Doctor/ Health Care Provider to Release Information:

I, _____ (Resident/Patient), request that Dr. _____ immediately release any medical information requested below to the housing facility (owner/agent/manager/employee/LLC member/corporate officer/legal representative) listed below. I request this information be delivered to the same.

_____
Resident/Patient

Medical Information Requested by Resident/Patient

Do not indicate the severity or type of disability, but rather, only whether (Resident/Patient) has a physical or mental impairment that is debilitating to the extent that the disability substantially limits one or more major life activities that has/have been documented and diagnosed by you as a treating health care provider.

□ No / □ Yes **If so, please explain (attach additional sheets, if necessary):**
_____
_____
_____
_____

The date of the last consultation with the patient _____.

If you classify the Resident/Patient listed above as having such a limiting impairment, is it your medical opinion that Resident/Patient is in medical need of a reasonable accommodation for the disability? □ **No / □ Yes**

_____
Doctor/Health Care Provider
Address:_____
_____
Phone:_____
E-Mail Address: _____

PLEASE RETURN COMPLETED FORM TO:

_____
_____
_____

FORM FOR A REQUEST FOR OR A SERVICE ANIMAL OR AN ASSISTIVE ANIMAL

If the Resident claims the need for modification of a policy and an accommodation a service animal, assistive Animal, therapeutic animal or emotional support animal the Landlord/Property Manager should provide the following form to the Resident to give to the medical provider to fill out at the exam:

MEDICAL VERIFICATION REQUEST FOR
A REASONABLE ACCOMMODATION FOR AN ANIMAL

Doctor/Health Care Provider:_____ Phone #:
_____

Address:_____

Reference:_____

Patient's Name:_____

Patient's Date of Birth:_____

Patient's Address:_____

_____

Patient's Phone Number:_____

Request for Doctor/Health Care Provider to Release Information

I, _____ (Resident/Patient), request that Dr. _____ immediately release and respond below to this "Medical Information Request" to the housing provider listed below regarding my need for a service or support animal to assist me with my disability. I request that this information be delivered to the housing provider listed below.

_____

Resident/Patient

Medical Information Requested By Resident/Patient

Please do not indicate the type or severity or the disability, but rather, only:

1.) Whether your patient has a physical or mental impairment that is debilitating to the extent that the disability substantially limits one or more major life activities that has been documented and diagnosed by you as a treating Doctor/health care provider, and;

2) Whether your patient needs an animal(s), a _____(list specific type of animal), because the animal does work, provides assistance, or performs at least one task that benefits your patient because of your patient's disability, or because it provides therapeutic emotional support to alleviate a symptom or effect of the disability of the patient and not merely as a pet.

☐ No / ☐ Yes If yes, please explain (attach additional sheets, if necessary):

_____

_____

_____

_____

Additionally, if the animal is not a dog, cat, small bird, rabbit, hamster, gerbil, other rodent, fish, turtle, or other small, domesticated animal that is traditionally kept in a home for pleasure rather than for commercial purposes, please provide the following additional information.

1. The date of the last consultation with the patient _____.
2. Any unique circumstances justifying the patient's need for the particular animal or particular type of animal, if already owned by the patient.

_____

_____

_____

3. Whether you have reliable information about the specific animal or whether you specifically recommended this type of animal. ☐ No / ☐ Yes

If you classify the Resident/Patient listed above as having such a limiting impairment, is it your medical opinion that Resident/Patient is in medical need of a reasonable accommodation for the disability? ☐ No / ☐ Yes

_____
Doctor

PLEASE RETURN COMPLETED FORM TO:

_____

_____

_____

For either form, to request an accommodation, non-animal accommodation or animal accommodation, the Landlord/Property Manager needs to verify that the Resident was seen by the medical care provider on the date indicated on the form, that the Resident has a disability, and that the accommodation is necessary for the Resident. So, once you receive the form(s) back from the doctor/healthcare provider, simply call and ask the doctor/healthcare provider if they actually saw the patient on the date indicated and if the completely filled-out form is true and accurate. Do not inquire into the nature of the Resident's disability. You are only verifying that the completed form is actually and legitimately from an actual doctor/healthcare provider.

Sometimes Residents play games with the forms and do not really take the forms to a doctor/healthcare provider for diagnosis and signing. Sometimes they get internet certificates. However, you have a right to have the form filled out by a true doctor/healthcare provider who actually saw the Resident as a patient.

Sometimes Residents play games with the forms and do not really take the forms to a doctor/healthcare provider for diagnosis and signing. Sometimes they get internet certificates. However, you have a right to have the form filled out by a true doctor/healthcare provider who actually saw the Resident as a patient.

10. MILITARY STATUS:

The Soldiers' and Sailor's Relief Act governs (SSRA) Military Status and prohibits discrimination against any service member in the Armed Forces or Veteran with an honorable or general administrative discharge.

EXAMPLE Just because someone is in the Armed Forces, a Landlord/Property Manager cannot ask how long before they deploy or how long they will be in the area. The best way to handle someone in the military is to perform all the other functions of a Landlord/Property Manager while pretending the individual or family is not in the military.

NOW, TO CHANGE PACE A BIT, PLEASE COME ON A CHRONOLOGI-AL JOURNEY WITH ME AS A LANDLORD/PROPERTY MANAGER ATTORNEY FROM SHOWING THE PROPERTY TO THE RESIDENT VACATING THE PROP-ERTY. THIS BOOK IS MEANT TO WALK YOU THROUGH THE WHOLE LAND-LORD/PROPERTY MANAGER PROCESS IN THE HOPE THAT YOU WILL NOT MAKE MISTAKES OTHER LANDLORDS/PROPERTY MANAGERS HAVE MADE THAT COST THEM A LOT OF MONEY, TIME AND EMOTIONAL TURMOIL.

Principle # 4

THE PROPERTY TOUR
An Additional Screening Tool

Today, many tours of the property are completely on-line. I am going to take you through a property tour as if the applicant was physically touring the property. Much of the physical tour crosses over to the virtual tour. Use the principles to strengthen your virtual tour as well.

When a prospective applicant decides they want to see a unit/home/etc., before you take them on the tour, have them fill out a guest tour card. Do the same for the virtual tours.

REQUIRE A GOVERNMENT ISSUED PHOTO IDENTIFICATION BEFORE AN INPERSON SHOWING OF THE PROPERTY

For security purposes, tell the applicant that one of your criteria for renting is to go on a tour and that before going on a physical property tour the applicant must provide you with a government issued photo ID that will be secured in a safe place during the tour. Then, upon completion of the tour (or before), make a copy of the ID which will be kept in company records. Return the actual physical ID only after the tour is completed.

Although many Landlords/Property Managers today handle the tour on the internet, when performed virtually, the Landlord/Property Manager loses the ability to use the tour as an additional screening tool to observe how the applicants act on the tour.

If the applicant decides not to take a physical tour because they do not want you to hold their ID or make a copy of their ID, that is their choice. However, you have been up front with them about the tour procedure and criteria. Remember, if the applicant does not want to give you their ID to hold in a safe place while on tour, or does not want you to copy their ID, then don't show the property to them. You have to decide if you want this level of protection. You only need to follow this step if you want security and if you want to use the tour as an additional and practical screening tool.

Landlords/Property Managers performing tours online do not need to worry about safety issues of the physical tour. But if you do go to the unit/house with the applicant, then all of the safety precautions come into play.

IF YOU FEEL AFRAID AT ANY TIME

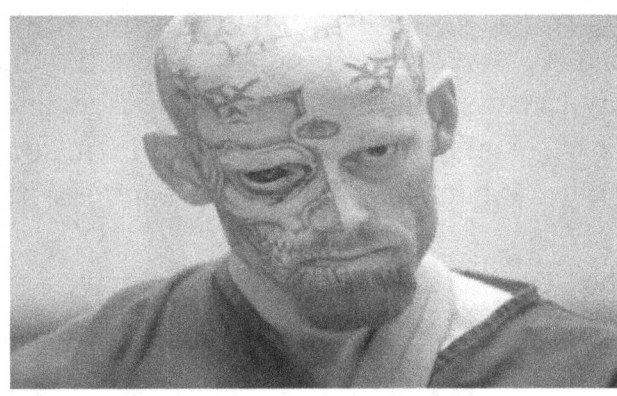

If you feel afraid or even uncomfortable about going into the unit/house with the applicant, don't go into the unit. Instead, get someone else to go on the tour with you, cancel the tour, or reschedule the tour with someone else. (remember to document your fear[s] in the file that you will create for all applicants) It is not worth taking a chance with your safety. I have found that most tour guides are female. So, you have to use extra caution. These are safety precautions just in case the potential applicant poses a risk or harm. Requesting the photo ID helps act as a deterrent to a would-be assailant as well. If the applicant has nefarious intent, this demand will help stop criminal activity.

As unlikely as it may be for a criminal act to occur on the tour, it does happen. By securing the photo ID, if a criminal event did occur, the perpetrator(s) could not go back to the office (or other safe place) to retrieve their ID since they would not know where you put it. Make sure you are out of their sight when you secure the photo ID. If the applicant fills out an application and enters into a lease, then transfer the copy of the photo ID into your property file of that Resident. This secret securing of the ID may not be practical in some settings so you will have to improvise if that is the case. You could simply take a photo of the ID and send it to your company email. At least that is something and in this digital world that may be all you need for a deterrent effect.

HAVE A PHONE WITH YOU

Make sure that you have some type of communication device with you when you go on the tour. If you do not have a walky-talky where you can talk to maintenance or other office staff, or 911, be sure to have a cell phone with you. Be sure to have the cell phone already and dialed into 911 in case you need to push an emergency panic button push. Again, if you have concerns about your safety with whoever may be touring, do not go into the unit/home. Stay outside. Document your concerns in writing in the file or on the guest tour card.

Thinking about personal protection and doing it the same way every time will be hard at first, but it could prove vital – even if it is just taking a picture of a photo ID and emailing it to your office email. Get in the habit. Most of us think, "It could never happen to me". Until it does. Never let the applicant have a key to go and do the tour alone. Arguably, you have then given possession of the unit to them, although it is a weak argument in court. Unfortunately, I have seen it happen where they have to be evicted when the police said it is a "civil matter" and not a criminal issue, and they will not take any action to remover the now squatter. You do not want them locking the door and then having to evict them, and yes it happens. It can take a month or more to get them out

Also, never give possession (the keys) before you have verified the entire application, all parties have signed the lease, you have received the security deposit, you have received verification of renter's insurance, and you have received the first month's rent in certified funds. Yes, certified funds or cash. That is the best way to start off the relationship, especially if you do not know them. Make it a policy and blame it on the attorneys. You do not want a personal check for the first payment – you do not know these folks and there is no need to take a chance with no history with the Resident. This may seem strange and even onerous, but it could save you big time if their check bounces and you have to go to court to get possession of your unit/house back – with no income.

Some attorneys take the position never to have a copy of a photo ID in the file because it could be used to show discriminatory practices. I have handled numerous discrimination cases and do not agree with that position and believe from my experiences that having a government issued photo ID in the file can actually help you. Who comes to look at a property, is who comes. It is what it is. You don't care who comes. It just is what it is. You have little control over who actually wants to view the property. Make this procedure part of your written procedures. Do the same for everyone and you are protected.

Having a copy of a photo ID proves you have a good and duplicatable procedures, good security reasons for the procedures, and that you do the same thing for every person, every time.

It has also been suggested by some attorneys that if a discrimination allegation is made, the prosecuting agency will subpoena your files, and try to show a disparate impact violation by suggesting that you did not rent to people of certain races or ethnic origins based on the ID photos and the population demographics in the area. I have never seen that happen. However, if it did happen, your actions would actually show just the opposite. Your actions would demonstrate that you show the property to all sorts of people – everyone and anyone who wants to rent. Your records of who you actually rent to will show that you do not discriminate against any protected class. The records will show that you rent to those who meet your criteria and that you treat everyone the same. You have many supporting documents including rental criteria such as FICO/rental scores, rent to income ratios, criminal history, work history, and safety reasons why you did or not rent to a particular person.

I also believe a photo ID is critical to have in the file in case a Resident loses a key or remote, for police/safety purposes and for potential future collection purposes. Again, your personal safety and the risk of liability is not worth compromising when a photo ID deterrent is so easy to obtain and to defend.

Showing the property is not a game. It is serious business. It is often the only time you will interact with the applicant before you process their application. You want to have evidence of who was visiting the property. You want the file to be complete, with information on everyone who is being allowed to have access to and control of your investment. This way you have evidence of everyone who toured and leased. The key to avoiding problems with your tour and application criteria is that you use it the same way, for every person, every time. Be consistent.

Also, if you are concerned about this issue, you could have a procedure or policy to destroy the photo ID after the tour. Then, any allegation regarding the issue is averted. However, I like having all of the information in the file.

Whatever you decide to do, write it in your policy manual and then do it the same for everyone.

Principle # 5

THE RESIDENT APPLICATION

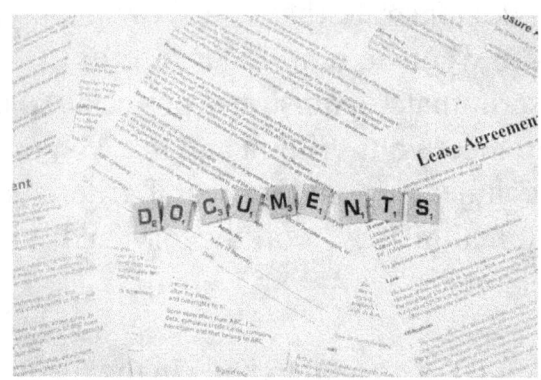

MORE IS BETTER. Let me say this again. MORE IS BETTER!!!

PURPOSE OF THE APPLICATION

There is but one purpose for the application – to gather relevant information about the applicants in order to make an informed and educated determination as to whether the applicant can meet the Landlord's/Property Manager's written criteria. You don't want to just throw the dice. You want good Residents for a long time.

The only way to perform a proper Resident screening is to have an adequate and complete application. A sample application is provided later in this chapter. It is a long and comprehensive application. I have found that having a long application is an additional screening tool. Applicants that want to hide something in their background do not want to fill out a long application. It is also true though that busy people do not want to fill out a long application. But the more information you demand and obtain on the application the better your applicant screening will be. You don't want to miss anything, so you ask for everything that is important for you to make a vital leasing decision about your investment. You do not have to use the long application as there are many short form applications, but you just take more risk when using a shorter application. However, for purposes for this chapter we will discuss the benefits of a comprehensive application and then you can use the long form or develop your own shorter form. Regardless, make it part of your policies and procedures and use it for all applicants.

The application itself is your dominant screening tool. A properly drafted application is a deterrent to potential Residents that simply do not care about other people's property, that may have ill intent, that may not qualify or that provide false information. So, make it meaningful.

The application itself is your dominant screening tool. A properly drafted application is a deterrent to potential Residents that simply do not care about other people's property, that may have ill intent, that may not qualify or that provide false information. So, make it meaningful.

Some applicants look at longer application and say, "This application is too long", and they do not want to fill it out. You may have just saved yourself from possible problems. Good risks who want to live at the property will generally fill it out – no matter how long it is. Some applicants, when seeing a long application, have inquired about the application length and asked if all applicants are required to fill out the same application. When most applicants are told that all applicants must complete the same application, they comment that they feel really good because now they know that the Landlord/Property Manager is thorough, they realize the Landlord/Property Manager really cares about the property and the Residents, and that the Landlord/Property Manager performs deep due diligence on everyone.

The question by a potential Resident about the application length should be answered by explaining that management does the best job it can to screen applicants based on practicalities, time and financial constraints. Further, management should explain that one of the reasons that the application is longer than shorter is because management wants to do the best job possible to keep those away from the property who may pose a risk of future potential harm due to criminal background or multiple other reasons. When the rationale behind the application is explained to the applicant, the applicant is usually supportive and fills out the application as it is seen as an additional deterrent to would be criminal or other harmful activity that could occur on or about the property. Many applicants are actually not only supportive, but even excited to fill out the application as they recognize it as an additional protection.
tion as they recognize it as an additional protection.

Sometimes, potential Residents refuse to fill out the application. Of course, that can be a big advantage to having a comprehensive application. That is part of the weeding out process. There is no law that governs how long an application can be. If the applicant does not want to fill out and sign the application, it tells you something may be wrong from the beginning. Better to know now than later, when it is too late.

If you have not already provided all of the rental criteria to the applicant, now is the time to do it. The reason for this is that the full criteria is an additional screening tool. If a bad guy, or one that is looking for an easy Landlord/Property Manager mark, (and they come in all flavors, sizes and personalities) sees the written criteria, that applicant may just move on. One more problem avoided. There is obviously a fine line to walk. You do not want the application so hard to fill out that good people who will pay the rent timely and will not cause problems, just walk away. However, I can promise you that if you are picky as to whom you rent to (strong rental criteria and comprehensive application), you will be much happier in the long run and much more profitable because renters will absolutely remain longer, and their awesome friends will also want to live at your properties. You just can't cave, because using a longer application seems a little bit harder than you are used to. You have to hold out, believe in the principle of a longer application, rather than shorter application, and it will be of great benefit to you in the long run.

Here is a **SAMPLE** comprehensive application.

You can add to it or take away from it, as desired. It is better to ask for too much information, than not enough information. There is criminal history information requested on this application – remember that in some jurisdictions you cannot ask about criminal history until after the financial evaluation is completed, and in some jurisdictions, you cannot ask about criminal history at all.

APPLICATION FOR OCCUPANCY

This application __must__ be filled in __completely__ to be considered for occupancy

PROPERTY _____

ARE YOU A FULL TIME STUDENT?   Yes ☐   No ☐

Are you a United States Citizen   Yes ☐   No ☐   **OR,** do you have the legal right to reside in the U.S.A.

Yes ☐ No ☐

Failure to __complete__ __ALL__ sections and for every Adult Resident and Responsible Party to sign will result in delay or denial of this application (Any co-signer or guarantor is also required to fill out an application as well)

The Landlord/Property Manager does not discriminate on the basis of race, color, religion, national origin, familial status, gender, sexual orientation, age, military status, or disability.

1. Name: _____
    SSN: _____   Date of Birth: _____
    Maiden Name: _____   Work phone #: _____
    Home phone #: _____   Description: _____
        Weight: _____ Height: _____ Eye color: _____ Hair color: _____
        Distinguishing Marks _____ Copy of Driver's License ☐ Copy of Social security card ☐
    Marital status: Married _____ Divorced _____ Single _____

2. Spouse: _____
    SSN: _____   Date of Birth: _____
    Maiden Name: _____   Work phone #: _____
    Home phone #: _____   Description: _____
        Weight: _____ Height: _____ Eye color: _____ Hair Color _____
        Distinguishing Marks _____ Copy of Driver's License ☐ Copy of Social Security Card ☐

In case of emergency, notify: _____ Phone #: _____

How did you hear about us: Apt. Guide: ☐ For Rent Mag.: ☐ Newspaper: ☐ Drive By: ☐ Other_____

If pets allowed: Type: _____ Weight: _____ Has this pet __ever__ bitten or attacked anyone: Yes ☐ No ☐

List names, social security numbers, and dates of birth of each and every applicant and occupant who will be residing at the premises:

Name: _____ SSN: _____ Date of birth: _____
Name: _____ SSN: _____ Date of birth: _____
Name: _____ SSN: _____ Date of birth: _____
Name: _____ SNN: _____ Date of birth: _____
Name: _____ SSN: _____ Date of birth: _____

1

Residential History

Please provide the following information for yourself

1. Present Landlord
   Name: _____

   Address: _____ Apt.#: _____ City/State/Zip Code: _____

   Phone #: _____ Rent Amount: $_____

   Dates Rented/ From: _____ To: _____

   For Office Use
   Only
   VERIFIED: Date: _____ Who verified with: _____

2. Present Landlord Name: _____

   Address: _____ Apt.#: _____ City/State/Zip Code: _____

   Phone #: _____ Rent Amount: $_____

   Dates Rented/ From: _____ To: _____

   For Office Use
   Only
   VERIFIED: Date: _____ Who verified with: _____

3. Present Landlord Name: _____

   Address: _____ Apt.#: _____ City/State/Zip Code: _____

   Phone #: _____ Rent Amount: $_____

   Dates Rented/ From: _____ To: _____

   For Office Use
   Only
   VERIFIED: Date: _____ Who verified with: _____

Provide the following information for your spouse, roommate(s) and every other Lessee (signer(s) of the lease):

1. Present Landlord Name: _____

   Address: _____ Apt.#: _____ City/State/ZIPCode: _____

   Phone #: _____ Rent Amount: $_____

   Dates Rented/ From: _____ To: _____

   For Office Use
   Only
   VERIFIED: Date: _____ Who verified with: _____

2. Present Landlord Name: _____

   Address: _____ Apt.#: _____ City/State/ZIPCode: _____

   Phone #: _____ Rent Amount: $_____

   Dates Rented/ From: _____ To: _____

   For Office Use
   Only
   VERIFIED: Date: _____ Who verified with: _____

3. Present Landlord Name: _____

   Address: _____ Apt.#: _____ City/State/ZIPCode: _____

   Phone #: _____ Rent Amount: $_____

   Dates Rented/ From: _____ To: _____

2

Employment

Provide the following information for yourself:

1. Name of Employer: _____
    Address: _____
    Phone #: _____   Position: _____   Direct Supervisor: _____
    Income: $ _____   Per: _____   Employed From: _____   To: _____

2. Previous Employer: _____
    Address: _____
    Phone #: _____   Position: _____   Direct Supervisor: _____
    Income: $ _____   Per: _____   Employed From: _____   To: _____

3. Previous Employer: _____
    Address: _____
    Phone #: _____   Position: _____   Direct Supervisor: _____
    Income: $ _____   Per: _____   Employed From: _____   To: _____

Provide the following information for your spouse, roommate(s) and every other Lessee (signer(s) of the lease):

(Use the back of this form if additional space is needed)

1. Name of Employer: _____
    Address: _____
    Phone #: _____   Position: _____   Direct Supervisor: _____
    Income: $ _____   Per: _____   Employed From: _____   To: _____

2. Previous Employer: _____
    Address: _____
    Phone #: _____   Position: _____   Direct Supervisor: _____
    Income: $ _____   Per: _____   Employed From: _____   To: _____

3. Previous Employer:

3

Address: _____
Phone #: _____ Position: _____ Direct Supervisor: _____
Income: $ _____ Per: _____ Employed From: _____ To: _____

For Office Use
Only
VERIFIED: Date: _____ Who verified with: _____

Provide the following information for all other occupants of Majority: (**Use the back of this form if additional space is needed**)

1. Name of Employer: _____
   Address: _____
   Phone #: _____ Position: _____ Direct Supervisor: _____
   Income: $ _____ Per: _____ Employed From: _____ To: _____

   For Office Use
   Only
   VERIFIED: Date: _____ Who verified with: _____

2. Previous Employer: _____
   Address: _____
   Phone #: _____ Position: _____ Direct Supervisor: _____
   Income: $ _____ Per: _____ Employed From: _____ To: _____

   For Office Use
   Only
   VERIFIED: Date: _____ Who verified with: _____

3. Previous Employer: _____
   Address: _____
   Phone #: _____ Position: _____ Direct Supervisor: _____
   Income: $ _____ Per: _____ Employed From: _____ To: _____

   For Office Use
   Only
   VERIFIED: Date: _____ Who verified with: _____

Other Income – *Self*

Other Income: (Verification will be requested). Please list any SSI, Pension, Disability, Student Grants, Dividends, etc.
Name: _____
Type of Income: _____ Amount: $ _____
Name: _____
Type of Income: _____ Amount: $ _____

Financial – *Self*

Bank Name: _____ Phone #: _____
☐ Checking   Acct. #: _____
Bank Name: _____ Phone #: _____
☐ Savings   Acct. #: _____
☐ Other Accounts   Phone #: _____
Bank Name: _____ Acct.#: _____

Other Income -- *Self*: (Verification will be requested). Please list any SSI, Pension, Disability, Student Grants, Dividends, etc.
Name: _____
Type of Income: _____ Amount: $ _____
Name: _____

4

Type of Income: _____ Amount: $ _____
Bank Name: _____ Phone #: _____
    ☐ Checking / ☐ Savings   Acct. #: _____
Bank Name: _____ Phone #: _____
    ☐ Checking / ☐ Savings   Acct. # _____

Other Income -- *Spouse/Roommate(s)and every other Lessee (signer(s) of the lease)*

Other Income: (Verification will be requested). Please list any SSI, Pension, Disability, Student Grants, Dividends, etc.
Name: _____
Type of Income: _____ Amount: $ _____
Name: _____
Type of Income: _____ Amount: $ _____

Financial -- *Spouse/Roommate(s) and every other Lessee (signer(s) of the lease)*

Bank Name: _____ Phone #: _____
    ☐ Checking   Acct. #: _____
Bank Name: _____ Phone #: _____
    ☐ Savings   Acct. #: _____
☐ Other Accounts   Phone #: _____
 Bank Name: _____ Acct.#: _____
Other Income -- *Spouse/Roommate(s)*: (Verification will be requested). Please list any SSI, Pension, Disability, Student Grants, Dividends, etc.
Name: _____
Type of Income: _____ Amount: $ _____
Name: _____
Type of Income: _____ Amount: $ _____
Bank Name: _____ Phone #: _____
    ☐ Checking / ☐ Savings   Acct. #: _____
Bank Name: _____ Phone #: _____
    ☐ Checking / ☐ Savings   Acct. # _____

Other Income -- *Occupant(s)/Roommate(s) and every other Lessee (signer(s) of the lease)*

Other Income: (Verification will be requested). Please list any SSI, Pension, Disability, Student Grants, Dividends, etc.
Name: _____
Type of Income: _____ Amount: $ _____
Name: _____
Type of Income: _____ Amount: $ _____

Financial -- *Occupant(s)/Roommate(s) and every other Lessee (signer(s) of the lease)*

    Phone #: _____
Bank Name: _____
    ☐ Checking   Acct. #: _____
Bank Name: _____ Phone #: _____
    ☐ Savings   Acct. #: _____
☐ Other Accounts   Phone #: _____

5

Bank Name: _____ Acct.#: _____

Other Income -- *Occupant(s)/Roommate(s) and every other Lessee (signer(s) of the lease)*: (Verification will be requested). Please list any SSI, Pension, Disability, Student Grants, Dividends, etc.

Name: _____

Type of Income: _____ Amount: $ _____

Name: _____

Type of Income: _____ Amount: $ _____

Bank Name: _____ Phone #: _____

    ☐ Checking / ☐ Savings   Acct. #: _____

Bank Name: _____ Phone #: _____

    ☐ Checking / ☐ Savings   Acct. # _____

General Questionnaire -- Answer All Questions (Adults Applicants and Juvenile Occupants)

1. Have you, or <u>any</u> (including all potential occupants) person that will be living in the premises (including any potential occupant – that includes juveniles), ever been evicted, asked to leave or move from a property, moved to avoid eviction, or moved because of any problem with another Resident or the Landlord/Property Manager?   ☐ Yes   ☐ No
If yes, please explain: _____
(write on the back side of this page if more room is needed)

2.   A. Have you, or <u>any</u> (including all potential occupants) person that will be living in the premises, ever plead no contest to, plead guilty to or been convicted of a felony involving a person, property or drugs in the past ten (10) years; or been released from custody for a felony in the last five (5) years, or been released from parole for a felony in the last five (5) years. *(Remember – check your jurisdiction if you can ask about criminal history at this point.)*
     B. Have you, or <u>any</u> (including all potential occupants) person that will be living in the premises ever plead no contest to, plead guilty to, or been convicted of any misdemeanor in the last five (5) years - (this question includes any misdemeanor or felony for which any juvenile plead guilty to, plead no contest to, was convicted or determined by a court or entered into a plea agreement and found to be or adjudicated a juvenile delinquent.)
     C. Have you, or <u>any</u> (including all potential occupants) person that will be living in the premises ever plead no contest to, plead guilty to, or been convicted of any sex crime or crime against a child?
☐ Yes   ☐ No
If yes, please explain in detail, including date of disposition, date of release, copy of disposition and jurisdiction.: _____ (write on the back side of this page if more room is needed)

3. Are there any criminal cases currently filed, open, pending, looming, awaiting final disposition, or in an indictment or pre-indictment stage for you or any person that will be living in the premises; OR are there any pending warrants or outstanding warrants for you or any person that will be living in the premises:
☐ Yes   ☐ No
If yes, please explain: _____
(write on the back side of this page if more room is needed)

Are there any criminal cases for which you, or any person that will be living in the premises, will be on probation or parole during any part of the term of the lease?
☐ Yes   ☐ No
If yes, please explain: _____
(write on the back side of this page if more room is needed)

4. Vehicles   A)
    #:_____   Make: _____ Model: _____ Year: _____ Color: _____
         Registered owner: _____ License Plate #: _____

6

B) Make: _____ Model: _____ Year: _____ Color: _____
Registered owner: _____ License Plate #: _____
C) If additional vehicles please list on back of this page.

5. **Your Driver's License #: (Attach a copy of the applicant(s) driver license to back)** *Driver's License #* _____
   Spouse's/Roommate(s)Name: _____

                                                        Driver's License # _____
   Each Occupant's/Roommate(s)Name: _____

For Office Use Only
VERIFIED: Obtain copy of driver's license for file
6. Character Reference -- *Self:* (List two references):

Name: _____	For whom: _____	(name)
Address: _____	Phone #: _____	
Name: _____	For whom: _____	(name)
Address: _____	Phone #: _____	

Character Reference -- *Spouse or Roommate(s) or other lessees* (list two):

Name: _____	For whom: _____	(name)
Address: _____	Phone #: _____	
Name: _____	For whom: _____	(name)
Address: _____	Phone #: _____	

Character Reference -- *Occupants/Roommate(s) for each occupant* (list two):

Name: _____	Phone #: _____	
Address: _____	For whom: _____	(name)
Name: _____	Phone #: _____	
Address: _____	For whom: _____	(name)

If additional space is needed for references or any other requested information, use the back of this page.

False Statements or Incomplete Information Will Be Grounds for Denial of this Application, and for Eviction if Information Provided is Later Learned to be False or Misleading

This application must be signed by all adults who will occupy the premises before it can be considered by Landlord/Property Manager. Acceptance of this application, and any monies deposited herewith, is not binding upon Landlord/Property Manager until approved by Landlord/Property Manager in writing. The Application fee is <u>non</u>-refundable. If anything in this application is found to be false or misleading, even if the residency is approved, Residents will be subject to immediate termination.

7

Non-Refundable Application Processing Fee: $_____

In compliance with the FAIR CREDIT REPORTING ACT this notice is to inform you that the processing of this application including, but not limited to, making any inquiries deemed necessary to verify the accuracy of the information herein, including procuring consumer reports from consumer credit reporting agencies and obtaining credit information from other credit institutions, may be performed by Owner/Landlord/Property Manager or its agents or vendors. The undersigned agrees that this application and any information reported to the Owner/Landlord/Property Manager will remain the property of Owner/Landlord/Property Manager. I/we hereby grant the Owner/Landlord/Property Manager and their representatives, affiliates, agents and vendors, the right to process this application and to obtain my consumer reports, including my credit, social media and criminal history information from any credit reporting agency, or any other source, now and at any time during my tenancy, if my tenancy is approved. Owner/Landlord/manager/assignee may also obtain my credit reports thereafter for collection purposes at the sole discretion of Owner/Landlord/manager whether a judgment is obtained or not. I/we agree that at all times during the lease should Owner/Landlord/Property Manager require a new application to be filled out, I/we agree to fill out a new application within ten days after a written request is made. Failure to do so shall subject me/us to immediate termination at the Owner's/Landlord's/Property Manager's sole discretion. Additionally, I/we authorize all corporations, companies and law enforcement agencies; academic institutions; lending institutions; current and former employers; Landlords; Owners; Property Managers; Courts; mortgagees; lenders; courts; and character references to release information they may have about my/our credit, criminal history, employment history, banking history, financial history, rental/ownership history, academic history, character history or any other information needed by Owner/Landlord/Property Manager/Assignee. Applicant hereby releases Owner/Landlord/Property Manager, their agents, attorneys, associates, affiliates, members, employees, vendors, stockholders, and all others performing any investigation regarding this application or for any other purpose from any and all liability or claims whatsoever, including class action participation of any kind. A photographic or faxed copy of this authorization shall be as valid as the original. Lastly, I have also signed a separate one-page Federal Disclosure and Authorization for said investigation. (see below for a copy of the separate, one-page Federal Disclosure and Authorization)

The signatures below authorize the Owner/Landlord/Property Manager to obtain a credit/consumer report for analyzation purposes for housing.

Owner, Landlord, or Property Manager

X_____

Signature of All Applicants and Guarantors

X_____

X_____

X_____

X_____

ABOUT THE FOLLOWING ADDITIONAL AUTHORIZATION FORM:

The next authorization form is a federal authorization form set forth below and it changes from time to time. Therefore, you must run this document through your attorney for approval before use. You need to follow the advice of your own attorney regarding this federally mandated authorization form to ensure you have an up-to date authorization form.

FEDERAL REQUIREMENT: SEPARATE, SINGLE-PAGE, WRITTEN DISCLOSURE TO CONSUMER AND AUTHORIZATION BY CONSUMER

FOR PROCUREMENT OF INVESTIGATIVE CONSUMER REPORT INFORMATION THROUGH A CREDIT REPORTING AGENCY

1. **CLEAR, ACCURATE AND CONSPICUOUS DISCLOSURE** pursuant to the Federal Fair Credit Reporting Act 15 U.S.C. Section 1681b:

I am a consumer and understand that this document represents formal notice to me that _____, a housing provider or its agent, shall obtain an investigative consumer report (background investigation information) for housing purposes.

2. **AUTHORIZATION** pursuant to the Federal Fair Credit Reporting Act 15 U.S.C. Section 1681b:

I authorize my prospective housing provider to obtain any information regarding me to complete a background investigation (consumer report) which may include, but is not limited to, information about my: character; general reputation; history of payments; driving record; drug screenings; credit bureau reports from any credit reporting agency; workman comp claims; social security number, addresses and date of birth verifications; judgments; criminal history; public records; social records; private records; and, evictions.

_____   _____
Applicant Signature   Date

OR --- you can do the following instead:

If the Owner/Landlord/Property Manager uses a company like Rent Perfect, then the Owner/Landlord/Property Manager does not need to worry about any authorization at all (AND THIS IS A CRAZY COOL WAY TO AVOID ANY ISSUES WITH THE FAIR CREDIT REPORT ACT COMPLIANCE) to obtain the applicant's consumer report because Rent Perfect will accomplish the authorization for the Owner/Landlord/Property Manager directly with the applicant and share it with the Owner/Landlord/Property Manager based on the applicant's written instruction as follows:

CONSUMER'S WRITTEN INSTRUCTIONS FOR RELEASE AND USE OF MY CONSUMER REPORT

I authorize and instruct Rent Perfect to obtain and instruct Rent Perfect to release and deliver my consumer report to ABC Property Management Company, LLC.

_____   _____
Applicant Signature   Date

KNOW YOUR JURISDICTION

In some jurisdictions, you cannot ask about criminal history or eviction history at all. Yes, the government has and continues to pass rules to protect criminals. As a result, these governmental actions throw the burden of societal problems on Landlords and Property Managers. There are more jurisdictions that do not allow a housing provider to discuss criminal issues before the financial analysis is completed. KNOW YOUR JURISDICTION.

As of February 2020, be careful in Seattle, Cook County Illinois, D.C., Minneapolis, Kansas City and New York City. There is a push by some government entities to protect those with criminal history so that the public can't even know anything at all about criminal history - ever. This is similar to States and Cities that have "banned the box" for employment screening – but much worse.

Ban-the-box means there is a prohibition for an employer asking an applicant anything to do with criminal history until after a conditional offer for employment is made with the idea that learning about criminal history in the application does not allow the employer to get to know the applicant first before the applicant is tainted with his/her own criminal history. It is in my opinion an exercise in stupidity at a terrible cost to the employer.

However, in the housing arena it is worse. In some jurisdictions, even after the Landlord/Property Manager makes a conditional offer of housing, the Landlord/Property Manager does not get to then run a criminal history and cannot use criminal history or evictions at all in the Landlord's/Property Manager's analysis for determining a applicant's worthiness to lease.

How does a Landlord/Property Manager deal with these crazy rules? First, again, know your State and local laws on the matter. If draconian laws do exist in your jurisdiction, you follow whatever they are until they are changed or a legal way around them is found. Or stop investing in areas that have such laws. If there are laws, rules or ordinances that do not allow the use for criminal history or eviction history, one thing you can do is raise your financial score requirements/criteria and not worry about criminal history at all because, generally, not always, people with recent (5-10 years) criminal history, or those that have recently been released from custody, have poor credit, usually not over a 550 FICO score.

There are also HUD implications for Landlords/Property Manager that we will cover later in this book.

When analyzing the application, and the applicant(s) actions while in your presence, be aware of a few issues that can help you avoid a rental disaster. We call these issues "Red Flags". Red Flags warn you of impending danger(s) that require additional questions and inquiry, and a need for a deeper investigation of the applicant(s). You need adequate time to ensure that you are properly screening/vetting your applicant(s) and digging deep enough into every applicant to protect your property, you, and your staff.

Applicants may have just been evicted, left the last landlord in the middle of the night without paying, damaged the last property, have criminal issues, or have other problems they may be trying to hide which would preclude them as a qualified renter(s). You need to know. Desperate people can resort to almost any tactic, any lie, or any fraudulent effort in an attempt to trick a Landlord/Property Manager. Don't be fooled.

Although these folks may be in dire circumstances and in serious need of help, they may also be smooth talkers   and may appear to be awesome potential renters at first appearance, stay the course to follow through with your applicant investigation. Follow your screening processes and don't cut corners. You don't want to end up with a non-paying Resident, or one that is going to otherwise be a headache just because you were trying to help. The following are some of the Red Flags to consider:

A. When an applicant wants to move in immediately – like today or tomorrow. They may be driving a U-Haul, Budget or Penske type truck trying to find a place to live right now. Either way, that should seem suspicious to you. Most people don't look for a place to live like that. They may be driving around in what appears to be a vehicle fully loaded with clothes and/or household goods. They may make you feel pressured to let them have possession of the unit by showing you their little children, or whatever, to pull at your heartstrings. They may even offer to pay you extra money to move in right away, to pay an additional security deposit, or to pay pre-paid rent - like a check for six (6) months of rent. They may have lots of compelling reasons why they want, or need, to move in right away. They may come across as genuine, humble, lovely and worthy. Don't do it. These are your signs that something is wrong; and maybe, terribly wrong. You need to move through your list for screening/vetting applicant(s) as youwould any other applicant, on your timetable, and carefully.

B. When the applicant is in a big hurry.

C. The applicant makes statements, or asks you questions, like:

 a. How far back does your screening process go?
 b. How long does your screening process take as we are in a bit of a hurry to find a new place,"with my new job and all", "because we already moved out of our old place", "because we just got to town", or whatever.
 c. What are your requirements regarding criminal "things"?
 d. Does it matter how long we have had our jobs, or how much money we make?
 e. Do you do a background check?
 f. "If you contact our landlord, he did not like us just because we had kids (or whatever). He wasa total jerk and constantly pestering us."
 g. They start trying to explain issues they have in life before you even provide them with an application or before they have even looked at the property.
 h. You notice that they treat each other, and/or their children, in a rough manner, and/or they shout or scream at each other, or at their children.
 i. They are driving a beater vehicle that looks like they are living in it or looks like everything they own is in the vehicle. Perhaps the tag for the vehicle is expired.
 j. Something just feels off with the way they act or the comments that they make.

D. When an applicant has a gap in where they lived or worked. These situations require additional questions.

E. When a 35-year-old applicant's last landlord on the application reads something like, "living with parents", you must dig deeper. Did they get evicted? Did they just get out of prison?

F. When the property is not available on online, yet the applicant does not want to take a tour of the property before signing a lease. Something is wrong.

G. When the social security number investigation finds no credit history for the applicant. That is common for an eighteen 18-year-old, but not for the 25-year-old.

H. When verifying employment income, the person answering the "business" phone does not sound like they are from a "Company" or from a real business. That can take many forms:

    a. They answer, "hello" instead of, "XYZ Company, this is Martha, how may I help you". Why? That sounds suspicious.

    b. You can tell that the person you are talking to has no idea what they are doing, yet they are supposed to be the Human Resources Manager or the applicant's boss. Why? That sounds suspicious.

    c. Most professional companies will not even verify income on the phone and demand a written request signed by the applicant, yet the supposed large company you are calling has no such requirement. Why? That sounds suspicious. Or, the company does not have an email address, fax number or website. Why? That sounds suspicious.

And the list goes on. If at any stage of your application analysis something feels or sounds off, or sounds suspicious, that is a Red Flag warning you that you need to dig deeper and ask more questions. Screening/Vetting an applicant is as much of an art as it is a science. You need to watch and listen to what is happening regarding the dynamics of your prospect(s). You get better at it with time and experience – like anything.

Principle # 6

RENTAL CRITERIA

Qualifying Criteria of an Ideal Tenant

Good financial history   Clean background check   Clean eviction check   Stable employment   Sufficient income   Positive reference checks

The rental criteria are simply the factors you use to determine if an applicant will qualify for possession and control of your hard earned, expensive asset such as: a person's rental history, employment history, criminal history, financial history, credit history, social media history and other history. History is the best determining factor of how someone is acting now or will act in the future.

Once you have set your criteria for renting in place a copy of your rental criteria in your policy and procedure manual. Each property can have different criteria, depending on the demographic of the property and other factors. Provide a copy of the rental criteria to the applicant at the first possible opportunity, post it to be seen, email a copy before a property tour is scheduled, at the tour of the property, but not later than the application phase. Why? Because the criteria provides the applicant with the critical factors that will be considered to make a determination for their occupancy approval or denial. The criteria is an additional, important and, of course, critical screening tool for the Landlord/Property Manager. It sets the stage for the Resident to know that the Landlord/Property Manager has control of the property, will be hands on, and that the property is not a place where a Resident will be able to go unnoticed. It is a significant deterrent to someone that wants to live in a property where there are no rules or weak rules, and where the Landlord/Property Manager really does not pay attention or does not care. It sets forth what is important to the Landlord/Property Manager and gives the applicant a pretty good idea of whether or not he/she/they will qualify to reside in the property or even want to live at the property. It is a form of security for the applicant and Landlord/Property Manager.

There is no sense for the applicant to waste a non-refundable application fee when he/she/they does not think they will qualify under the criteria, or for you or your agent to waste time showing a property or processing an application if the applicant does not think they will qualify or does not want to try to qualify.

Additionally, once the applicant reads the rental criteria, the applicant can see that the Landlord/Property Manager has straightforward, clear rental standards; that the Landlord/Property Manager is serious and thoughtful; and that the applicant can weigh out the criteria to determine if the property is right for them, without pressure. And generally, someone who knows they will not qualify based on the written criteria will not take a tour and will not fill out the application. It cuts down on both of your wasted time and money. This kind of communication helps everyone and sends a message to those that do fill out the application that there is structure at the property, and that the Landlord/Property Manager cares about the property. It also cuts down on the number of people who will have interest in your property. That can be good and bad depending on the property location and the market.

The following are items you can chose from to form your own rental criteria:

Rental Criteria Elements

1. Criminal History

Again, know your jurisdiction and its limitations regarding how you must deal with this issue. But you have to develop your own criteria upon which to judge an applicant. I will go through a simplified version of what to do at the end of this criminal history section and provide an article I wrote that will provide you greater insight on this issue at a deeper level.

Here a set of criteria to consider use; but run it by your attorney first.

A. Felonies: No felony involving persons, property, drugs, gangs, weapons, honesty, violence for the past ten (10) years.

You should also analyze the ten (10) years not just from the date the criminal act was committed, but from date of release from custody and/or release from parole, which ever occurred last. Someone could have committed a felony fifteen (15) years ago and have just been released from prison or just released from parole. In that case the person would have had little or no time in society to see how they would act or respond to life outside of prison or court ordered supervision. That may not be a risk you want to take, especially with the high recidivism rates that inmates experience. But it is something you need to consider and be prepared for from a policy standpoint. You will need to set your own criteria with your attorney, and place it in your written policies and procedures manual.

Be careful not to set a policy of "no felony of any kind, ever". The AGs and HUD have made it clear in their guidelines that having such a policy with those or similar words can be indicia of discrimination because such a policy does not allow for an individualized assessment of the applicant based on the nature and seriousness of the crime, the time that has passed since the crime occurred and the degree of danger or type of impact that that type of crime may have upon the property, the manager, the staff or other residents.

B. Misdemeanors: No misdemeanors involving persons, property, drugs, gangs, weapons, honesty, violence within the last five (5) years.

C. Diversions: An issue with misdemeanors and felonies is that many times a person does not plead guilty to the charge but is offered some type of diversion to avoid a conviction and/or jail time. A diversion can take many forms. The main ingredient of a diversion is that the defendant must do something for the Court and/or the Prosecutor in order to get the matter dismissed. It does not mean the defendant did not do the criminal act. It means that a deal was cut that if the defendant took classes, paid a fine, did community service or a combination thereof, that the matter would be dismissed upon successful completion of the probation terms.

So, you should consider limiting occupancy to applicants with diversions for felonies and misdemeanors depending on the nature and seriousness of the criminal activity, the time since criminal activity occurred, the age of the applicant when the activity occurred, and the impact of the type and seriousness of the criminal activity regarding renting your property to the applicant.

Some States, like California, prohibit Landlords/Property Managers from using diversions in their analysis, but rather only allow actual convictions to be used for evaluation purposes. I say it a lot - know your jurisdictions.

D. Sex and Children: No felonies or misdemeanors involving children, or sex offenses – ever!

Again, generally, under the HUD guidelines, a Landlord/Property Manager needs to avoid the word "ever" when analyzing criminal history and a prohibition standard. But in cases of children and sex offenses, a strong argument has been made that such crimes may be a risk so severe, a Landlord/Property Manager just cannot take such a high risk.

Beware here, it is common for those who have committed sex crimes or crimes against children to try and hide their crimes by changing their name, social security number, birth date, addresses, etc. You should also always check your state's sex offender registry and the National Sex Offender Registry at https://www.nsopw.gov/ to see if your applicant is on it.

E. Two or more DUI's in the last five (5) years.

F. No open, pending or looming criminal cases in the categories of offenses mentioned above.

G. No diversion cases of any kind in the categories of offenses listed above.

H. No cases for which the applicant is on probation or parole.

J. No open warrants.

Below is a more in depth look at criminal history criteria in relationship to HUD.

HUD GUIDELINES FOR PRIVATE HOUSING PROVIDERS: The following is an article that I wrote regarding the 2016 HUD Guidelines (the most comprehensive modifications in many years) for using criminal history in your analysis for residency, which includes my updates and re-publishing by the Idaho State Bar Magazine the "Advocate" in 2019.

How to Comply with the April 4, 2016, HUD Fair Housing Standards When Landlords Use Criminal History for Rental Analysis

The U.S. Department of Housing and Urban Development (HUD) issued Guidelines on April 4, 2016, addressing what providers or operators of housing (Landlords, owners, management companies, real estate agents, etc. that rent or lease residential property) must do to avoid discriminatory effects and disparate treatment of Tenants when a Landlord refuses to rent or renew a lease based on a Tenant's criminal history. I have found that many attorneys and Landlords are not familiar with HUD's Guidelines. This article summarizes HUD's Guidelines and provides helpful suggestions for attorneys to use in advising Landlord clients.

The Good News

Landlords can, and must, still use criminal history in their analysis to determine if an applicant qualifies for residency, unless their jurisdiction prohibits the same. However, HUD's Guidelines require that Landlords avoid discrimination in doing so. Good Landlords have been doing what HUD set forth in its Guidelines long before 2016. Good Landlords don't discriminate based on any of the reasons set forth in the HUD Guidelines. Good Landlords already do the right things for the right reasons. The reasons why good Landlords must use criminal history as part of the application process (when not jurisdictionally prohibited) is to do the best they can to avoid risk, protect other Tenants, protect their investments, avoid legal liability for failure to provide reasonably safe premises, avoid having neighbors sue them for placing a bad element next door, and protect their employees and agents.

The Bad News (if any)

Attorneys should advise their Landlord clients to do a better job of documenting why they denied an applicant and revisit their Landlord's policies and procedures (especially the rental criteria) to ensure those policies and procedures are supported by legal justification. HUD has suggested several steps Landlords can take to avoid discrimination and to treat Tenants fairly. I will set forth these steps with specificity below. Employers have been taking most of these steps for years. It is not difficult for good Landlords to do the same. As attorneys, we can teach Landlords how to find a safe harbor in the HUD Guidelines.

First, it is important to understand the basic background and reasons why HUD claims the Guidelines have been implemented. HUD cites statistics that African Americans comprise about 36% of the total U.S. prison population, but only 12% of the Nations' total population. Hispanic Americans account for 22% of the prison population, but only 17% of the total population. White Americans comprise 34% of the prison population and 62% of the total population. Consequently, HUD opines that criminal records-based barriers to housing (criminal background checks) are likely to have a disproportionate impact on minority housing seekers. Most people understand that being released from prison or having a criminal record presents obstacles to finding a good job and good housing, regardless of race or national origin. While those obstacles are not the fault of Landlords, Landlords have to be mindful not to discriminate against people with criminal history based on race or national origin. Therefore, while HUD recognizes that having a criminal record is not a protected characteristic under the Fair Housing Act, criminal history-based restrictions on housing opportunities violate the Act if, without justification, their burden falls more often on renters or other housing market participants of one race or national origin over another (i.e., discriminatory effects liability). Additionally, intentional discrimination in violation of the Act occurs if a housing provider treats individuals with comparable criminal history differently because of their race, national origin or other protected characteristics (i.e., disparate treatment liability).

HUD sets forth three steps to analyze for determining whether a claim that a housing provider's use of criminal history to deny housing results in a discriminatory effect in violation of the Act.

Step One: Whether the Criminal History Policy or Practice Has a Discriminatory Effect.[vii]

The complaining party (or HUD) must prove that the Landlord's criminal history policy actually or predictably resulted in a discriminatory effect or resulted in disparate impact due to race or national origin. This step will depend on the facts. Since this step is not something specifically for the Landlord to accomplish, we will move to step two (2).

Step Two: Evaluating Whether the Challenged Policy or Practice is Necessary to Achieve a Substantial, Legitimate, Non-discriminatory Interest.[viii]

If a complaint has been made against the Landlord, the Landlord must prove that the challenged policy or practice of using criminal history in its application process is justified or necessary to achieve a substantial, legitimate, non-discriminatory interest. This means proof showing the challenged policy actually achieves that interest. So, what is a substantial, legitimate, nondiscriminatory interest? HUD does not provide a litmus test or list of what is acceptable and what is not acceptable. Generally, the interest must be real, not hypothetical or speculative, or a pretext. Such an interest is usually for the protection of property (the Landlord's investment), of other Residents, or from risk of liability of some sort (for Example, an owner's or Landlord's duty not to put its neighbors at risk of harm)or for other important reasons. The Landlord must also produce reliable evidence that the policy or practice actually assists in protecting Resident safety, the property, or other important and legitimate reasons.

Landlords, with the help of experienced Landlord attorneys, should draft criminal history policies with substantial, legitimate, non-discriminatory interests in mind. Attorneys should advise Landlords to consider the following points in drafting written criminal history policies:

First, do not exclude anyone because of an arrest record alone. However, an open or pending case is more than just an arrest. If a case that may pose risk is being litigated, then such an issue or interest in that case may well be substantial, legitimate and non-discriminatory. It will always depend on the facts.

Second, do not include a blanket prohibition, such as, "No felonies ever", or "No criminal convictions ever". There is one exception that HUD has made. A Landlord may discriminate for a conviction of illegal manufacture or distribution of a controlled substance as set forth in 21 U.S.C. § 802. [x]

Third, look at the nature and gravity of the conviction. What kind of crime was committed and how bad was it? What poses unacceptable risk and what does not? Even here you will need to be careful. For Example, a conviction for sexual misconduct with a minor when the applicant was nineteen and the minor was sixteen. Now the applicant is thirty-one. He married the minor when she turned eighteen. They have three children. Consider the nature and gravity of the conviction, not just that the conviction exists. Although you cannot re-litigate a case, you can to some degree often evaluate whether the applicant's conviction actually poses a risk of harm. HUD recognizes that Landlords can generally rely upon a court conviction record for what is stated in the case disposition. However, HUD also states, "Bald assertions based on generalizations or stereotypes that any individual with an arrest or conviction record poses a greater risk than any individual without such a record, are not sufficient to satisfy this burden." Therefore, the criteria must be specific when looking at the nature and gravity of the crime and the assessment of risk from that crime regarding whether or not to rent to that applicant.

Unfortunately, what the HUD Guidelines do not explain is that if a Landlord does not do what the Landlord is able to do (what is commercially available) to obtain criminal history records information (a criminal background investigation or at least some kind of serious background check), then the Landlord may well become civilly liable for the criminal act of a third party. Such liability would not be for discrimination, but for negligence. A Landlord may be found negligent if the Landlord rents to a person that poses a risk that the Landlord should have, and could have, known about and that applicant later causes harm to another for which the Landlord was responsible to provide reasonable safety. So Landlords must walk a fine line not to discriminate while still trying to ensure protection for liability claims.must be specific when looking at the nature and gravity of the crime and the assessment of risk from that crime regarding whether or not to rent to that applicant.

Crimes	Nature & Gravity	Time Elapsed	Substantial, Legitimate, & Non-discriminatory Landlord Interests
Felonies	Murder, manslaughter, robbery, burglary, theft, arson, violence of all types, drug-related crimes, crimes against persons, crimes against property, (list all that pose a risk to persons or property).	Ten years from the date of conviction or release from custody or release from parole, whichever occurs last.	To protect the Residential unit from harm; unknowing neighbors, Tenants; Protect management from harm; Protect owners from premises liability and other potential risks regarding responsibilities for reasonable safety.
Crimes Against Children & Sex Crimes	Case-by-case evaluation. The applicant may need to provide Landlord with a police report and other documents for review.	Case-by-case evaluation (but in some instances a long time period because the risk can be much higher). In many cases the crime may be so heinous or repugnant that "never" may be the answer.	To protect the Residential unit from harm, unknowing neighbors, Tenants; protect management from harm; Protect owners from premises liability and other potential risks regarding responsibilities for reasonable safety.
Misdemeanors	Assault, disorderly conduct, theft, violence of all types, crimes against persons, drug-related crimes, crimes against property, (list all that may pose risk to persons or property)	Five years from the date of conviction or release from custody, whichever occurs last.	To protect the Residential unit from harm, protect unknowing neighbors, Tenants; protect management from harm; Protect owners from premises liability and other potential risks regarding responsibilities for reasonable safety.

Fourth, consider how long has it been since the conviction occurred. For felonies and misdemeanors, how long is long enough that the applicant no longer poses a risk for which the Landlord may be held responsible? Obviously, it is legitimate to have a longer prohibition for felonies than for misdemeanors since the nature and gravity of a felony is worse than it is for a misdemeanor. Even in court, felonies can be used against a witness to impeach the witness's propensity for truth and honesty. Most jurisdictions allow a witness to be impeached for up to ten years after conviction of a felony. HUD has not stated what timelines are reasonable to use in assessing felonies or misdemeanors in the rental application process. HUD has only offered that after six or seven years without reoffending, the risk of new offenses by a person with a prior criminal history begins to approximate the risk of new offenses among persons with no criminal history.[xiii]

Fifth, Landlords need to determine what interests are substantial and legitimate, so they do not discriminate. I suggest a tailored approach where the Landlord determines:

- what crimes pose a risk and why.
- what constitutes a reasonable time period of no criminal involvement after which the applicant no longer poses a risk.
- and the substantial, legitimate, and non-discriminatory interests involved.

With any tailored approach such as listed above (list of crime and for a time period), a Landlord/Property Manager must be able to prove that the Landlord's/Property Manager's policies are necessary to serve a substantial, legitimate, non-discriminatory interest. Policies must accurately distinguish between criminal conduct that indicates a demonstrative risk to Resident, staff and property safety, and criminal conduct that does not. Of course, such a determination must be made on a case-by-case basis.

Sixth, if an applicant feels his or her application should not have been denied based on the applicant's criminal history, the Landlord/Property Manager must provide an individualized assessment. This means that the Landlord/Property Manager should look at other information such as mitigating information beyond that contained in the applicant's criminal record such as inaccuracies, incompleteness, or circumstances surrounding the conviction, the age of the applicant at the time of the criminal conduct, evidence that the applicant has maintained a good Tenant history before and/or after the conviction or conduct, evidence of rehabilitation efforts, and any other mitigating information provided by the applicant.

Finally, pursuant to their policy, Landlords/Property Manager's should provide a copy of their criteria to Tenants early in the application process so that the Tenant will know what to expect for the criminal history evaluation.

Step Three: Evaluating Whether There is a Less Discriminatory Alterative.

If the Landlord/Property Manager proves that its criminal history policy is necessary to achieve its substantial, legitimate, non-discriminatory interest, then the burden of proof shifts back to the plaintiff, or HUD, to prove that such interests could be served by another practice that has a less discriminatory effect. What does that mean? HUD would evaluate the elements in the sixth point of step two to determine if the applicant received a complete evaluation of all mitigating factors. By addressing these elements by policy and in the initial evaluation of an applicant, a Landlord/Property Manager can proactively defend against any potential action by a complainant or HUD.

As with all discrimination issues, the purpose for the HUD Guidelines is to further ensure that Landlords/Property Managers treat everyone equally without respect to any protected characteristics to help ensure that decisions concerning housing are not made pursuant to arbitrary or overbroad criminal history related bans. Although these rules may be used to file frivolous claims and be a source of unnecessary litigation, Landlords/Property Managers should comply to protect against potential claims. Attorneys representing Landlords/Property Managers need to be thoroughly familiar with HUD's Guidelines to properly advise clients and to help them avoid discrimination claims. I have found that when attorneys help Landlord/Property Manager clients draft and understand the foundational principles surrounding the steps outlined above, it becomes much easier for clients to properly use and analyze criminal history in the rental application process.

Denny's firms have represented over 120,000 rental units and have handled over 250,000 evictions. He has handled hundreds of bench trials and over twenty-five jury trials, defended dozens of discrimination complaints, and authored a great deal of Landlord-Tenant legislation. He is a co-founder of the Crime Free Association and wrote the Crime Free Lease addendum for private housing. He is the general counsel for Rent

By Denny Dobbins
Attorney at Law
General Legal Counsel
Rent Perfect, Inc.
CrimShield, Inc.

U.S. Dep't of Hous. & Urban Dev., Office of General Counsel Guidelines on Application of Fair Housing Act Standards to the Use of Criminal Records by Providers of Housing and Real Estate-Related Transactions, 1–10 (April 4, 2016), https://www.hud.gov/sites/documents/HUD_OGCGUIDAPPFHASTANDCR.PDF.
Id.at 3.
Id.at 3–4.
Id.at 4.
Id.at 10.
Id.at 2.
Id.at 3–4.
Id.at 4–7.

See Martinez v. Woodmar IV Condo. Homeowners Ass'n, Inc., 189 Ariz. 206, 941 P.2d 218 (1997).
U.S. Dep't of Hous. & Urban Dev., Office of General Counsel Guidelines on Application of Fair Housing Act Standards to the Use of Criminal Records by Providers of Housing and Real Estate-Related Transactions, 8 (April 4, 2016), https://www.hud.gov/sites/documents/HUD_OGCGUIDAPPFHASTANDCR.PDF.
Id.at 5.

See Dep't of Hous. & Urban Dev. v. Rucker, 535 U.S. 125 (2002); Martinez v. Woodmar IV Condo. Homeowners Ass'n, Inc., 189 Ariz. 206, 941 P.2d 218 (1997). See also Katy Moeller & Cynthia Sewell, Mass stabbing suspect flew under the radar in Memphis. Then, he came to Boise., Idaho Statesman, December 16, 2018, available at https://www.idahostatesman.com/news/local/crime/article222603405.html; Tommy Simmons, Mother of 3-year-old Boise mass stabbing victim sues apartment complex owners, Idaho Press Tribune, Dec. 26, 2018, available at https://www.idahopress.com/news/local/mother-of--year-old-boise-mass-stabbing-victim-sues/article_767e2c05-e8f4-5a86-a4cd-6fa1838554b7.html.

U.S. Dep't of Hous. & Urban Dev., Office of General Counsel Guidelines on Application of Fair Housing Act Standards to the Use of Criminal Records by Providers of Housing and Real Estate-Related Transactions, 7 n.34 (April 4, 2016), https://www.hud.gov/sites/documents/HUD_OGCGUIDAPPFHASTANDCR.PDF.
Id. at 7.
Id.
Id.

I suggest that you talk to your experienced Landlord attorney before you decide on how you will handle criminal history regarding your applicants. You can find a list of potential Landlord attorneys in various cities by going to the Rent Perfect Website at rentperfect.com. There should be an experienced landlord attorney in or near your city that will not charge you an arm and a leg for advice.

Doing what you legally can do to keep those with criminal history of harm, as set forth above, away from your rental is critical to your property being successful.

2. Residents Must Sign a Crime Free Lease Addendum Prior to Resident Receiving Keys.

All occupants must sign a Crime Free lease addendum promising that they and their occupants, and invitees will live a crime free lifestyle during the lease term. It is an extra deterrent to a would-be bad-guy applicant and sends a crystal-clear message that criminal behavior during the lease will not be tolerated whether or not the criminal conduct is committed by the Resident or one of its occupants or invitees.

Since the Crime Free Programs ("CFP") began in 1992 CFP have been teaching Landlords/Property Managers/Owners/Police Departments/Police Officers/Cities how to detect and deter criminal activity in and from any kind of rental property. CFP provide training for Landlords/Property Managers in all aspects of security, including how to screen potential Residents in regard to past criminal activity. CFP help Landlords/Property Managers gain education about gangs, drugs, weapons, prostitution, landlord law, credit history, employment history and rental history. Call your local police department to see if it has Crime Free Programs available for you and your properties.

Too often, Landlords/Property Managers fail to properly screen their Residents in the areas of credit, criminal background, rental history and employment history. It is easy to forget to get it all done in the midst of the daily battle of property management. Applicants with problems in their credit, criminal, employment and/or rental history can be extremely charming and persuasive, even to the extent to entice you into letting them lease from you. There is no need to let an applicant slip through the cracks because if you follow my advice there will be no cracks. A copy of the crime free lease addendum can be found in Chapter 1, "Landlord Philosophy."

3. Insurance. Where permissible under the law, the Resident(s) should maintain a minimum of thirty thousand dollars ($30,000.00) in renter's insurance; a policy that also names the Landlord/Property Management as an additional insured and loss payee. The Resident must provide you with proof of purchase of the same before the Resident receives the keys.

4. Income Rent Ratio. The income to rent ratio must be _____ times rent; whatever you want it to be for your property for your screening purposes. The higher the income to rent ratio, the less applicants you will have in your renter pool and generally, the less likely you will have rent or damage issues.

5. Financial Score. A FICO Score is a credit score created by the Fair Isaac Corporation. It is the score that lenders and housing providers use, along with other details on borrowers'/Tenant's credit reports to assess credit risk to determine whether or not to extend credit. A FOCO score ranges from 300-850. The higher the score, the better the risk.

Therefore, the higher the financial score the better chance the renter will timely pay the rent, and generally, the less you will see criminal activity in an applicant's background. It is common in the rental industry rule that an applicant should have a FICO score of at least 550. The nicer the property the higher the financial score requirement might be. However, this standard can be fairly elastic depending on the Resident pool available in the demographic.

FICO financial scores are the predominant financial analysis tool today for deciding whether or not to rent to an applicant. There are other similar scoring methods. You have to decide what FICO, or other financial information, is the lowest acceptable standard you will accept. This will vary depending on your property and your market. But, if you chose to use only a FICO, or other similar financial score, once you set it, stick with it. If you don't generally stick with the score you chose, you could wind up with discrimination issues.

Many Landlords/Property Managers use an "approve" or "disapprove" for the financial section of the applicant analysis based on a FICO type score. A FICO type score is easy to obtain and you don't really have to think much about it. It is a pass or fail test. But you are responsible for it and to know what it means.

However, when you use a FICO type score as the ultimate financial test you could be losing some good prospects, depending on how high you set your acceptable standards. Some people rent because they want to avoid home and yard maintenance, live an active lifestyle, just need a quick place to crash, or just don't see the value in owning. Many people rent because they have to rent and can't afford to purchase. And there are lots of reasons why a person may have a low FICO type score.

It is inevitable that you will have folks with credit problems and other financial problems. Depending on how nice your property is and how high the rents are, I suggest not just looking at the FICO type score, but also looking at why the FICO type score is what it is. If the score is low because a parent signed for a student loan for a child where the student defaulted, or due to an emergency medical procedure, perhaps that FICO type score is not giving a true picture of what kind of Resident the applicant will be. Perhaps there was a short sale that lowered the FICO score because the real estate market tanked. Maybe the FICO type score took a dive due to a foreclosure five years ago when the market tumbled, and the applicant lost his/her job. Maybe the applicant was recently discharged in bankruptcy due to medical bills or other issues that we not based on negligent or uncontrolled spending.

The real credit issues you want to be careful of are consumer spending, still in bankruptcy, recklessness, failure to make car payments or rent payments. You may think about a hybrid of both the FICO type scores and taking into consideration reasons for those credit scores in order to get a better idea of whether a Resident is too financially risky to accept. However, whatever you do, you need to pick your method and then stick to it every time for everyone. Just be consistent. And, put your decision on process and procedure on the matter into your written policies and procedures manual.

6. Rental History. No past evictions in the last five years.

You absolutely need to know if the applicant has been evicted, and when, and why. Some courts have started hiding eviction records from the public. Some jurisdictions prohibit the Landlord/Property Manager from knowing or using eviction information. But in the majority of jurisdictions that allow a Landlord/Property Manager to know about and use rental history, remember that if the applicant is a bad Resident then their current Landlord/Property Manager will likely only tell you if they paid their rent timely or not – if even that much. If the applicant is a bad current Resident, the current Landlord/Property Manager wants to get rid of them. For reasons of a possible lawsuit for defamation, it is unlikely that the current Landlord/Property Manager will say much at all. However, the current Landlord/Property Manager may say all kinds of great things about your applicant like they hate to see them go. If the current Landlord/Property Manager wants to get rid of them, all bets are off because it is possible that the current Landlord/Property Manager would say anything to get rid of a bad Resident and send them packing your way.

The better previous Landlord/Property Manager to talk to about your applicant is not the current Landlord/Property Manager, but rather, the Landlord/Property Manager just before the current Landlord/Property Manager. If your applicant was a problem that Landlord/Property Manager is not worried about getting rid of them and is more likely to tell you much more about the applicant.

Here are some questions you should ask each applicant about eviction at the end of the application set forth above. If you have been evicted or threatened with eviction in the last five (5) years you must answer the following questions:

- *In what city were you evicted?*
- *Where were you evicted from?*

- *Who was the Landlord/Property Manager that evicted you?*
- *Why were you evicted or threatened with eviction?*
- *In what court did the eviction take place and what is the case number?*
- *Did you have an attorney represent you in the eviction?*
- *Did the sheriff get involved to remove you from the premises?*
-

If you learn that the applicant was asked to leave a property to avoid an eviction, ask?

- *Have you ever been given a notice to terminate a tenancy?*
- *Have you ever been asked to leave a leased property?*
- *Have you ever moved to avoid an eviction?*
- *Have your ever moved due to a problem with another Resident or the Landlord/ Property Manager?*
- *Describe the circumstances why the Landlord/Property Manager gave you notice to vacate or that the lease would be terminated.*

7. Other Credit Issues. No charge offs, no failure to pay as agreed on any credit report (consumer debt). The idea here is that you are looking for bad credit issues that show that the applicant is not a good financial risk.

8. Foreclosures. No foreclosures within the last three (3) years, (but check out the whole circumstance).

9. Repossessions. No repossessions within the last five (5) years, (but check out the whole circumstance).

10. Occupancy Standards. The occupancy standard is generally safe at two persons per bedroom; bedrooms being those rooms designated by management as bedrooms. A more restrictive standard can get you into trouble with the Attorney General. Check your local rules. States have different rules on what is a reasonable restriction on the number of occupants for which a Landlord/Property Manager may legally limit the Resident. Most states and Government Housing Authorities generally have a presumption that a reasonable limitation is two (2) persons per bedroom with a bedroom being designated by the Landlord/Property Manager. It is important to remember that a pregnant woman only counts as one person even if she will deliver during the occupancy. Once the infant arrives the Landlord/Property Manager should not count the child as an occupant until the renewal of the lease term. Be sure to have a diagram of the unit with a designation of what is a bedroom and what is NOT a bedroom.

11. Smoking. No smoking. Smoking is NOT a protected class. Marijuana smoking, or its use, is a Federal crime, even though it may not be State crime in your state. However, many states have rules on this issue that you need to be aware of in your own jurisdiction. The general rule is that if the Federal government prohibits it, then the Landlord/Property

Manager can prohibit it. In government, government funded or assisted housing, marijuana use is not allowed.

There is the issue of Residents with a medical marijuana prescription. That is too long of a subject to cover here. Suffice to say that you should contact a Landlord attorney in your local area regarding this issue as it could take some time to explain the ins and outs of this issue.

12. Pets. No pets. (Of course, saying no pets does not immunize you from therapy/service/support animal issues and reasonable accommodation issues – and a therapy/service/support animal is technically NOT A PET). If you accept pets see the pet section under the Lease clauses below for several suggestive ways to deal with pets, i.e., pet addendum or revocable pet license. I personally like the revocable pet license that you can terminate at your discretion. It is clean and gives you the right to have the pet removed as you see fit or pursuant to the conditions of the license.

13. Bankruptcy. Not currently in bankruptcy and not contemplating bankruptcy (of course they will not tell you if they are contemplating BK but asking is at least some deterrent). If an applicant is currently in a bankruptcy, you could be drug into the bankruptcy if you lease to them. If the Resident files bankruptcy after signing a lease, stops paying rent and claims bankruptcy protection, you cannot evict (or do anything else to collect rent or remove the Resident) unless, and until, you have the automatic bankruptcy "STAY" lifted and obtain permission from the court. This takes time and money. When bankruptcy is filed basically the court takes over and creditors cannot do anything to that debtor unless and until the court approves. Failure of the Resident to pay rent while in bankruptcy would force you into bankruptcy court to petition the judge that rent be paid or that you be able to proceed to remove the Resident from the property.

Therefore, you need to ask if the applicant is contemplating bankruptcy. Then, if you rent to that Resident and they file bankruptcy, and they warranted that their statements were true, those statements will be additional ammunition to evict them out of your property if they file for bankruptcy after they move in and stop paying rent.

14. Verifiable current and past employment.

- *What kind of job does the applicant have? Does the stated income match the job?*
- *How long has the applicant been on the job?*
- *What does the current job pay per month?*
- *Require pay stubs AND bank statements to verify income.*
- *Be sure to verify the job with the employer. Doing so is an art and a science depending on the size of the employer.*
- *Get at least the last three years with the name of employer and supervisor, addresses and phone numbers. This will help you better know the stability of your*

applicant.

- *Why was the applicant terminated from employment or why did the applicant change employment?*

Perhaps all that matters to you is that they have a job and make enough money to pay the rent. However, I suggest that you call the current employer and at least find out what is the likelihood of continued employment, and for how long.

Red flags occur when verifying employment when the phone is not answered by the company on the application or the person on the phone sounds suspect.

You call ABC company and whoever picks up the phone answers "hello". That is generally a problematic greeting. It tells the called that perhaps this is not a real business. Don't be afraid to ask pointed questions. If the job is real, often the company will say that they first need written authorization from the employee before they will talk to you. That is actually a good sign. Further, applicants with bad pasts know that they have problems renting and as a survival mechanism they will lie to you and have their friends lie for them posing as a current or past employer, or current or past Landlord/Property Manager. Do your due diligence and make the calls.

15. Verifiable income. See paragraph #19 above and do the same.

16. Verifiable bank information. See paragraph #19 above and do the same.

17. Personal References. Obtain at least three that are not related in any way. Then, see paragraph #19 above and do the same.

Principle # 7

RESIDENT/TENANT SCREENING

Now that you know what you are looking for in a Resident, what should the tenant screening investigation consist of, and how do you go about performing the investigation in an effort to screen out bad risks?

WHY IS PROPER SCREENING CRITICAL AND WHAT IS IT?

Proper, thorough Resident screening is the most important process that you will do in an effort to ensure a good quality Resident who pays the rent on time and treats the premises with respect. This is not magic. It is common sense and factual. Just like the FBI would not want someone in its ranks that did not pass a rigorous background investigation, a Landlord/Property Manager is in a similar position. As a Landlord/Property Manager, you are about to hand over an investment worth many thousands of dollars to someone you may do not even know. The property you are renting out may be your retirement, or you may have a fiduciary duty to the Owners to do all in your power to help ensure a good Resident. Therefore, you have a duty to yourself and possibly to others to be as careful as you can before delivering possession of this asset to someone whom you ultimately know little about. Furthermore, it is not difficult to do. It just takes some time and knowledge on where to look for who to use to help you. It is unlikely that you have the resources or know how to do tenant screening on your own. No worries. There are companies that can help you. You just have to make a few changes. Then make those changes a habit and get used to it.

If you have been in the housing providing industry for any time at all you may already have a background screening company that you use. In my experience, most background screening companies are fairly useless and just make a bunch of money off of you, delivering an inferior, inept product to you that does little to protect you. We will explore some of what I am talking about below.

You may have heard of the 80/20 rule. In property management the odds are better than 80/20 if you do things right. Resident screening is where the 97/3 rule comes into play in a major way. If you want to limit your headaches as a Landlord/Property Manager, you must – let me repeat this – YOU MUST properly screen your potential Residents. If you want to avoid a bad Resident 97% of the time, then do a proper screen 100% of the time. If you fail to properly screen, then you will run into the 80/20 rule experiencing 80% of your overall tenant problems as a Landlord/Property Manager with at least 20% of Residents that you failed to properly screen. There are too many nightmare stories about Landlords/Property Managers who rented to bad Residents because they did not perform a comprehensive, deep and proper Resident screen.

The following is a story out of the employment sector with direct cross over application to the housing sector.

 I was an expert witness in two rape cases against two (2) large, well-known, National hotel chains a few years ago. The first hotel hired a man as the night-time manager. The night-time manager watched the cameras to see when a young woman came in for the night that was drunk. The night-time manager used his master key and went into the room and raped the young lady while she was unconscious. While he was under investigation and on leave for the allegation that he raped her, he took a night-time manger job at another well-known, National hotel and did the exact same thing.

When I got the case facts to review, I was stunned. In both cases, with both hotels, not only did both of the hotels do a sub-par (less than the National Standards for a Hotel) for an employment screen for that job at the hotel, they did not do ANY background investigation at all. Had the hotel simply put the night-time manger applicant's name in the National Sex Offender Registry at https://www.nsopw.gov/ (a compilation of every State's sex offender registration list), and NOTHING else, they would have seen a picture of their applicant and seen that he was a registered sex offender.

The Hotels should have done much more to meet the minimum requirements for the National Standards for a background investigation for a hotel manager of any kind, but they literally did NOTHING. They did not even follow their own background investigation procedures and policies. Needless to say, that case did not go to trial and settled fairly quickly.

It has been my experience, and for good reason, that good Landlords/Property Managers would rather have a unit/house sitting empty for several months, rather than get a bad Resident living in the unit/house. I know many Landlords/Property Managers that have done just that. Recently on a property, a Landlord/Property Manager screened several potential Residents and found no one who met their rental criteria. The home sat empty for three months. The Landlord/Property Manager felt that that was better than taking a chance on a potentially bad Resident. The risk of the cost of new carpet, countertops, flooring, repairing drywall, harm to neighbors, legal fees, emotional and mental

110

stress, time wasted, whatever the case may be, is just not worth the hassle in many cases. In some cases, it is better just to have the unit/house off the market and wait to get a good Resident.

So, you may be saying, I am not like that. I do a background check. Well, here is the rub. Many so-called background checks are just about the same as doing no background at all. Let me explain.

Instant Background Check or Background Investigation

Yep, that's right. An instant background check does not work, and for many reasons. To protect your investment, you don't want to miss anything about your applicant. You want an accurate and complete investigation performed, not just a simple or "instant" background check. There is a huge difference.

A background check has become somewhat meaningless because a "background check" is now synonymous with an internet search and whatever information is in some data base somewhere. Or you pay some company $10 to $20 for literally nothing. I know, you did not know you were likely getting garbage or old and incomplete information about your applicant. It is ok. There are better ways to go about it.

Today, a background check is too often thought of as accessing the internet, typing in a name, SS#, DOB and address with the expectation that now the magic will happen where you will get all the information on that person that exists; whether you input the data into some website or whether you give the data to some background check company. Unfortunately, getting accurate and complete background information on an applicant simply does not work that way – though many will tell you otherwise. You only get what is in the database that is going to be searched. You do not know who put the database together, when it was assembled or how comprehensive it was - or anything about its accuracy.

For all intents and purposes, you cannot perform an actual background investigation on your own. You don't have the knowledge or experience. You need to hire a company that can do it for you. But remember, you get what you pay for. Or perhaps it is better said that your applicant gets what they pay for. You chose who performs the investigation, and the applicant pays for it. You need the background information quickly, but the problem is that quickly produced research/investigative products are usually called instant background checks and are for the most part, unreliable. An instant background check just searches purchased or subscribed to databases. They **_do not_** contain all current court record information. An instant background check will generally cost between $6-$20. An instant background check is not complete and almost NEVER accurate.

To protect your investment, you need a background investigation performed by licensed private investigators that researches directly in the courts with real and experienced hands and eyes on your applicant's information. You may now be saying that this guy is way overboard. I'm not. You may also be saying that this sounds way too expensive. It's not. Again, remember, you are not paying for it – the applicant is paying it. But a real investigation is not "expensive anyway". Does it cost a little more? Yes. I use a company called Rent Perfect at rentperfect.com. or CrimShield. My friends and I use them not because I am the attorney for these companies – but because I know exactly what is done and I know the industry. I helped create these companies to combat all of the inferior work that Landlords and Property Managers are unknowingly relying upon that wind up later getting them in trouble and costing them hard earned money. Does it cost a little more to have licensed private investigators find information by going directly to the courts where the applicant has lived over their lifetime, review all of the file information about an applicant and product a reliable product? Only a little bit more. But what good is spending any money on a background that does not protect you. Besides, the applicant is paying the fee to protect you. You should go ahead and do it right and get the best protections possible.

I know this sounds self-serving to put this in my book – promoting a company that is a client. However, I do not know how else to discuss this critical topic. I have done this work a long time. I am heavily involved in the industry and I understand it inside and out. I won't lie to you like many so-called "background" companies that will gladly sell you a joke of a product that does not have trained eyes analyzing all of the information. The fact is, there are some real background investigation companies around the country that can produce a true product – most background check/investigation companies cannot provide you with a product that will protect you, thereby leaving you hanging with liability you do not if know is present. Most of these so-called background check companies are frauds. They are uneducated, uncaring, in it for a quick buck, and ready to take full advantage of an unsuspecting Landlord or Property Manager.

Unless the Landlord/Property Manager is trying to create a profit center off of background, i.e., charge $40 and keep $20, the applicant pays for the background. All of the money the applicant pays for the background should be used on the background. Otherwise, you short yourself with inferior information and place yourself at risk of legal

112

action for not using all of the money collected for the background on the background. Unfortunately, I have had the misfortune of dealing with some unethical Landlord/Property Managers that trade the comfort of more a complete and accurate information that is much more thorough and reliable for a few pieces of silver.

THE FOLLOWING ARE JUST A COUPLE OF IMPORTANT DIFFERENCES BETWEEN A BACKGROUND CHECK AND A BACKGOUND INVESTIGATION.

A background investigation company as opposed to a background check company identifies and researches: maiden names, misspelled names, misstated or fraudulent social security numbers that just don't match up or are not real, attempts at using someone else's ID, false addresses, small changes of a date of birth or a name, and the list goes on. Background checks and instant checks don't do that.

Further, applicants with bad (criminal and financial) pasts know that they have problems renting and as a survival mechanism they will lie to you, lie on the application, and try to trick and confuse you and any background or investigation company. They can be very successful in doing so, especially if you are only using a database background check because, the information some applicants provide to you to run through a background check cannot be recognized by database background checks. Such companies cannot deal with the details and nuisances of the lies. Private Investigator performing a background investigation are uniquely qualified to handle all of the ins and outs or lies, half-truths and nuisances with their eyes and hands on the files to help them catch those kinds of shenanigans, where background checks cannot.

Background Investigations Should Not Be a Profit Center for a Landlord/Property Manager – Legal Considerations.

Don't make the mistake of making background checks/investigations a profit center where you charge the applicant more than the cost of the background check and pocket the difference. That can come back to haunt you legally. It is a liability you do not want. Not only are you shorting yourself on protection, but if an issue arises in court later due to a Resident causing damages to someone else, and you would have caught the disqualifying criminal history in an actual background investigation where you paid out all of the money received from the applicant for the investigation as opposed to pocketing some of the money, you are toast because you did not follow the National Standard of care for background investigations in a Landlord/Property Manager and Resident relationship. The National Standard of care is to do what can be reasonably done to protect those for whom you have a duty to protect. There is simply too much liability for you to cut corners and try to make money off your applicants while providing less than you could have, and should have, provided for the money received. If fact, it is fraud and theft. Just charge a tad more for a real investigation, and get the job done right the first time. Don't take a chance on background check databases missing information that could cause you a lot of harm and a lot of money.

TOO MANY BACKGROUND COMPANIES PROVIDE BAD
(Inaccurate and Incomplete) INFORMATION

There are hundreds of of background check companies that will take your money and give you less than what you asked for. They know that most Landlords/Property Manager do not know what the National Standards are for a background investigation, or even what background investigation is supposed to entail. You are the one left holding the liability bag if the information was not good, not accurate and/or not complete, and you did not use a company that provides information that meets the National Standards. Sure, they may get sued as well, but do you really want to be in that position? There are a number of background investigation companies out there that that will give you current, accurate and complete information. Unfortunately, there are multitudes of "background check" companies, and unfortunately Landlord/Property Managers do not have any idea which company to choose for the best information at the best price. They just use who their colleagues use or who they hear about at an association meeting.

Also, in my experience that Landlords/Property Managers do not know what National Standards are or what they are liable for regarding screening. Their attorneys should know what the National Standards are and what elements meet those National Standards for liability issues. However, I have found that many attorneys, even attorneys deeply involved in the industry, do not know. If your attorney does not know that information, you need a new attorney.

Database or instant background check companies have flooded the internet, most of which claim to give you great information, but don't. But it is still your responsibility as a Landlord/Property Manager to understand the National Standard about where and how to obtain complete and accurate information. As the U.S. Department of Justice said in its 2006 study on background information, the only place to find current, complete and accurate information on a person is found directly in the courts, not on an internet website or vendor that uses database subscription and does not physically go to the courts when a court is not online. Only a background investigation company that goes directly into the courts for information at the time the order is made should be trusted by you. If you use a database background search instead of a real background investigation, you do not know who researched the data that is in the database, where the data came from, if the data was verified with the courts, when the data was assembled or how current the data may be. It is simply not worth the risk to use a company that uses only databases to provide you information to rely upon to protect your hard-earned asset.

Database background check companies will try to lure you with low prices. Why do you think their prices are so low? There are few costs involved for them because they do not provide anything that is current and do not send anyone to the courts for information. Ask them who put their databases together, when were the databases compiled, how accurate are the databases (impossible for them to know) and do they catch all the nuances mentioned above. They will not be able to articulate a coherent answer. If the background check is instantaneous or comes back very quickly, you know that that company is not going to the courts in real time research of your applicant's name, aliases, maiden names, similar names, dates of birth and various social security numbers. And I guarantee there is no seasoned private investigators helping ensure that the person who filled out the application is actually the person that they say they are. Furthermore, no trained eyes or hands have seen or touched that file to look for strange or intentional inconsistencies when applicants try to game the system. For just a few dollars more you can get the real deal and sleep better at night knowing that you had every rock turned over, and that you met the National Standards to do what could be, and should be, done so you are not relying on a completely inferior database background check product. This is just stuff you don't know unless you are in the industry. Now you know. Besides, the applicant pays the cost.

Today, it is becoming more and more important, from a legal standpoint, to perform a complete and accurate screening for potential Residents and employees.

Unless you are highly trained and have lots of time to perform a comprehensive Resident screen you should be using a professional Resident screening company that verifies information directly at the courts in real time, through the hands on and eyes on seasoned private investigator, especially since you are not paying for it and it does not cost much more than the typical inferior background check.

Principle # 8

THE LEASE AGREEMENT

Now that you have what you consider to be a good rental applicant based on your written criteria, what will be the terms of your agreement? The lease is simply a contract between the parties. The lease provisions are slightly different in the way they are worded and a bit different in structure between a multi-family lease agreement and a single-family lease agreement, but the content and purpose are essentially the same. The following will be a dissection of a residential lease agreement.

Commercial – retail, office and industrial leases can get complex and will not be analyzed in this book. First, what are the basic obligations of the Landlord/Property Manager and the Resident?

GENERAL LANDLORD/PROPERTY MANAGER OBLIGATIONS

Statutory provisions need not be set forth in the lease as they exist as a matter of law. However, you can expound upon them. Many states have a Landlord and Tenant act. Other states have at least some statutory guidelines regarding Landlord and Tenant relationships. In all States, the statutes, guidelines, rules, ordinances, etc. usually refer to Residents as TENANTS or TENANT. I like the word "Resident" better as "Tenant " sounds so subservient.

It is incumbent upon all Landlords/Property Managers to become very familiar with all obligations and to ensure compliance at all times, whatever they may be. When you have to start spending money for legal fees, you can kiss your cash flow goodbye. Develop an inspection and maintenance schedule and stay on top of your obligations. When things break down all at once and Residents are complaining, life as a Landlord/Property Manager is not fun. It is just like a car. If you put all of the little things off until later, soon you have a costly disaster staring at you like a money-gobbling monster. Just make a decision now to take care of things proactively. Do not delay. The following is typical language from a state Landlord/Property Manager and Tenant act setting forth Landlord/Property Manager basis obligations to Residents.

A. The Landlord/Property Manager shall:

1. Comply with the requirements of applicable building codes materially affecting health and safety.

2. Make all repairs and do whatever is necessary to put and keep the premises in a fit and habitable condition.

3. Keep all common areas of the premises in a clean and safe condition.

4. Maintain in good and safe working order and condition all electrical, plumbing, sanitary, heating, ventilating, air-conditioning and other facilities and appliances, including elevators, supplied or required to be supplied by the Landlord/Property Manager.

5. Provide and maintain appropriate receptacles and conveniences for the removal of ashes, garbage, rubbish and other waste incidental to the occupancy of the dwelling unit and arrange for their removal.

6. Supply running water and reasonable amounts of hot water at all times, reasonable heat and reasonable air-conditioning or cooling where such units are installed and offered, when required by seasonal weather conditions, except where the building that includes the dwelling unit is not required by law to be equipped for that purpose or the dwelling unit is so constructed that heat, air-conditioning, cooling or hot water is generated by an installation within the exclusive control of the Resident and supplied by a direct public utility connection.

B. If the duty imposed by subsection A, paragraph 1 of this section is greater than any duty imposed by any other paragraph of this section, the Landlord's/Property Manager's duty shall be determined by reference to that paragraph.

C. The Landlord/Property Manager and Resident of a single family residence may agree in writing, supported by adequate consideration, that the Resident perform the Landlord's/Property Manager's duties specified in subsection A, paragraphs 5 and 6 of this section, and also specified repairs, maintenance tasks, alterations and remodeling, but only if the transaction is entered into in good faith, not for the purpose of evading the obligations of the Landlord/Property Manager and the work is not necessary to cure non-compliance with subsection A, paragraphs 1 and 2 of this section.

D. The Landlord/Property Manager and Resident of any dwelling unit other than a single-family residence may agree that the Resident is to perform specified repairs, maintenance tasks, alterations or remodeling only if:

1. The agreement of the parties is entered into in good faith and not for the purpose of evading the obligations of the Landlord/Property Manager and is set forth in a separate writing signed by the parties and supported by adequate consideration.

2. The work is not necessary to cure noncompliance with subsection A, paragraphs 1 and 2 of this section.

3. The agreement does not diminish or affect the obligation of the Landlord/Property Manager to other Residents in the premises.

If the Landlord/Property Manager purchases utility services from a public service corporation for distribution through a system owned or operated by the Landlord/Property Manager and imposes separately stated utility or similar charges on the Residents, the aggregate amount of the separately stated charges shall not exceed the actual cost paid by the Landlord/Property Manager to the public service corporation for the utility services. The Resident is not required to pay any other separately stated charges for provision of the utility services.

Think of being a Landlord/Property Manager like being an owner of a restaurant. The Landlord/Property Manager is providing good service to its customers for an agreed upon price. The menu items are the state, and local laws and ordinances, and the lease agreement. If your state or local rules are silent on issues that may arise, you need to cover those areas in your own lease agreement before they occur, so the parties can refer to the lease to determine how the parties are required to deal with the situation, should it occur. In this way the parties are not left to wonder what course of action is necessary to remedy the situation because they likely won't agree.

It is important for you to be completely familiar with all of the obligations and rights of both you as Landlord/Property Manager and those of the Resident. Like most things in life, this knowledge itself is power. With any power comes responsibility. Seldom does a Resident understand either party's obligations or rights. Literally, most

Residents are quite ignorant. Judges know that and at times are going to offer some protection to Residents, especially if the judge feels the Landlord/Property Manager is taking advantage of the Resident. Therefore, a Landlord/Property Manager has a very special duty to do the right thing and use the power of their knowledge with wisdom with prudence. If you fail to do so, your rights will be legislated away, and it will be ever more difficult and expensive to be a Landlord/Property Manager. It is inherent in every Landlord/Property Manager to know everything there is to know about both parties obligations and rights to ensure that no genuine issue of law or fact ever arises such that any reasonable person think the Landlord/Property Manager violated any Landlord/Property Manager obligation, Resident right or abused a Landlord/Property Manager right. Simply put, Landlord/Property Manager must use their knowledge fairly for protection of their property and at the same time for the service of their Residents.

GENERAL RESIDENT OBLIGATIONS

Just as with Landlord/Property Manager Obligations, Resident Obligations are imposed as a matter of law in many jurisdictions. However, I like to expand upon many of them in the lease so that the Resident has something to refer to, or something a Landlord/Property Manager can easily refer them to. Remember, expectations are a key to a good relationship and a powerful tool to obtain compliance. Go over these Resident obligations with the Resident at the lease signing to help solidify those obligations in the Resident's mind from the start. The following set of basic Resident obligations come from a state Landlord/Property Manager and Tenant act:

The Resident Shall:

1. Comply with all obligations primarily imposed upon Residents by applicable provisions of building codes materially affecting health and safety.

2. Keep that part of the premises that he occupies and uses as clean and safe as the condition of the premises permit.

3. Dispose from his dwelling unit all ashes, rubbish, garbage and other waste in a clean and safe manner.

4. Keep all plumbing fixtures in the dwelling unit or used by the Resident as clean as their condition permits.

5. Use in a reasonable manner all electrical, plumbing, sanitary, heating, ventilating, air-conditioning and other facilities and appliances including elevators in the premises.

6. Not deliberately or negligently destroy, deface, damage, impair or remove any part of the premises or knowingly permit any person to do so.

7. Conduct himself and require other persons on the premises with his consent to conduct themselves in a manner that will not disturb his neighbors' peaceful enjoyment of the premises.

In general, Residents have just as serious obligations regarding the premises as does the Landlord/Property Manager; they are just a bit different. All of the obligations go to good faith for Residents and to use the facilities in a reasonable manner.

Also, it is important to note that most states recognize that the Resident shall be held responsible for the actions of the Resident's guests that violate the lease agreement or rules or regulations of the Landlord/Property Manager if the Resident could reasonably be expected to be aware that such actions might occur and did not attempt to prevent those actions to the best of the Resident's ability. The Crime Free Lease Addendum will strengthen those Resident responsibilities. Many state statutes also indicate that Residents are responsible to require other persons on the premises with Resident's consent not to disturb neighbors.

So, what EXACTLY should be in the lease agreement? As a Landlord/Property Manager, what are the elements or clauses of a great lease agreement? About everything a Landlord/Property Manager could need can be found in this chapter in one place, and you can pick through the clauses contained in this chapter and use what you like and what works for your jurisdiction. Meet with your attorney and pick the clauses that work for you.

But before we look at the clauses of a good lease let's get a little more housekeeping out of the way to get you ready.

Most Landlord/Tenant laws incorporate all of the principles of fraud, duress, undue influence, unconscionability, lack of capacity, illegality, mistake, and good faith are part of the lease contract regardless of the lease language. Therefore, you need an agreement that covers as many of the events that can occur during a tenancy as possible, so that when the event arises you already have that event addressed in your agreement as to how it will be handled by both parties. If you have been a Landlord very long, you know that the kinds of events can occur on a property are many. Over the years I have added language to my lease to cover as many events as possible that come up during a lease term.

If you use an agreement from a copy center, not only are you doing a disservice to yourself and the Resident, you are making a statement that you like to pay attorney's fees and enjoy going to court. You are saying that you like putting the fate of your property and money in the hands of a judge that did not "live the event" that got you in front of him/her. If you are going to spend thousands or millions of dollars on a property, then get the lease right, make it thorough and expansive to help keep you protected from legal problems with Residents. From thirty (30) years of trial experience, I can tell you that a short, or off-the-shelf lease, can only get you in deep trouble.

This lease section is like the magician that recently came on television and showed the public how the allusions are performed. I am giving away many thousands of dollars by revealing to you some of the important elements of the trade. I have been working on my lease for 30 years. Every time an issue arises that was not covered in the lease or in the statutes, I add a section to the lease so my clients have more control over the issue than does a judge. Still, you want to consult your attorney before you start using a Residential lease agreement like the one I am going to discuss, in an effort to make sure that the clauses will be legally sufficient in your particular jurisdiction.

EVERYTHING A LANDLORD/PROPERTY MANAGER AND RESIDENT RELATIONSHIP MUST BE IN WRITING – *ALWAYS - PLEASE*

You want the lease to be written in such a way that it cannot be misunderstood. Please do not enter into an oral lease. In fact, never do anything with a Resident verbally. Make it your policy from this day on to do everything, EVERYTHING, with a Resident IN WRITING. After the Resident has indicated that they have carefully and completely read the lease, then review the lease with your Resident before they sign it so that you have extra ammunition if they come back later in front of a judge and claim they had no idea what was in the lease. Document the meeting in your file regarding reviewing the lease with the Resident. This review could be an important step if the Resident later claims they did not understand they were entering into a lease and a myriad of other claims they may make. The idea is that you want your Resident to have the same understanding and expectations as you have.

ENGLISH LANGUAGE – OTHER LANGUAGES

What if you have an applicant who wants to apply that does not speak or read English? You have two choices. You do not have to provide an interpreter, and therefore, do not have to deal with such an applicant if they do not have their own interpreter. However, if it is clear that they cannot read the lease and have no interpreter, it will be impossible for you to come to a meeting of the minds regarding the terms lease, and the lease will be voidable by the Resident if you enter into it under those conditions. It is a matter of understanding and fairness.

On the other hand, you could have it translated into their language. In the Southwest we have a large Spanish speaking only population. In other pockets of the Country there are high populations of various languages spoken. The idea is to help your Residents understand the lease terms. If you have the lease translated into Spanish, my dealings with the Offices of the Attorneys General office in various States on the subject indicate that not only would such a translation be permissible, but it would be seen as a good approach. Whenever you have a high population of foreign language speaking applicants in your area, it could be helpful to translate the lease into that language, but you are not required to do so. However, make sure that you also have a signed lease in English as well indicating in both of the leases that if there are any contradictions, discrepancies or translation problems between the leases that the English version will control. Besides, the courts can and do demand contracts in English. This happened to me in Court with a Spanish lease where the judge would not move forward with the case because "American Courts use only the English language". In that case the lease was only in Spanish and the judge could not read it.

Landlords/Property Managers have asked if they put their lease in Spanish, do they also have to translate the lease into Slovene if a Slovenian seeks residency? My dealing with the Attorneys General offices have indicated that such a translation would not be required under the fair housing laws. The fact that Arizona's Spanish speaking population is so large and growing creates special circumstances. Again, the idea is to help the Resident understand before entering into the lease. If they do not understand, then there is no meeting of the minds and that is a good defense to a lot of issues. However, translating the lease into another language can be costly. It would obviously become cost prohibitive to have to translate the lease into every language that any person might speak. Be careful though, if you translate the lease into Spanish you are setting a pattern for yourself to put all documents for that Resident into their language, including, but not limited to, notices, letters and any other communication to that Resident in Spanish and English as well.

If the lease was only in English and you enter into a lease with a Spanish or Russian only speaking Resident, be sure there is a translator and obtain plenty of information about the translator.

PROHIBITED PROVISIONS IN THE LEASE

Remember, the Law trumps the lease. If when the lease is not in compliance with the law, the law governs the agreement between the parties in those particular respects.

Some States have statutes that specifically set forth prohibitions from being a lease agreement. You must know your own state and local laws and ordinances.

EXAMPLE: In more than one State you will find the following, or similar, prohibitions to lease terms:

A. A rental agreement shall not provide that the Resident does any of the following:
1. Agrees to waive or to forego rights of remedies under this chapter.

2. Agrees to pay the Landlord's/Property Manager's attorney fees, except an agreement in writing may provide that attorney's fees may be awarded to the prevailing party in a contested forcible detainer action is eligible to be awarded attorney fees regardless of whether the rental agreement provides for such award.

3. Agrees to the exculpation or limitation of any liability of the Landlord/Property Manager arising under law or to indemnify the Landlord/Property Manager for that liability or the costs connected therewith.

B. A provision by subsection (A) of this section included in a rental agreement is unenforceable. If a Landlord/Property Manager deliberately uses a rental agreement containing provisions known by him to be prohibited, the Resident may recover actual damages sustained by him and not more than two months periodic rent.

THE ACTUAL LEASE TERMS OR LEASE CLAUSES FOR INCORPORATION INTO YOUR LEASE

1. RESIDENT SIGNATURES

Your property may be in a community property state. If the Residents are husband and wife, always have both husband and wife sign the lease to be safe. In community property states if the lease is for one year or more, and only one party to the community signs the lease, then you cannot hold the community responsible for the lease. So always have both the husband and the wife sign. If you cannot hold the community liable for the lease, you cannot collect from community funds for the obligations if the Residents are later in breach of the lease.

The following is a typical Community Property Statute on the Matter:

Either spouse separately may acquire, mange, control or dispose of community property, or bind the community, except the joinder of both spouses is required in any of the following cases:

A. Any transaction for the acquisition, disposition or encumbrance of an interest in real property other than an unpatented mining claim or a lease for less than one year.

B. Any transaction of guaranty, indemnity or suretyship.

2. MATERIAL FALSIFICATIONS OF INFORMATION FROM RESIDENT

Non-Curable False or Misleading Information:

If the Resident provides any information to the Landlord/Property Manager that is materially false or misleading in the application process or in the lease, Landlord/Property Manager may terminate the lease upon a ten (10) day written notice from Landlord/ Property Manager for Non-Curable false information such as, but not limited to:

    A. Criminal background information.
    B. Prior evictions history information.
    C. Information regarding current criminal activity.

In such a case the Resident shall be responsible for all damages including, but not limited to, cleaning and repairing the property, the remainder of the lease rent and all costs, including, but not limited to, marketing and re-renting the property.

Curable False or misleading Information:

On the other hand, if the Resident provides any information to the Landlord/Property Manager that is materially false or misleading in the application process or in the lease, Landlord/Property Manager may provide Resident with a ten (10) day written notice to cure the false or misleading information. Curable false or misleading information shall consist of, but not limited to, the following:

    A. Number of occupants in the dwelling.
    B. Number or type of pet(s) in the dwelling.
    C. Income of the Residents.
    D. Residents' social security number(s).
    E. Current employment information.

If the Resident provides truthful information to Landlord/Property Manager within thirty (10) days after receipt of the ten (10) notice and Landlord/Property Manager, Landlord/Property Manager may investigate the information to determine if Resident qualifies for residency based on Landlord's/Property Manager's rental criteria. If Resident fails to provide truthful information to the Landlord/Property Manager within the ten (10) day period, then the aforementioned curable false or misleading information shall immediately become non-curable. If it is found in Landlord's/Property Manager's further investigation that the information provided to Landlord/Property Manager would not allow Resident to qualify for residency based on Landlord's/Property Manager's rental criteria, then Landlord/Property Manager may deliver to Resident a ten (10) day notice setting forth why the Resident did not qualify for residency based upon the new information provided to Landlord/Property Manager as analyzed against Landlord's/Property Manager's rental criteria. In such a case, the Resident shall be responsible for all damages including, but not limited to, cleaning and repairing the property, the remainder of the lease rent and all costs, including, but not limited to, marketing and re-renting the property.

3. GUARANTIES

Do not use a guarantee or guarantor agreement. Just have the guarantors also sign the lease. You may ask why?

In college towns it is common to have the parents sign a guarantor agreement basically setting forth that if the parent's childommon to have the parents sign a guarantor agreement basically setting forth that if the parent's child, who is an adult with no credit, wants to live in the community, then the parent must sign a separate agreement that if the child violates the lease, or does not pay rent timely, that the parent will be liable. I have seen many Landlords/Property Manager caught in this trap. You may ask why it is a trap. If the lease is for a year or more, and the rental community is located in community property State, both mom and dad must sign of the guarantor agreement, or the actual lease, in order to bind the community to the obligations of the lease.

I realize that the reason guarantee agreements are used is for ease when dealing with Residents who do not qualify on their own and need help from parents or others that may live out of town. But beware of this time bomb. With the use of Fed-X, UPS, and similar companies, or even email through various signature programs, it is easy to get both parent signatures on the lease.

Here is another key factor in this regard. Be sure to verify that the person signing does so in front of you if in town, or in front of a notary who will verify that the person signing is in fact that person, if they reside out of town. Lots of games are played with this issue. And verify who signs in front of you with other forms of ID like driver license and/or passport.

4. JOINT AND SERVERAL LIABILITY - SIGNITURES

Always make the lease a joint and several obligations if there is more than one responsible party.

126

This LEASE AGREEMENT , (hereinafter referred to as the "Agreement") made and entered into as of the _____ day of_____ 20____, by and between ABC Properties, LLC, a Texas Limited Liability Company (hereinafter referred to as "Landlord" or "Property Manager"), and _____ _____, as community property (if community property applies), jointly and severally, (hereinafter referred to as "Resident").

5. DISCLOSURES TO RESIDENT AND TENDER OF LEASE

Many States require disclosure of the owner, and/or manager, of the property be spelled out in the lease. It does not matter if your State requires it or not. Just add it in.

SAMPLE STATUTORY LANGUAGE:

A. The Landlord/Property Manager or any person authorized to enter into a rental agreement on his behalf shall disclose to the Resident in writing the name and address of each of the following:

1. The person authorized to manage the premises.

2. An owner of the premises or a person authorized to act for and on behalf of the owner for the purpose of service of process and for the purpose of receiving and receipting for notices and demands.

B. At or before the commencement of the tenancy, the Landlord/Property Manager shall provide Resident with a free copy of the current Residential Landlord/Property Manager and Resident act.

C. A person who fails to comply with subsections A and B becomes an agent of each person who is a Landlord/Property Manager for the following purposes:

1. Service of process and receiving and receipting for notices and demands.

2. Performing the obligations of the Landlord/Property Manager under this chapter and under the rental agreement and expending or making available for the purpose all rent collected from the premises.

3. A written rental agreement shall have all blank spaces completed.

4. Landlord/Manager shall provide a copy of the executed lease agreement to the Tenant in a reasonable time frame. Therefore, *to simplify*, put the following in the lease:

1. Manager name.

2. Statutory agent or person authorized to accept service of process, notices and demands.

3. Provide the Resident with a copy of your state Landlord/Property Manager and Resident act or any other applicable statutes, or ordinances.

4. Fully execute the lease filling in all blanks.

5. Provide Resident a copy of the written lease agreement as soon as possible.

6. USE OF THE PROPERTY

You need to define how the premises may be used and how it may not be used. The premises should not be used for business purposes or for any illegal activity. Agree as to who will be a Resident and what constitutes an unauthorized occupant. I see too many lease agreements that do not discuss the specifics about what constitutes an unauthorized occupant. If the rules are not in the agreement, then how is the Resident to know what crosses the line?

Just the other day I got a letter from the homeowner association telling me that my grass in my yard was "too" high. Of course, it was not "too" high. The letter cited a rule that had nothing to do with how high the grass could be before it was a considered a violation, leaving me to wonder how I had violated the rule. So, I called the HOA office and asked where in the rules it states how high the grass can be before the height of the grass is a violation. The young man I spoke with said, "Well, it's about six (6) inches". I said, "About? Is that written in the rules or just a guess? Is that what the standard reads?" He said, "Well, no. But that is kinda of what we go by." Then we had a long discussion about the lack of specificity. It was a lot of fun, at least for me.

Another similar area for Landlords/Property Managers deals with what constitutes guests vs. occupants. Agree in the lease what constitutes guests vs. occupants in order to control the use of the premises by guests and occupants. Also, agree up front what the premises can and cannot be used for.

The premises may be used for Residential purposes only and shall be occupied only by the lessee and the named individual(s) stated in this lease. The premises shall be used so as to comply with all state, county and municipal laws and ordinances and shall be kept in a clean and orderly condition. Lessee shall not use the premises or permit it to be used by anyone for any commercial or industrial purpose, retail purpose, disorderly or unlawful purpose or in any manner so as to interfere with the quiet enjoyment by neighbors. Lessee shall be responsible and fully liable for the conduct of Lessee's occupants, guests and invitees. Acts of occupants, guests and invitees in violation of this Agreement or Lessor's rules and regulations may be deemed by Lessor to be a material breach by lessee. Lessee shall at all times supervise its occupants, guests and invitees in the unit and on the property. The premises shall be used only as a family residence by the Lessee. The premise will not be used or allowed to be used for any purposes deemed hazardous by the Lessor's insurance company because of fire or any other risk.

The only individuals that may reside in the premises shall be:

_____

_____

No other individual may reside in the premises. Anyone, not listed above, visiting over 14 calendar days in any twelve-month period is an unauthorized occupant.

7. THE PREMISES, OR PROPERTY

Explain exactly what is being leased.

SAMPLE LEASE PROVISION

In consideration of the rents and mutual covenants herein set forth, Lessor and Lessee agree:

The Lessor leases to the Lessee and the Lessee rents from the Lessor the premises located at _____, (City, State, Zip Code), (herein referred to as the "premises"), under the following terms and conditions.

8. THE TERM OF THE LEASE.

Next, you must set forth how long the lease will extend. Do you want a month-to-month lease, or a fixed-term lease that will turn into a month-to-month lease only if either party fails to provide the other party a 60 or 30 day written periodic notice prior to the termination of the initial term? A month-to-month tenancy provides you with the ability to say goodbye upon proper notice but robs you of any long-term commitment. Once you enter into a long-term lease, you cannot simply give the Resident a thirty-day notice to vacate. The Resident has a right to the premises until the end of the lease term, or until a material breach of the lease occurs and is not, or cannot, be cured.

SAMPLE LEASE PROVISION

The initial term of this Agreement shall commence on the ___ day of _____, 20___ and continue through the ___ day of _____, 20___ (the initial term). Upon the completion of the initial term, this lease will automatically turn into a month-to-month lease agreement upon the same terms and conditions and continue from month to month thereafter until one party delivers proper written notice of non-renewal to the other party at least thirty (30) periodic days (periodic means a full 30 days of a single month or twenty-eight (28) days in February) prior to the end of that period (a full month) in which the party wants the lease to terminate. For Example, if either party wants to terminate on July 31st, the party wanting to terminate the lease must deliver a written termination notice to the other on or before July 1.

SAMPLE 30-DAY TERMINATION NOTICE

How to terminate the month-to-month residency:

The following form is the one used to notify Resident that you are terminating their month-to-month lease agreement. You only use this notice if the Resident has actually completed the initial term and is now on a month-to-month lease agreement

30-DAY TERMINATION NOTICE

TO: Residents

        _____

        _____

        _____

FROM: Landlord or Property Manager

        _____

        _____

        _____

DATE: _____ ___ 20__.

30-DAY NOTICE

PERIODIC THIRTY (30) DAY NOTICE OF INTENT TO TERMINATE MONTH-TO-MONTH RENTAL AGREEMENT

Please be advised that your tenancy will terminate on the ___ day of _____ 20___. Please be advised that prior to your tenancy terminating, you will be required to vacate the subject premises described above and have a joint move-out walk through . If you fail to vacate the premises as demanded, a special detainer and/or forcible detainer proceeding will be initiated against you. Please contact the office to schedule a move-out walk through and inspection.

By_____

Title:_____

❑ Hand Delivered
❑ Certified Mail, Return Receipt Requested
   on the _____ day of
   _____, 20___, to:

By: _____
Title:_____

9. RENT, LATE FEES, SERVICE OF NOTICE CHARGES, NSF OR OTHER CHARGES

The amount of rent, late charges and all other charges need to be agreed to and specifically set forth in the lease agreement. In the following provision you will notice that the rent is due, delivered to you not later than 5:00 pm on or before the first day of the month, or it is late. It is not a legal requirement to grant a grace period, at least not in any jurisdiction that I am aware of. Then, if rent is not paid timely, a notice for failure to pay rent can be served on the Resident on the night of the 1st. This gets the clock ticking so you can get to court quicker, if in fact, the Resident fails to pay rent and late fees.

SAMPLE LEASE PROVISION

Lessee agrees to pay to Lessor rent for the premises during the term hereof in monthly installments on the 1st day of each month in advance and without notice, which rent shall be payable to lessor in the amount of $_____ at _____(address), or at such other location as Lessor may later specify in writing. Said installment shall be paid for each and every month during the "Term" of this Agreement. MAILING THE RENT BY THE DUE DATE DOES NOT CONSTITUTE PAYMENT. RENTS MUST BE RECEIVED AT THE OFFICE OF THE LESSOR BEFORE 5:00 P.M. ON THE DUE DATE OF EACH MONTH TO BE CONSIDERED PAID. MONIES RECEIVED ARE APPLIED FIRST TO CLEAR OUTSTANDING BALANCES, IF ANY, AND THEN TO THE CURRENT RENT. CASH WILL NOT BE ACCEPTED. Rent shall be paid for each and every month during the "Term" of this Agreement. Rent must be received at the office before 5:00 pm on or before the first day of the month, otherwise the payment is late and late fees shall immediately begin to accrue. Late fees shall accrue at the rate of *$_____.00 per day. If rent is late Lessor shall deliver to Lessee a *_____ day notice to pay or vacate the premises by hand delivery or certified mail. (whatever your jurisdiction requires) If Lessee fails to pay all of the rent, all of the late fees and an additional *$50.00 for the preparation and delivery of the notice, then Lessor may evict Lessee. Both parties agree that the venue of any eviction or forcible detainer proceeding shall be held in the *_____ Court or Court of Lessor's choosing. Both parties waive their rights to a jury trial and agree that the matter be heard by a judge in a bench trial. If Lessee is ever late with any payment, then Lessee agrees to pay all further rent, late fees and other charges for the remainder of the lease by certified funds only. If lessor serves/delivers to Lessee any notice for any breach of this Agreement, Lessee shall be charged and agrees to pay *$50.00 for and such service/delivery of such notice, which shall be paid by Lessee as additional rent.

10. SECURITY DEPOSITS

Experienced Landlords/Property Managers typically do a good job managing their properties. Security deposits, however, is an area that can give fits to even a seasoned Landlord/Property Manager. Usually, the market and government dictates what, if any, security deposit you can charge a Resident. Let's look at the law and then discuss it.

TYPICAL LAWS ON THE MATTER:

A Landlord/Property Manager shall not demand or receive security, however denominated, including, but not limited to, prepaid rent in an amount or value in excess of one and one-half month's rent. This subsection does not prohibit a Resident from voluntarily paying more than one and one-half month's rent in advance.

A Landlord/Property Manager can only ask for or accept from a Resident the amount of security deposit as allowed by law. Do NOT take more security deposit than is allowed. This is one area where Landlords make mistakes. Generally, Landlord's do not screw up but when they do this is one of the areas and judges are merciless when it happens. So do not accept more than is authorized in your jurisdiction. Even if your jurisdiction allows you to accept more security deposit if volunteered by a Resident, which I have seldom seen happen, only do so with an agreement where the Resident explains their rational for volunteering additional security deposit.

Sometimes Residents, for various reasons, want to pay three, six or twelve months up front. If you take more than the monthly rent, use the following form in an effort to provide added protection for yourself. Be careful accepting rent in advance. You can accept rent in advance, and Landlords/Property Managers love when that happens. But to ensure that accepting advanced payment of rent never becomes an issue where a Resident later wants the advanced payment of rent back or claims that it was a security deposit. For your protection be sure that the Resident signs the following form.

RESIDENT'S VOLUNTARY
PAYMENT OF ADVANCE RENTS

I/We the applicant(s) voluntarily desire to pay more than one month of rent to begin my/our lease. I/We desire to make payment of rent in advance. This advance payment of rent is NOT a security deposit. I/We make this payment of $_____ voluntarily as advanced rent. I/We agree that Landlord/Property Manager may account in Landlord's/Property Manager's accounting and bookkeeping that advanced rent has been paid and applied to my obligations under the lease agreement and that the amount paid is NON-REFUNDABLE. I/We warrant that none of the amount of the advanced rent paid is any kind of a security deposit. I/We have not been asked or coerced to pay said sum of advanced rent. I/We have our own reasons for doing so and realize that Landlord/Property Manager will have control of said monies. I/We have entered into a binding lease agreement and this payment pays for ____ months of rent. I/We have signed my/our name(s) to this document to indicate that the money that I/we have paid was paid as a free, conscious and voluntary choice and without coercion of any type.

_____   _____
Owner/Landlord/Property Manager   Resident
Date: Date:

                                                   _____
                                                   Resident
                                                   Date:

ADDITIONAL LAWS OF CONCERN:

Many states have statutory language like:

The purpose of all non-refundable fees or deposits shall be stated in writing by the Landlord/Property Manager. Any fee or deposit not designated as non-refundable shall be refundable.

This is very important, but easy to comply with. Some of the possible deposits you may find in a lease are deposits for pets, redecoration, cleaning, early termination and administrative fees. Therefore, you must call out all monies received as non-refundable or refundable, as the case may be. You want them to be non-refundable. Otherwise, any fee or amount you think is non-refundable that does not clear state it is non-refundable, is refundable. However, remember if there is a statutory cap on how much security deposit you can collect each non-refundable deposit you collect must be calculated in the total collected security deposit. Also, trying to call something a "FEE" or other name to avoid the fact that it is a security deposit will not work. If walks like a duck....

For example, the following typical statutory language has bearing on security deposits in this regard:

ADDITIONAL LAWS IN SOME STATES:

"Security" means money or property given to assure payment or performance under a rental agreement. "Security" does not include a reasonable and non-refundable fee or charge for redecorating or cleaning, a lease break fee or an agreed early termination of a lease agreement or an administrative fee.

PRACTICAL POINT: non-refundable redecorating or cleaning deposit is not counted in the definition of security deposit. Be very careful how you deal with security deposits come termination time. This is one area where judges hammer bad Landlords/Property Managers, Landlords/Property Managers who give a bad name to good Landlord's/Property Mangers by not being fair in the Security Deposit calculations and in getting the Security Deposit returned to the Resident timely.

Let's say the Resident vacates leaving $500 of damages. The lease set forth $200 that was non-refundable fee for redecorating and a $100 non-refundable cleaning deposit. The $500 in damages are related to cleaning and redecorating. Therefore, you use the non-refundable $300 of redecorating and cleaning first. In other words, do not pocket the $300 of non-refundable redecorating and cleaning deposit first and then charge the $500. Many Judges look at that practice as taking advantage of the Resident and as a windfall to the Landlord/Property Manager. And it is. It is wrong. If you do that kind of sharp/shrewd/deceptive manipulation, you will lose the trust of the Judge forever, and you will get hammered by the Judge as well. Remember, be fair and reasonable. Also, be careful in that you cannot charge a resident for normal wear and tear. However, Landlords and Residents have very differing ideas of what constitutes "normal" wear and tear.

I once had a trial regarding damages caused by the Resident's children. The damages were around $4,000. Those damages included, fans torn from the ceilings, the inside of the dishwasher destroyed (no idea how or why that happened), areas of carpets were burnt, counter tops were pulled apart, and vinyl flooring was torn to shreds. My client filed suit as the security deposit did not cover the damages. The defendant, former tenant, filed a counter-claim for failure to return the security deposit. The former tenant's defense was that the damages were "ordinary and normal" wear and tear. Specifically, the former tenant claimed their children caused the damages and that those kinds of things normally happen as a matter of everyday living. They actually took this case to trial. Of course, this case cost the owner even more money to go to trial. During the trial, the judge, after hearing what the tenants considered everyday living, and normal and ordinary wear and tear, gave the former tenants and their attorneys (all three attorneys) not only a reprimand and scolding, but a rebuke and a lecture, and threaten to turn them into the bar for ethics violations for such a "cockamamie" defense. The owner was out all of the repair costs and court costs, because the former tenants were judgment proof and would never have any money or job from which to collect.

Therefore, if you want to avoid a deposit problem, use a "non-refundable fee" as a separate category, such as a non-refundable fee for administration to get the unit back on the market, office staff costs to re-rent the property fee, etc. If something is designated as a security deposit as opposed to a fee, whether non-refundable or refundable, it counts as a security deposit. If you have a non-refundable fee of some kind, that is clearly not a security deposit, that is fine. Just be sure it is not a security deposit and agree to it in the lease. If it goes to damages – it is a security deposit. Interestingly, most states do not require you to pay the Resident interest on the security deposit.

SAMPLE LEASE PROVISION

Security Deposits.   Lessee agrees to pay Lessor as a security deposit the sum of $ _____ as security for the prompt payment of the rent and other sums due, or which may become due hereunder, and for the performance of all agreements between the parties. Further, Lessee shall pay a non-refundable cleaning fee in the amount of $ _____ as part of the security deposit. Lessee shall pay a non-refundable pet license fee in the amount of $ _____ in addition to the security deposit, if Lessee has an animal. Refundable deposits are to be refunded to Lessee only upon: 1. termination of tenancy; 2) delivery of possession of the property (including all keys), and; 3) Lessee's written demand for the return of the re-fundable security deposit which written demand must be delivered to the Lessor by certified mail return receipt requested or by hand delivery. If *there is unpaid rent, other charges or damages, any refundable security deposits shall first be applied to unpaid rent, charges and damages. In the event the sums due hereunder by Lessee to Lessor exceed the amount of the refundable security deposit for damages or under any provisions hereof, then Lessee agrees to pay any additional sums due over and above said security deposit to Lessor within thirty (30) days after notification by Lessor to Lessee of such sums due. The deposit shall bear no interest and shall be kept in such place as the Lessor designates.*

11. CONDITION OF PROPERTY UPON MOVE-IN

Now that the move-in walk-through has been completed, it is important that part of the lease contain an acknowledgment that the premises are in safe, habitable and good condition.

SAMPLE LEASE PROVISION

Lessee has inspected and examined the premises and finds the premises to be in good, safe and habitable condition. Lessee and Lessor have walked the property and Lessee has filled out a move-in walk-though report which is made part of the Lessor's file and a copy has been received by Lessee.

12. UTILITIES

The key regarding utilities is to specifically describe all the utilities and set forth who will pay what utility and when, regardless of whether the billing goes directly to the Resident, to the Landlord/Property Manager or is Sub-Metered.

Set forth you will pay each of the utilities:

A. Water
B. Sewer
C. Electric
D. Wastewater
E. Gas
F. Garbage Collection
G. Cable/Satellite TV
H. Internet
I. Pool and Spa
J. Pest Control
K. Outside Lawn Maintenance
L. Maintenance for any repairs or replacement of the unit, including, but not limited to, fixtures, appliances, windows, sheet rock, carpet, grout, etc. If utilities are sub-metered there may also be statutory provisions to be aware of in your jurisdiction.

Lessee is responsible for payment of all utilities including, but not limited to, water; sewage; garbage collection; cable TV; satellite; electricity; gas; internet services; satellite services; and phone services, even if the bills remain in Lessor's name. Failing to pay the utility bills timely is a material default hereunder and a violation of this Agreement. Any installation costs are the responsibility of Lessee. Any wall jacks, telephone or cable installation shall remain with the premises.

13. ATTORNEY FEES

You must have an attorney fees section if you want to get your attorney's fees included in a judgement. I remember in a law school class years ago where the professor, on the first day of class, made for an interesting fiasco. He was a very old, nice gentleman. His name was Dr. Smith, and he wrote the book we were using. He told the class that there were two golden rules to be a successful lawyer. He had the entire class on the edge of their chairs. He said the first rule is to never have more than one file opened on your desk at the same time. He continued, indicating the second rules was like unto the first, always remember Section 12-341.01. Then, he walked out of the class. Everyone looked around at each other for a few seconds, and then, all at the same time, everyone swarmed the library to try and find the statute (we did not have cell phones in those days). It was a statute explaining all about attorney fees. This is a simple thing to do and here is a sample.

SAMPLE LEASE PROVISION

In the event of any controversy or claim concerning this Agreement, the prevailing party shall be entitled to recover from the other party, all of its costs and expenses, including attorney fees, paralegal fees and all other costs. If Lessor engages an attorney, or if suit is brought to enforce any covenant of this Agreement, or for a breach of any covenant or condition herein contained, the Lessee agrees to pay all of Lessor's fees and costs and other sums due hereunder, regardless of whether a suit is brought.

14. PETS

There are three (3) ways to deal with pets.

    A. NO PETS. Do not allow pets. This language is simple and clear. But, it cuts down on your applicant pool.

"No pets of any kind are allowed on or in the premises at any time whatsoever."

B. PET AGREEMENT. Allow a pet, or pets, as you choose. However, if you can avoid having a petliving in your property, you will save money. In general, it is not whether you will have damage in the home if you allow a Resident to have a pet, rather it is a matter of how much damage you will have. That has been my experience. I do not hate pets. It is just a fact that I have run into many, many times with many clients. Pets in a rental cost the Landlord/Property Manager headaches and money. I realize that not allowing pets limits your renter pool. That is your choice. It is your money. The following is a provision you could put in your lease if you allow pets. One thing about pets you want to cover is EVERYTHING.

SAMPLE LEASE PROVISION

PET AGREEMENT
(Landlord – this is NOT for Use with Service or Assistive Animals)

I/WE understand if I/WE choose to have a pet after I/WE move-in, I/WE must get written approval from management prior to getting the pet. I/WE must also pay an additional, non-refundable deposit and additional rent as listed below. If a pet is found on the premises belonging to me/us, my/our guest(s) or any occupant of the premises without prior written permission, I/WE agree that the Rental Agreement may be terminated and that I/WE must immediately vacate the premises and pay all damages. All penalties shall attach for such a breach of the Rental Agreement.

Breed Restrictions are: NO Doberman, Chow, Rottweiler, German Shepherd, Mastiff, St. Bernard, Newfoundlander, or Pit Bull. No reptiles ever, with the exception of a turtle.
Pet Description (Only one pet will ever be allowed):

Name	Breed/Color/ Description	Weight	Age	Color

1. I/We agree to pay $_____.00 as a pet deposit of which $_____ is refundable. I/We understand that $_____ of the said deposit is non-refundable which is NOT part of the security deposit and is applied to sanitize the apartment after I/WE vacate. If, in the sole opinion of management, there is an odor or other damage, I/WE agree to pay the actual cost of returning the apartment to its original condition less the $_____ refundable deposit paid.

2. I/We agree to pay an additional $_____ per month as additional rent for having the pet.

3. I/We agree to keep my/our pet inside my/our apartment or walked on a leash not longer than six (6) feet long by a responsible adult. I/We will immediately remove pet droppings while walking my/our pet. Any damage done by my/our pet will be reported to management immediately, and I/We agree to pay for repairs no later than the next rental period. It is a violation of these policies if any Lessee simply "turns out the pet" and recalls it at his/her convenience. I/We will provide documentation from my/our veterinarian that my/our pet's mature weight is _____ lbs. or less and that it has received all shots and vaccine that should be recommended by a vet. Lessee shall ensure that the pet's shots are always current and shall provide proof of the same to the Lessor in writing, prior to move in, and every six months thereafter.

4. If my/our pet is a cat, I/we will also provide documentation that my/our cat is neutered/spayed and declawed. Exotic animals, including, but not limited to, rodents or reptiles are not permitted.

5. Patios/balconies shall be kept clean of pet droppings and urine. Pet food is not allowed to be left outside the unit at any time.

6. If, in management's sole opinion, my/our pet disturbs my/our neighbors in any way (i.e., barking, etc.) or if the agreement is violated, management may immediately revoke my/our pet agreement and I/We will immediately and permanently remove my/our pet from the property.

7. Pets are NOT allowed in the pools or pool areas at any time.

8. I/We am/are responsible for immediately cleaning up after my/our pet. Failure to do so will subject I/we to eviction proceedings.

9. Lessee(s) hereby acknowledges that his/her pet is safe, and that Lessee(s) will indemnify and hold the Lessor harmless from any injuries inflicted by his/her pet. Lessee(s) hereby warrants and discloses that his/her pet has never attacked, bitten, or injured another person, and that Lessee(s) indemnify and hold Lessor harmless, including the payment of court costs and attorney's fees incurred by Lessor, if a court orders the Lessor to pay damages to a third party injured by Lessee(s) pet.

DATED this _____ day of _____, 20____.

Lessee(s)   Lessor:

Signature(s):_____
        Signature(s):_____

C. A PET LICENSE

I do not allow any pets in my properties nor do many of my clients. But for those clients that did allow pets wanted better control over pet issue. Therefore, instead just allowing a pet in the lease, the parties would enter into a separate pet license agreement. Here is the pet license agreement language.

SAMPLE LEASE PROVISION

Lessee must obtain written approval from management prior to obtaining any pet. Lessee must also pay a revocable and non-refundable pet license fee which fee in not part of any security deposit. This pet license is a separate agreement from the lease agreement. If a pet is found on the premises belonging to Lessee, Lessee's guest(s) or any occupant of the premises without permission, Lessee agrees that the Rental Agreement may be terminated and that Lessee shall immediately vacate the premises, and that Lessee shall still be responsible for the monthly rent until the property is re-rented. A pet license may only be approved once the Lessee completes the following information and the Lessor agrees to the pet license in writing.

REVOCABLE PET LICENSE

**(THIS LICENSE MAY BE REVOKED AT ANY TIME BY LICENSOR
FOR ANY REASON OR NO REASON)**
Pet Description (Only one pet will ever be allowed):

Name	Breed/Color/Description	Weight	Age	Color

Breed Restrictions: NO Doberman, Chow, Rottweiler, German Shepherd, Mastiff, St. Bernard, Newfoundlander, or Pit Bull. No reptiles ever, with the exception of a small turtle.

1. Licensee shall pay a $_____.00 non-refundable, revocable pet license fee. If, in the sole opinion of Licensor, there is an odor or other damage, Licensee agrees to pay the actual cost of returning the premises to its original condition.

2. Licensee shall pay an $_____.00 per month to Licensor as a pet license.

3. Licensee shall keep Licensee's pet inside Licensee's premises or in its yard (*as Licensor chooses). Licensee's pet shall be walked only on a leash not longer than six (6) feet long by a responsible adult. Licensee will immediately remove pet droppings while walking Licensee's pet. Any damage done by Licensee's pet will be reported by Licensee to Licensor immediately and Licensee agrees to pay for and have repairs professionally made no later than Licensee's next rental period under Licensee's lease with the Landlord. It is a violation of these policies if any Licensee simply "turns out the pet" on the Landlord's property and recalls it at his/her convenience.

4. Licensee will provide documentation from Licensee's veterinarian that Licensee's pet's mature weight is, or will be less than 20 lbs. If Licensee's pet is a cat, Licensee will also provide documentation that Licensee's cat is neutered/spayed and de-clawed. Exotic animals, including, but not limited to, rodents or reptiles are not permitted. Licensee agrees to ensure that the pet's shots are always current and shall provide proof of the same to the Licensor in writing, prior to move in, and every six months thereafter.

5. Patios/balconies must be kept clean of pet droppings and urine. Pet food is not allowed to be left outside the unit at any time.

6. If, in Licensor's sole opinion, Licensee's pet disturbs Licensee's neighbors in any way (i.e., barking) or if this agreement is violated, Licensee's Landlord who is also Licensee's Landlord, and Licensee may immediately revoke Licensee's pet license and Licensee will immediately and permanently remove Resident's pet from the property. If Licensee fails to do so, then Licensor or Licensee's Landlord may do so, the Licensor and the Landlord being one in the same entity.

7. Pets are NOT allowed in the pool or spa at any time.

8. Licensee is responsible for immediately cleaning up after Licensee's pet. Failure to do so will subject Licensee revocation of the pet license and to eviction proceedings.

9. Licensee hereby acknowledges that his/her pet is safe, and that Licensee indemnifies and holds the Licensee and Landlord harmless from any injuries

inflicted by his/her pet to any person or property. Licensee hereby warrants and discloses that his/her pet has never attacked, bitten, or injured another person.

10. Licensee's pet is never allowed inside the house/unit or garage. (optional language at your discretion)

DATED this _____ day of _____, 20____.

RESIDENT(s)   LANDLORD/PROPERTYMANAGER:

Signature(s):_____   Signature(s):_____

RULES AND REGULATIONS

You can develop any rules that suit the needs of your property that are also compliant with law. The following are few to consider:

15. SAMPLE RULES AND REGULATIONS

A. Locks and Burglar Alarms. Lessee is prohibited from adding locks to or changing, or in any way altering locks installed on the doors of the premises without prior written permission of Lessor, and upon written permission. It is mandatory for Lessee to provide Lessor immediately with keys to such locks if allowed to modify the same. Lessee is prohibited from installing a burglar alarm, or changing or in any way or altering any existing burglar alarm installed on the premises, without prior written permission of Lessor. If the installation or changing of such burglar alarm is permitted, it is mandatory that Lessee shall immediately provide Lessor with all codes/keys to such burglar alarm/door.

B. Telephones. Lessee shall obtain a cell or home telephone and must supply Lessor with a cell or home phone number, and a work telephone number immediately and shall notify Lessor within forty-eight (48) hours of any change of any numbers during the term of this Agreement.

C. Storage. Goods or materials of any kind or description which are combustible, such as gasoline, propane, kerosene, starter fluid, acetone, fuel oil and etc., or that which may or would increase fire risk, shall NOT be stored in the premises within fifteen feet (15) from any structure on the property. Any storage shall be at Lessee's risk and expense and Lessor shall not be responsible for any loss or damage to anything or anyone.

D. Good Housekeeping by Lessee. Lessee agrees to keep the premises in a clean and sanitary condition and to remove from the property any trash or rubbish as it accumulates.

E. Pest control. Lessee shall provide pest control as needed, and no less than on a monthly basis, at Lessee's sole expense. Any infestation shall constitute a material default of this Agreement.

F. HVAC maintenance. Lessee shall change HVAC filter(s) monthly during the heating and cooling seasons, at Lessee's sole expense.

G. Space Heaters. Lessee shall not use any form of Kerosene, gasoline, propane, oil or electric space heater(s) in the premises.

H. Water-beds. No water-bed may be kept in the premises.

J. Yard Care. Lessee is responsible for maintaining the lawn, bushes, and trees in a neat and attractive manner at Lessee's sole expense. If not cared for, Lessor may cause the same to be maintained professionally and Lessee shall pay for same immediately upon delivery of an invoice.

K. Gutters. Lessee shall keep gutters cleaned as needed. Lessee is responsible for all costs for failure to do so. Lessee permission to Lessor to inspect the gutter at any time without further notice.

L. Basements. Lessor in no way warrants the basement, if one exists, against any leakage of any kind at any time. Further, Lessor does not warrant against any water leak at anytime, anywhere, nor is Lessor liable for damages to any person or property due to any water leak.

M. Septic. If the premises have a septic tank, Lessee shall not abuse or misuse the septic system, e.g., Lessee shall not deposit cooking oil, tobacco, coffee grounds or unnecessary food or other wastes or materials, including diapers, sanitary napkins, tampons, chemicals or other products, down sinks or toilets that are not specifically safe for the septic system. Lessee shall add septic tank treatment regularly, at least monthly. Such septic tank treatments are available at home supply stores (such as Ridx) at Lessee's cost, and Lessee shall keep the septic system operating properly and efficiently. Lessee is prohibited from adding a garbage disposal to the house if there is a septic system.

O. Grills and BBQ. Using any open flames such as gas grills or charcoal barbecues on balconies, patios and porches are prohibited. All such devices must be used at least fifteen (15) feet away from any structure on the property.

P. Vehicles. Vehicles shall NOT be parked on the lawn, dirt, sidewalks or walkways at any time and are never allowed inside the unit. Non-operative vehicles are not permitted on the premises. Any non-operative vehicle may be removed by Lessor at the expense of Lessee, for storage or public or private sale, at Lessor's option, and Lessee shall have no right of recourse against Lessor thereafter.
It is agreed that only the vehicles listed herein may be parked at the premises:

1. Year:____ Make: ____ Model: ____ Color: ___ License Plate #: _____
2. Year:____ Make: ____ Model: ____ Color: ___ License Plate #: _____
3. Year:____ Make: ____ Model: ____ Color: ___ License Plate #: _____
4. Year:____ Make: ____ Model: ____ Color: ___ License Plate #: _____

If a vehicle, in the reasonable opinion of the Lessor, is inoperable; abandoned; unmaintained; unauthorized; unregistered; unlicensed; uninsured, impedes the progress of a vendor or utility provider; is being, or has been, repaired on the property; is parked on the grass, dirt, walkways or sidewalk at the property, then that vehicle may be towed at the Lessee's expense without any additional notice or warning to Lessee, notwithstanding and superseding any city, state or county ordinance to the contrary. Lessee agrees that Lessee shall have no right of recourse whatsoever against Lessor thereafter. Lessee's sole recourse shall be against the tow company that towed the vehicle. Should Lessee violate these rules more than one time, in addition to any other rights of Lessor, Lessee shall pay a non-refundable fee to Lessor in the amount of $200.00 with Lessee's next monthly rent payment as additional rent for each occurrence and such act(s) shall be deemed a material breach of the lease agreement. Payment of said amount shall not limit Lessor's right to also evict Lessee for the violation.

Q. Bedbugs. Lessee has received educational materials on bedbugs, including information and physical descriptions, prevention and control measures, behavioural attraction risk factors, information from federal, state, and local centers for disease control and prevention, health or housing agencies, non-profit housing organizations, or information developed by the Lessor.

R. Changing a Rule During a Lease Term:

There is only one way to change and rule during the term of a Resident's lease. It is a statutory procedure and different states have different rules.

A. A Landlord/Property Manager, from time to time, may adopt rules or regulations, however described, concerning the Resident's use and occupancy of the premises. Such rules or regulations are enforceable against the Resident only if:

1. Their purpose is to promote the convenience, safety or welfare of the Residents in the premises, preserve the Landlord's/Property Manager's property from abusive use or make a fair distribution of services and facilities held out for the Residents generally.
2. They are reasonably related to the purpose for which adopted.
3. They apply to all Residents in the premises in a fair manner.
4. They are sufficiently explicit in prohibition, direction or limitation of the Resident's conduct to fairly inform the Resident of what the Resident must or must not do to comply.
5. They are not for the purpose of evading the obligations of the Landlord/Property Manager.

B. A rule or regulation adopted after the Resident enters into the rental agreement is enforceable against the Resident if a thirty-day notice of its adoption is given to the Resident and it does not constitute a substantial modification of the Resident's rental agreement.

C. If state, county, municipal or other governmental bodies adopt new ordinances, rules or other legal provisions affecting existing rental agreements, the Landlord/Property Manager may make immediate amendments to lease agreements to bring them into compliance with the law. The Landlord/Property Manager shall give a Resident written notice that the Resident's lease agreement has been amended, and the notice shall provide a brief description of the amendment and the effective date.

It is not often that you will need to modify a rule. The statute above is very clear on the procedure to make a change. The change of rule form below is considered a notice to a Lessee and must be properly served upon the Lessee. The notice may only be hand delivered or sent certified mail, depending on your State rules. There are no other ways to effectuate service. The following notice is a thirty (30) calendar day notice. Remember, if you send it certified mail, return receipt requested, add the mailing time and get it in the mail by the 24th of the month so it will be effective after a full monthly period.

TO: _____
    _____
    _____

FROM: _____
    _____
    _____

DATE: _____

**30-DAY NOTICE OF ADOPTION OF
NEW RULES OR REGULATIONS**

Pursuant to [whatever rule applies in your jurisdiction] and for the purpose of providing for the convenience, safety and/or welfare of the Lessee(s) in the premises, preserving the Lessor's property from abusive use or making a fair distribution of services and facilities held out for the Lessees generally, the following rules/regulations which have been adopted for this property (attached hereto).

This (these) new rules/regulations shall take effect on the _____ day of _____, 20_____. If you have any questions, please contact management.

By:_____

Title:_____

- Hand delivered
- Certified mail

on the _____ day of _____, 20___:

By: _____

Title:_____

16. RESIDENT DEFAULT

Both parties need a clear understanding as to how and what acts on the Resident's part constitute a default or breach of the Landlord and Tenant Act (or rules in your jurisdiction) and the other lease terms. This section can be modified for your particular lease needs. We will discuss how to enforce the default section later.

SAMPLE LEASE PROVISION

If Lessee fails to pay any installment of rent as provided herein within ____ (__) days from the date due, or if the lessee fails to timely cure any other default under this Agreement after receipt of written notice of such default by the lessor, then Lessor may terminate this Agreement without further notice and may (i) recover immediately from Lessee all rent and other sums due hereunder; (ii) cure such default and the expense of the curative action be added to the rent otherwise due; and/or (iii) enforce performance in any manner provided by law.

In any such event of default, Lessor may (i) take all legal remedies without being liable for trespass and without prejudice to any right or remedy for arrears of rent or breach; (ii) resume possession of the property and re-lease the same for the remainder of the then operative term; (iii) terminate Lessee's right to possession of the premises by any lawful means, in which case this lease shall terminate, and Lessee shall immediately surrender possession of the premises to Lessor.

In such event, Lessor shall be entitled to recover from Lessee all damages incurred by Lessor by reason of Lessee's default, including, but not limited to, the cost of recovering possession of the premises; any concessions given; early termination fees; all costs of collection pre and post judgement, including, but not limited to attorney fees and cost; and any leasing commission paid by Lessor for the defaulting Lessee lease and for any new Lessee lease obtained; all expenses for utilities until the time of re-letting the premises; and compensation for all damages to the premises. Unpaid installments of rent or other sums due shall bear interest from the date due at the rate of ____% interest per annum.

If rent is not paid when due, then Lessor may assert immediately any and all legal, equitable and contractual remedies to enforce this Agreement. Lessor may file a complaint in special detainer and evict and remove Lessee and any other occupants. Should Lessee answer the complaint, Lessee shall pay into the registry of the trial court all monies and all rent due. Whenever Lessor is entitled to possession of the premises: (i) Lessee will surrender same to Lessor in as good condition as at present and Lessee will remove all Lessee's effects. Lessor may re-enter the premises and repossess the premises and remove all persons and effects there from using such force as necessary without being guilty of forcible entry or detainer, trespass or other tort. Lessee is hereby advised if such action is necessary, a judgment may be rendered against Lessee for full damages including rent, eviction costs, and any additional costs and fees. If said costs and fees are not paid as ordered, monies may be collected through garnishment against wages and/or assets and judgments may be recorded with credit bureaus and may be assigned to a collection agency for collection with all costs of collection being the responsibility of Lessee.

OTHER IMPORTANT LEASE PROVISIONS TO CONSIDER

There are many areas of everyday workings of a Landlord/Property Manager and Resident relationship that are not set forth in statutes, guidelines or ordinances. Therefore, I have included some additional lease provisions that will be useful in constructing a lease agreement to fit your particular needs.

ADDITIONAL SAMPLE LEASE PROVISIONS

17. SMOKE DETECTORS. Lessee acknowledges the requirement for working smoke detectors/alarms in the premises and agrees to install, if necessary and in all events, and test all detectors/alarms weekly for proper operation. Lessee further agrees to replace any batteries (if so equipped) when necessary at Lessee's sole expense. Lessee also acknowledges Lessee's ability and understanding of how to test and operate smoke detectors/alarms. Lessee agrees to repair or replace any inoperative smoke detector/alarm immediately should it fail to operate properly during any monthly test and do so at Lessee's sole expense.

18. INDEMNIFICATION. Lessee shall indemnify and hold Lessor harmless from and against any and all penalties, claims, demands and liability of whatsoever kind or nature including attorneys' and paralegals' fees, all as may be made or sought against Lessor or the premises arising out of or in any way connected with Lessee's repair(s), occupancy, use, maintenance or operation of the premises, and Lessee shall defend Lessor from and against each and every such claim.

19. RENTERS' INSURANCE. Since Lessor's insurance **DOES NOT** cover Lessee, Lessee's occupants or Lessee's property for any reason, Lessee shall purchase a comprehensive Renter's Insurance Policy, against all perils, including, but not limited to, insurance on personal property and property of other persons for protection of loss due to or caused by theft, vandalism, bursting or breaking pipes, by or from fire, wind storm, hail, acts of God, malfunction of furniture/equipment and fixtures, flooding, leakage, steam, smoke, snow and ice, by or from running water, backing up of drainage pipes, seepage and the overflow of water or sewage on the premises, or from any other peril. Said policy shall include general liability coverage for in and in the amount of a minimum of $30,000.00. A copy of said policy shall be delivered to Lessor prior to move-in. With respect to any renewal policy, a duplicate original policy shall be provided to the Lessor by Lessee not less than ten (10) days prior to the expiration date of the then existing policy. Said policy shall be in force at all times during the tenancy or any renewal thereof.

20. EXCULPATORY CLAUSE. The Lessor's liability under this Agreement shall be limited to Lessor's ownership interest in the premises.

21. EMINENT DOMAIN. If all of the premises are taken under the power of eminent domain or conveyed by voluntary deed in lieu of condemnation proceedings, or if only a part of such premises is so taken or conveyed and the remainder thereof is inadequate or unsatisfactory for Lessee's purposes (the determination of which shall not be made arbitrarily or capriciously) then, in either such event, this Agreement shall terminate effective as of the date Lessee is required to vacate the premises. The termination of this Agreement as above provided shall not operate to deprive Lessee of the right to make claims against the condemning authority for any damage suffered by lessee, but Lessee possesses no right to make any claim against Lessor because of such termination. If this Agreement is not terminated as above provided, Lessor and Lessee shall agree upon an equitable reduction of rent for the remaining portion of the premises, but no reduction of rent shall occur if the taking does not include any of the building. If the parties fail to agree upon such reduction within sixty (60) days from the date of the final payment for the part of the leased premises so taken or conveyed, then either lessor or lessee may give thirty (30) day notice of termination.

22. ASSIGNMENT AND SUBLETTING. Lessee may not assign this Agreement nor sublease the whole or any part of the demised premises without the prior written consent of the Lessor. Any subletting, if granted, shall not release Lessee from the obligations outlined herein.

23. FIRE. If the premises are made uninhabitable by fire or other casualty, not the fault of Lessee, this Agreement shall be voidable by either party.

24. WILDLIFE. Lessee agrees and understands that the premises are located in area where wildlife of all types maintain a natural habitat. Lessee also understands that Lessee's can inadvertently bring various forms of wildlife into the premises upon move-in or when Lessee brings groceries or other items to the premises. As part of their natural habitat and as a matter of practicality in living in an apartment community, a single-family home or in a property of any kind, it is common that various forms of wildlife, including, but not limited to, animals, rodents, insects, bedbugs, lice, scorpions, birds and snakes may be present in, on, at and about the premises. Lessee understands that the presence of such wildlife is not the fault of the Lessor and that Lessee is responsible for Lessee's own safety regarding wildlife in and about the premises. If Lessee desires to limit Lessee's risk regarding wildlife, Lessee is hereby notified and accepts responsibility to contact the appropriate wildlife and/or health agencies for instructions for how to deal with wildlife of any and all kinds, and Lessee agrees to take whatever action is necessary to insure against potential loss resulting from wildlife. Lessee acknowledges that Lessor does not have any control over uninvited wildlife as such wildlife may relate to Lessee, Lessee's occupants, and Lessee's guests and invitees. Lessee hereby releases Lessor regarding any encounters or incidents with wildlife of any kind, including but not limited to, animals, rodents, insects, bedbugs, lice, scorpions, birds, snakes or any other wildlife. Lessee also agrees not to feed any wildlife on or near the premises. Lessor warrants that upon move-in, the unit has been sprayed with insecticide and is in good, safe and habitable condition. If Lessee encounters any wildlife, Lessee must notify Lessor in writing and reasonably work with Lessor to remedy the situation as practically as possible under the circumstances.

25. SATELLITE DISH AND ANTENNA. Under rules of the Federal Communications Commission (FCC), Lessee has a limited right to install a satellite dish or receiving antenna within the lease premises. Lessor is allowed to impose reasonable restrictions relating to such installation. Lessee is required to comply with these restrictions as a condition of installing such equipment. Lessee agrees to follow:

1. Number and size. Lessee may install only one satellite dish or antenna within the premise's boundaries that are leased to Resident for Lessee's exclusive use. A satellite dish may not exceed 39 inches in diameter. An antenna/dish may receive, but not transmit signals.

2. Location of the satellite dish or antenna is limited to (1) inside Lessee's dwelling, or (2) in an area outside Lessee's dwelling such as a balcony, patio, yard, etc. of which Lessee has exclusive use under Lessee's lease. Installation is not permitted on any parking area, roof, exterior wall, window, windowsill, fence, common area, wall, or in an area that other Lessees are allowed to use. A satellite dish may not protrude beyond the vertical and horizontal space that is leased to Lessee for Lessee's exclusive use.

3. Safety and non-interference. Lessee installation: (1) must comply with reasonable safety standards; (2) may not interfere with Lessor's cable, telephone, or electrical system or those of neighbouring properties; (3) may not be connected to Lessor's telecommunication systems; and (4) may not be connected to Lessor's electrical system except by plugging into a 110-volt duplex receptacle. If the satellite dish or antenna is placed in a permitted outside area, it must be safely secured by one of the three methods: (1) securely attaching it to a portable, heavy object such as a small slab of concrete; (2) clamping it to a part of the building exterior that lies within Lessee's leased premises (such as a balcony or patio railing); or (3) any other method approved in writing by the Lessor. No other methods are allowed. Lessor may require reasonable screening of the satellite dish or antenna by plants, etc. so long as it does not impair reception.

4. Signal transmission from exterior dish or antenna to interior of dwelling. Lessee may not damage or alter the leased premises and may not drill holes through the outside walls, door jambs, windowsills, etc. If Lessee's satellite dish or antenna is installed outside Lessee's living area (on balcony, patio, or yard of which Lessee has exclusive use under Lessee's lease), signals received by Lessee's satellite dish or antenna may be transmitted to the interior of Lessee's dwelling only by: (1) running a "flat" cable under a door jamb or windowsill in a manner that does not physically alter the premises and does not interfere with proper operation of the door or window; (2) running a traditional or flat cable through a pre-existing hole in the wall (that will not need to be enlarged to accommodate the cable); (3) connecting cables "through a window pane" similar to how an external car antenna for a cellular phone can be connected to inside wiring by a device glued to either side of the window, without drilling a hole through the glass; (4) wireless transmission of the signal to a device inside the dwelling; or (5) any other method approved in writing by the agent for Lessor.

5. Workmanship. For safety purposes, Lessee must obtain Lessor's approval of (1) the strength of materials to be used for installation, and (2) the person or company who will perform the installation. Installation must be done by a qualified person or company that has worker's compensation insurance and adequate public liability insurance. Landlord's approval will not be unreasonably withheld. Lessee must obtain required city permits for installation and comply with applicable city ordinances.

6. Removal and damages. Lessee must remove the satellite dish and/or antenna and all related equipment. Lessee may be required to remove the satellite dish and/or antenna if necessary, to make repairs to the building. Lessee is responsible for all damages regarding installation or removal during the lease or any renewal thereof. Upon vacating the premises Lessee shall put the premises back into the same condition it was in prior to installation. Lessor, or its agent, shall be the sole judge of the condition of the premises upon vacating. If Lessee fails to do so, Lessee shall be responsible to pay for any all damages.

7. Maintenance. Resident will have the sole responsibility for maintaining Lessee's satellite dish or antenna and all related equipment. Lessee may be required to remove the satellite dish and/or antenna if necessary, to make repairs to the building.

8. Deposit increase. A deposit increase (in connection with having a satellite or antenna) may be required by Lessor to help protect Lessor against possible repair costs, damages or any failure to remove the satellite dish or antenna and related equipment at time of move-out. A deposit increase does not imply a right to drill or alter the leased premises.

9. When Lessee may begin installation. Lessee may start installation of Lessee's satellite dish or antenna only after Lessee have: (2) provided management with written evidence of liability insurance and all other requirements referred to above; (3) paid management the additional deposit, if applicable, set forth above; and (4) received management's written approval of the installation materials and the person or company who will perform the installation.

26. PERSONAL AND PROPERTY LOSS & LIABILITY. Lessor is not liable for damage of any kind, including, but not limited to, theft, vandalism, or other loss of any kind to Lessee's personal property or the personal property of Lessee's occupants, guests or invitees. Lessor shall not be responsible or liable for any injury, loss or damage to any person or property of Lessee or any other person in or on the premises that is not a result of intentional misconduct by the Lessor. Lessee specifically agrees to look solely to Lessor's interest and ownership in the premises for obtaining or recovery of any judgment against Lessor. It is also agreed that Lessor and its officers, directors, managers, employees, partners, and members shall never be personally liable for any claim whatsoever by Lessee.

Lessor is not responsible for any injury to any person or any damage or loss to any property of Lessee, Lessee 's occupants, guests or invitees, caused by acts of God, fire, any criminal act by any third party, theft, burglary, malicious act, riot, smoke, explosion, sonic booms, insurrection, civil commotion, pandemic, the elements, failure or malfunction of furniture, fixtures or equipment in the premises or on the grounds in general. Lessor shall not be responsible for neglect, intentional acts or criminal acts of other Lessees, negligence of Lessor or Lessees of any contiguous property, or from any other cause outside the direct control of the Lessor.

Lessee understands and agrees that Lessee 's safety and security is Lessee 's own personal responsibility. Lessor does not provide any security devices or security mechanisms for the purpose of protecting Lessee except for the interior locks. Such services or mechanisms, if provided, are provided solely for the protection of the Lessor's property and not for the protection Lessees, Lessees' occupants, Lessees' guests, Lessees' invitees or for Lessees' personal property. Any benefit Lessee receives as a result of such services or mechanisms are only incidental to their existence. Lessee shall do whatever Lessee deems necessary to protect Lessee(s), Lessees' occupants, guests, and invitees from crime, accident or any natural catastrophe.

In the event of criminal activity, Lessee shall first contact the police department. Lessee recognizes that Lessor does not guarantee, warrant or assure Resident's personal security. LESSEE UNDERSTANDS THAT ANY PROTECTIVE STEPS LESSOR HAS TAKEN, OR MAY LATER TAKE, ARE NEITHER A GUARANTEE NOR WARRANTY THAT THERE WILL BE NO CRIMINAL ACTS ON THE PROPERTY OR THAT LESSEE WILL BE FREE FROM ANY VIOLENT ACTS OF THIRD PERSONS. LESSEE HAS BEEN INFORMED, AND UNDERSTANDS AND AGREES, THAT HIS/HER/THEIR PERSONAL

SAFETY AND SECURITY IS HIS/HER/THEIR PERSONAL RESPONSIBILITY.

Lessor strongly urges Lessee to keep all doors and windows locked while Lessee is inside the premises. Lessee shall always call the local law enforcement agency whenever Lessee is in need of security services; do not contact the management office for this will only delay the response time. In case of an emergency Lessee shall call "**911**".

Lessor shall not be responsible in any way for any accidental, negligent or intentional act involving any weapon, or discharge thereof, in, on, near or off of the property.

Lessor strongly urges Lessee to keep all doors and windows locked while Lessee is inside the premises. Lessee shall always call the local law enforcement agency whenever Lessee is in need of security services; do not contact the management office for this will only delay the response time. In case of an emergency Lessee shall call "911".

Lessor shall not be responsible in any way for any accidental, negligent or intentional act involving any weapon, or discharge thereof, in, on, near or off of the property.

27. TERRORISM WARRANT BY RESIDENT: Lessee warrants and represents to Lessor that Lessee is not and shall not become a person or involved with an entity with whom Lessor is restricted from doing business under regulations of the Office of Foreign Asset Control ("OFAC") of the Department of the Treasury (including, but not limited to, those named on OFAC's Specially Designated and Blocked Persons list) or under any statute, executive order (including, but not limited to, the September 24, 2001, Executive Order Blocking Property and Prohibiting Transactions With Persons Who Commit, Threaten to Commit, or Support Terrorism), or other governmental action, and that Resident is not, and Resident shall not, knowingly engage in any such dealings or transaction, nor be otherwise associated with such persons or entities. If Lessee is not a citizen of the USA, Lessee agrees to keep a current visa at all times or be subject to termination if Lessee fails to do so.

28. POOL/SPA. Lessee agrees that if there is a swimming pool/spa on the premises, Lessee shall use the pool/spa in a responsible manner and to ensure that Lessee's occupants, guests and invitees do the same. Lessee understands and agrees that pools and spas, like any pool or spa, carry with them the risk of injury and/or death. Lessee understands and agrees that no lifeguard is on duty and that Lessee, Lessee's occupants, guests and invitees may only use the pool/spa at their own risk. Lessor is not responsible in any way for damages regarding the pool/spa. Lessee understands that there may not be a gate around the pool/spa and that Lessee takes full responsibility for the prevention and care of all that occupy or visit the property to ensure their safety regarding the pool/spa. Lessee agrees to contact the County and City/Town authorities regarding pools/spas and the safe use thereof; and Lessee agrees to comply with all such rules, regulations,

156

codes and ordinances. Lessee understands that Lessor's insurance does not cover Lessee, Lessee's occupants, guests or invitees in regard to their use of the pool/spa.

29. MOLD

A. Mold consists of naturally occurring microscopic organisms, which reproduce by spores. Mold breaks down and feeds on organic matter in the environment. Mold spores may spread through the air and that the combination of moisture and organic matter allows for mold growth. Not all mold is readily visible, but when it is, it can often be seen in the forms of discoloration, ranging from white to orange or red and from green or blue to brown and black. Often there is a musty odor present. Reducing moisture by proper housekeeping significantly reduces the chance of mold and mold growth.

B. Mold is a significant portion of the earth's biomass and is a natural and essential part of the earth's biology as it is effective in digesting cellulose materials. Mold breaks such materials down into smaller substances that can then be recycled back into the ecosystems. After breaking down materials, mold engages in a reproductive cycle which is when spores are produced.

C. People react to mold spores in many ways including symptoms such as minor reactions like watery eyes or a runny nose, to possible illness. Because mold may also create toxic by-products, Lessee agrees to reduce the probability of any toxins or mold inside the property unit in an effort to avoid any possible negative health complications.

1. Effective Mold Prevention. In order to survive, mold must eat. Therefore, mold will attack almost anything inside a home in order to survive. However, there are two critical factors that must be present for mold to grow. These include water and food. Without water, either in the form of liquid or humidity in the air, mold cannot live and grow. Mold growth rates increase as ambient temperatures rise. Hot and humid weather is ideal for mold growth. Therefore, in order to prevent mold, the most important step must be to avoid the build-up of water and to keep the indoors dry and cool. Thus, Lessee agrees to keep the premises free from unnecessary moisture.

2. Climate Control. In order to prevent mold, Lessee agrees to control the climate of the premises. Therefore, Lessee agrees to use all air-conditioning, if provided, in a reasonable manner and use heating systems in moderation and to keep the premises properly ventilated by periodically opening windows to allow circulation of fresh air, during dry weather only. Lessee further agrees to accomplish the following measures to prevent mold in the premises:

A. Keep the premises clean and regularly dust, vacuum and mop.

B. Use hood vents when cooking, cleaning and dish washing.

C. Hang shower curtains inside the bathtub when showering.

D. Wipe down floors if any water spillage.

E. Open blinds/curtains to allow in light.

F. Keep closet doors ajar.

G. Avoid excessive indoor plant use.

H. Securely close shower doors when in use.

I. Use exhaust fans when bathing/showering and leave on for a sufficient amount of time to remove moisture after bathing/showering.

J. Leave bathroom and shower doors open after use.

K. Use ceiling fans, if present.

L. Wipe down windows and sills if moist.

M. Water all indoor plants outdoors.

N. Use dryer for wet towels.

O. Wipe down any moisture and/or spillage.

P. Use household cleaners on any hard surfaces.

Q. Wipe down bathroom walls and fixtures after bathing/showering.

R. Remove any moldy or rotting food.

S. Wipe down any vanities/sink tops.

T. Remove garbage regularly.

U. Regularly inspect for leaks under sinks.

V. Never dry clothes by hanging or drying indoors.

W. Regularly empty dehumidifier, if used.

3. *Notification.* Lessee must also be alert and on guard whenever there is a water leak. Plumbing leaks, roof leaks, foundations leaks, or any other source of water that penetrates into the home MUST be immediately reported in writing and by phone to Lessor. A prompt report in writing will give the Lessor the opportunity to repair the water penetration and thereby prevent the growth of mold. Lessee agrees to immediately report in writing and by phone to Lessor:

A. Visible or suspected mold.

B. All a/c or heating problems or abnormalities.

C. Leaks, moisture accumulations, major spillage.

D. Damp, warm, extending or sinking floors.

E. Shower/bath/sink/toilet overflows.

F. Leaky faucets, plumbing.

G. Any and all moisture and musty odors, (especially damp walls).

H. Loose, missing, failing or falling grout or caulk around tubs, showers, sinks, faucets, counter tops.

I. Clothes dryer vent leaks.

J. Moldy clothing.

K. Refrigerator and a/c drip pan overflows.

L. Discoloration of walls, baseboards, doors, window frames, ceilings.

4. Small Areas of Mold. If mold has occurred on a small non-porous surface such as ceramic tile, Formica, vinyl flooring, metal, or plastic and the mold is not due to an ongoing leak or moisture problem, Lessee agrees to clean the areas with soap (or detergent) and a small amount of water, let the surface dry, and then within 2 hours apply a non-staining cleaner such as Lysol Disinfectant, Pine-Sol Disinfectant (original pine-scented), Tilex Mildew Remover or Clorox Clean-up (make sure Clorox or other cleaners will not bleach/damage floor before using).

5. General Precautions. Lessee agrees as a precaution to using Lessee's air conditioner, whenever relative humidity is 60% or higher and temperatures are 80 degrees Fahrenheit or higher. Lessee agrees to keep humidity levels within the rented unit under 60%. Moving air with fans will help to facilitate drying, but high levels of humidity can only be effectively controlled through the use of an air conditioner or dehumidifier during periods of high temperature or humidity.

6. Default

A. A default under the terms of this mold section shall be deemed a material default under the terms of the Lease, and Lessor shall be entitled to exercise all rights and remedies at law, including eviction.

B. Resident agrees to be liable to Lessor or its Agent for any damages the premises sustains as a result of the Lessee(s) failure to comply with this mold section.

7. Acknowledgment. Lessee acknowledges that Lessee has a duty to keep the rental unit clean and take measures to retard and prevent mold from accumulating in the unit and/or on the surfaces of the rental unit. Lessee agrees to clean and dust on a regular basis and remove visible moisture accumulations on windows, wall and other surfaces. Lessee agrees not to block or cover any heating ventilation or air conditioning ducts in the rental unit. Lessee further agrees that Lessee shall be responsible for damage to the premises and Lessee's property as well as injury to Lessee, occupants, guests and invitees resulting from Lessee's failure to comply with the terms of mold section.

8. Defense and Indemnity. Lessee agrees to defend, indemnify and hold harmless Lessor and entities affiliated with Lessor against and from any and all actions, causes of actions, claims, demands, liabilities, losses, damages and expenses of any kind asserted against Lessor and its agents or its affiliates that arise out of or that are based upon any molds, mildew, or fungi brought into the premises or allowed to be brought into the premises, or that are allowed to grow in the premises, or that are caused in the premises, or that affect the premises as a result of the action(s), including inactions and/or omissions of Lessee or any guest or other person living in, visiting, occupying, using or residing in the premises.

30. MAINTENANCE AND REPAIRS. Lessee acknowledges the entire premises are in good, safe, habitable and properly working order. Lessee agrees to keep the inside and outside of the premises in clean, safe and habitable and properly working condition. Lessee agrees to spray for insects/bugs at least on a monthly basis at Lessee's own expense. Upon termination of this Agreement and/or upon vacating of the premises by Lessee, Lessee shall surrender possession of the premises in good, clean, habitable and properly working condition. Lessee shall change the HVAC filter(s) at least on a monthly basis at Lessee's expense. Failure to do so may result in serious damage and costly repairs or replacement of the HVAC equipment at the Lessee's expense. Lessee agrees to use all electrical fixtures, plumbing fixtures, heating, ventilating, air-conditioning, appliances, facilities, utilities, services and amenities in a reasonable manner without waste and without intentional or negligent damage, neither impairing or removing any part(s) of the equipment, nor permitting anyone else to do so.

Lessee agrees that Lessor has rented the premises to Lessee at below market value as adequate consideration for Lessee maintaining the inside and outside of the home and making all repairs to the property that are required to keep the premises and all of its equipment in good working order. Lessee shall also notify Lessor in writing of any needed repair before it is made. The parties agree that these provisions regarding maintenance and repairs are entered into in good faith and not for the purpose of evading any obligations of the Lessor.

**Access For Repair Requests By Lessee:** It is the duty of Resident that if there is any situation or occurrence in or about the premises that requires the Lessor to provide maintenance, or to make a repair(s) in order to keep the premises in a habitable condition. Therefore, Resident must deliver (by hand delivery or by certified mail – no other method shall be acceptable except in the case of an emergency) to the Lessor a written notice regarding the situation or occurrence that requires the Lessor to provide maintenance or to make a repair(s). Upon proper delivery of said written notice, Lessor, or its agent, shall have the right to access the premises after Resident's delivery of the forty-eight (48) hour notice to perform the maintenance or repair(s). However, if in the opinion of the Lessor the notice for Lessor to provide maintenance or repair(s) constitutes an emergency situation, then, the Lessor, or its agent, may enter the premises immediately, without further notice, in an effort to perform the maintenance or repair(s).

31. APPLIANCES. All appliances of any kind, including, but not limited to, window air conditioner(s), refrigerator(s), dishwasher(s), oven(s), washer, dryer, r/o and soft water system(s), etc., are excluded specifically from this Agreement. Such appliances remain as a convenience to Lessee and Lessor assumes no responsibility for their operation. No part of the monthly rent is attributable any appliance for rent or for Lessor to maintain. Lessor agrees to use any appliance in a safe manner and not to commit waste of any kind. Lessee also agrees to be responsible for making repairs to all appliances during Lessee's tenancy should any fail. Lessee shall also notify Lessor of any repair that is needed. Lessee agrees that Lessor may charge Resident for any repairs needed for appliances at time of termination and for any damages caused to appliances.

32. ACCESS GATES. Any gate on the property is for the purpose of access only. There are no security gates. Any access gates may be removed by Lessor at any time. In the event that any gate is damaged or becomes non-operational, Lessor agrees to immediately repair the same at Lessor's own expense, or in the Lessor's sole discretion, and the Lessor may remove the access gate all together. Lessor agrees not to rely on any access gate for any type of security or protection, as none is offered or provided.

33. ALTERATIONS. Lessor will not make, or allow to be made, any alterations, istallations or redecoration of any kind to the premises without prior written permission from the Lessor, including, but not limited to, nails holes, screws and screw holes, adhesive or hangers, shade brackets, or curtain rod brackets placed in or to walls or woodwork. No alternations or improvements to the exterior or interior of the premises shall be made by Lessor without written permission of the Lessor. Lessee is prohibited from adding, changing or in any way altering the locks in the premises without prior written permission of the Lessor. Lessor's response to any verbal request of the Lessor shall not waive the strict requirement for written notices to be delivered to the Lessor by the Resident. If Lessor requests additional security devices, such request must be in writing and Lessor shall provide keys and/or codes to all such devices should Lessor agree to the same.

If Lessor does consent to any alterations, installations or redecorations of any kind Lessor shall require such alterations, installations or redecorations to be made by a licensed contractor who is bonded and insured and who signs a written lien waiver/ release for the Lessor before starting any work. Lessee agrees all alterations, installations or redecorations including, without limitation, any items affixed to the premises, shall become the property of Lessor upon the termination of this Agreement. This includes, but is not limited to, appliances, HVAC system and units, ceiling fans, mini blinds, carpeting, fencing, lighting fixtures, shrubs, flowers, etc. Removal of these items shall be considered theft subject to civil and criminal prosecution.

34. RADON GAS AND LEAD PAINT DISCLOSURE AND DISCLAIMER. Radon is a naturally occurring radioactive gas that, when it is accumulated in buildings in sufficient quantities, may present health risks to persons who are exposed to it over time. Levels of radon that exceed federal and state guidelines have been found in public buildings. Additional information regarding radon and radon testing may be obtained from your county public health department. The lessor did not test for radon gas at the premises and therefore makes no representation regarding the presence or absence of such gas. Lessee hereby waives any and all actions against lessor related to the presence of such gas.

35. LEAD BASED PAINT NOTIFICATION AND ENFORCEMENT. For any apartment or for any single-family home built before 1978 the Lessor must comply with Federal Regulation regarding lead-based paint notification and enforcement. The following form provides prospective renters with information for people to protect themselves and their families form exposure or possible exposure to lead poison.

Housing built before 1978 may contain lead-based paint. Lead from paint chips and dust can pose health hazards if not managed properly. Lead exposure is especially harmful to young children and pregnant women. Before renting pre-1978 housing, lessors must disclose the presence of known lead-based paint and/or lead-based paint hazards in the dwelling. Lessees must also receive a federally approved pamphlet on lead poisoning prevention.

Lessor's Disclosure:

> **(1) Presence of lead-based paint and/or lead-based paint hazards.**
>> **(a) Lessor has no knowledge of lead-based paint and/or lead-based paint hazards in the housing**

> **(2) Records and reports available to the Lessor.**
>> **(a) Lessor has no reports or records pertaining to lead-based paint and or lead-based paint hazards in the housing.**

Lessee's Acknowledgement:

> **(3) Lessee has received copies of all information listed above, if any.**
> **(4) Lessee has received the pamphlet "Protect Your Family from Lead in Your Home".**

Certification of Accuracy

By evidence of their signatures below, the parties have reviewed the information above and certify, to the best of their knowledge, that the information they have provided is true and accurate.

36. FAILURE OF LESSOR TO ACT. Failure of Lessor to insist upon strict compliance with the terms of this Agreement shall not constitute a waiver of any violation, nor shall any acceptance of a partial payment of rent or partial acceptance of Lessor's repair, replacement, installation and/or maintenance, be deemed a waiver of Lessor's right to full amount compensation or full performance.

37. RIGHT OF ACCESS. During reasonable hours, Lessor may enter the premises upon delivery of a forty-eight (48) (check your jurisdiction to be safe here) notice to Lessee for inspection and maintenance. If locks were changed without providing Lessor with a key, Lessor may enter forcibly without being liable for damage or unlawful entry. Lessor may enter at any time in case(s) of emergency without notice of any kind to Lessee. During the last sixty (60) days of occupancy, or upon notification of intent to vacate, Lessor may place a sign on the premises and/or may install a lock box and show the premises during reasonable hours. During that time, Lessor will attempt to notify Lessee, but is not obligated to do so. (again, check your jurisdiction here)

38. HOLDING OVER. If Lessee remains in possession of the premises after expiration of the term hereof; Lessee shall be a "tenant at will" and there shall be no renewal of this Agreement. The monthly rent during any period beyond the term or after default hereof shall be twice the then monthly rent.

39. REMEDIES CUMULATIVE. All remedies under this Agreement or by law or equity shall be cumulative. In the event either Lessor or Lessee brings legal action to enforce the terms hereof or relating to the rental of the premises or whether suit be brought and whether incurred before, during or after any claim, notice of civil action, the appeal thereof on any Bankruptcy proceedings, the prevailing party shall be entitled to all costs incurred in connection with such action including attorneys' and paralegals' fees. If the services of a collection agency are necessary to collect any amounts due hereunder, Lessee agrees to pay any commissions for the same that Lessor contracts to pay with the collection attorney or collection agency or agent.

40. ENFORCEABILITY. If any term or provision of this Agreement, or application thereof to any person, is determined invalid or unenforceable, the remainder of this Agreement shall not be affected thereby.

41. NO ESTATE IN LAND. This Agreement shall create the relationship of Landlord-Tenant relationship between Lessor and Lessee. No estate shall pass out of Lessor. Lessee agrees that Lessee has no legal or equitable interest in the premises.

42. NON-RECORDATION. The Agreement shall not be recorded by Lessee or by any respective heirs and legal representatives.

43. ACCURACY AND RESPONSIBILITY. Lessor relied materially upon the information contained in Lessee's Application. It is agreed that the parties mutually negotiated this agreement and that Lessee warrants that the Lease Application is true, complete and accurate. If any statement in the lease application is false or misleading, Lessor may terminate this Agreement immediately. Lessor shall be entitled to retain any improvements to the premises, and any prepaid rents and/or security deposit. If Lessor terminates this Agreement for this cause, all persons and possessions may be removed from the premises after 24 hours of notification to Lessee by Lessor. Lessee further agrees to indemnify Lessor for any damages to the premises and Lessee waives any right of "set-off' and the same shall not be a charge to Lessor in any way. (Be sure to check your jurisdiction regarding this clause).

44. SUBORDINATION. The Agreement is automatically subordinate to any mortgage now or hereafter placed on the premises; provided, as a condition to such subordination as to mortgages hereafter entered into, such mortgagee shall expressly covenant, or such mortgage shall provide expressly, that so long as the lessee is not in default under the respective Agreement, the Lessee's quiet possession of the premises which shall remain undisturbed.

45. SEVERABILITY. If any part of this Agreement is construed as unenforceable, the remaining parts hereof shall remain in full force and effect as though the unenforceable part or parts were not written into this Agreement.

46. GENDER. All references to lessee herein employed shall be construed to include the plural as well as the singular, and the masculine shall include the feminine where the context of this Agreement may require.

47. COMPLETE AGREEMENT. This Agreement and all attachments and exhibits contain collectively the complete expression of the parties on the subjects herein and therein set forth and there are no promises, representations or inducements except such as are so provided, incorporated herein or referenced hereby.

48. MISCELLANEOUS. Subject to the provisions hereof this Agreement shall be binding upon the Lessee and all respective heirs and legal representatives and inures only to the benefit of Lessor and Lessee, and lessor's successors and assigns. This agreement is a _____ (state) contract and shall be construed in accordance with _____ (state) law.

Principle # 9

MOVE-IN WALK-THROUGH

Many Landlords/Property Managers do not perform a walk through with the Residents. This is a very, very bad idea. A lot of leasing is done on-line these days, but you have to do a walk through in person or through a representative. It is easy for a Landlord/ Property Manager to get lazy, or just not care, as properly managing can time-consuming if not set up right from the beginning. It takes effort to stay up on it. But remember, you have to take care of your investment and set the stage to show that you care. It is a perfect time to further explain more about the lease and expectations.

Advertising the property on websites is much different than the reasons why a move-in walk-through with the Resident is always needed – no matter what. If you want to avoid problems with security deposits and have proof of the condition of the property at the time of leasing, be smart and ensure a walk-through inspection with the Resident is performed. It really is critical.

I cannot tell you how many cases and trials I have had that have been over a security deposit return issues where there was no evidence of the condition of the property at move-in showing a move-in and move-out inspection check list. That always cuts against the Landlord/Property Manager. Residents many times say that they, "left the property in better condition when they left than it was when they moved in". You have to have evidence to prove the truth. If there is no move-in, move-out inspection check list with pictures and/or video then the judge sees you as a poor Landlord/Property Manager and the judge is left believing the Resident.

DO NOT just give the Resident a walk-through inspection form and tell them to fill it out in 5 or 10 days and return it. That is simply NOT good enough to protect you. You may never get it. You may get it after the Resident causes damage to the property and the Resident writes about the damage they caused after moving being present before they moved in. The move-in walk-through form completed in real time is vital evidence. If you want a judge to believe you when you testify regarding the condition of the unit before move-in and after move-out, you better have the evidence to support that testimony. And if you have the evidence, you may never have to go to trial at all because really, what's the point if the Resident knows they have nothing to prove their case.

The move-in walk-through needs to be performed together with your Resident and then kept as a contemporaneous record in your file for that Resident. There are other important evidential reasons for this that I will not go into here. Just trust me. Not only does having the move-in document help you avoid problems later, but you also get to see your Resident(s) demeanour, hear him/her/them talk, view their attitudes, see how they act, etc.

So, go on the move-in walk-through together. Together, list anything that is damaged with an explanation on the inspection form. Use a form similar to the one below. You will both sign that document.

It is imperative to take a detailed video of the property either before, or at the walk-through. It is good to get the Resident in the video so later at trial it can be seen that the Resident was there. In this way you can clearly document the condition of the property prior to giving possession to the Resident.

DO NOT, DO NOT give possession of the property before the move-in walk-through inspection is completed and signed. This form is very important because now the Resident knows you know the condition of the property and that you have evidence to back it up. The Resident will be much more likely to leave the property in the same condition received in order to get the security deposit back. It takes on more significance later when it is time for the move-out walk-through for comparison purposes. Following is the Move-in and Move-out walk-through inspection sheet.

Move-In and Move-Out Inspection Checklist

(B) = Blemish Found but no repair needed, (C) = Cleaning Needed, (R) = Repairs needed

Address:		Resident:			
Date:		**Time:**			

Item	B/C/R	Move-In Description	B/C/R	Move-Out Description	Charge
KITCHEN					
1. Stove/Range					
2. Oven/Hood &Fan					
3. Refrigerator					
4. Garbage Disposal					
5. Dishwasher					
6. Counters					
7. Sink					
8. Faucet					
9. Cabinets					
10. Light Fixtures/Outlets					
11. Walls/Ceiling					
12. Windows/Window locks					
13. Blinds					
14. Floor/ Molding					
15. Drains					
16. Other:					

Notes/Details:

_____

_____

_____

Item	B/C/R	Move-In Description	B/C/R	Move-Out Description	Charge
LIVING ROOM					
17. Heater					
18. Doors					
19. Walls Molding					
20. Floor/Carpet					
21. Ceiling					
22. Windows/Locks					
23. Blinds					
24. Light Fixtures/ Outlets					
25. Closets					
26. Other:					
HALLWAY					
27. Doors					
28. Light Fixtures/ Outlets					
29. Wall Heater					
30. Walls					
31. Floor/Carpet					
32. Windows/ocks					
33. Closet					
34. Other:					

Notes/Details:

_____

_____

Item	B/C/R	Move-In Description	B/C/R	Move-Out Description	Charge
1st BEDROOM					
35. Doors					
36. Walls/ Molding					
37. Floor/Carpet					
38. Ceiling					
39. Windows/Locks					
40. Blinds					
41. Lights / Outlets					
42. Heater					
43. Closets					
44. Other:					
2nd BEDROOM					
45. Doors					
46. Walls/ Molding					
47. Floor/Carpet					
48. Ceiling					
49. Windows/Locks					
50. Blinds					
51. Lights / Outlets					
52. Heater					
53. Closets					
54. Other:					
3rd BEDROOM					
55. Doors					
56. Walls/ Molding					
57. Floor/Carpet					
58. Ceiling					
59. Windows/Locks					
60. Blinds					
61. Lights / Outlets					
62. Heater					
63. Closets					
64. Other:					

Item	B/C/R	Move-In Description	B/C/R	Move-Out Description	Charge
BATHROOM					
65. Toilet					
66. Vanity					
67. Sink					
68. Towel Bars/Hook					
69. Tub / Shower					
70. Shower Rod					
71. Faucets/Shower					
72. Lights / Outlets					
73. Heater					
74. Toilet Paper Holder					
75. Vanity/MedCab					
76. Door					
77. Floor/Molding					
78. Windows/Locks Blinds					
79. Walls/Ceiling					
80. Hair Trap					
81. Other:					
MISCELLANEOUS					
82. Front Door Locks, Bar lock					
83. Phone Jack					
84, Doorbell/Intercom					
85. Cable Jack					
86. Smoke Detectors					
87. # of Keys issued/returned					
88. Unit defleaed? Debedbugged?					
89. Carpet steam cleaned?					
90. Hauling and Dumping?					
91. Other:					

Notes/Details:

_____

_____

_____

MOVE-IN WALKTHROUGH

By signing this move-in checklist Resident(s) agrees that other than noted on the checklist above, at the time of the move-in walkthrough there are no other items in need of maintenance or repair attention.

_____   _____
Landlord/Property Manager   Date

_____   _____
Resident Signature   Date

_____   _____
Resident Signature   Date

MOVE-OUT WALKTHROUGH

By signing this moveout checklist Resident(s) agrees that the property is in the condition set forth above in the move-out inspection report.

_____   _____
Landlord/Property Manager   Date

_____   _____
Resident Signature   Date

_____   _____
Resident Signature   Date

Principle # 10

HOW TO HANDLE LEASE VIOLATION AND OTHER ISSUES THAT ARISE WHILE RESIDENTS ARE LIVING IN THE PROPERTY

In this chapter we are going to look at the kind of notices that a Landlord/Property Manager may be required to deliver to a Resident for a variety of actions taken by the Resident that are in violation of the statutes, ordinances or the lease agreement or for other reasons. But, before we discuss the kind of breaches or content of the notices that need to be delivered, first we will discuss what a notice is and how you must deliver the notice to the Resident.

NOTICES AND SERVICE OF NOTICE TO A RESIDENT

1. WHAT IS A NOTICE?

A notice is generally a requirement pursuant to the law wherein a Landlord/Property Manager or Resident must make the other aware of a certain circumstance that materially or significantly affects the lease or occupancy.

The whole idea behind legislation about notice to a Resident or to a Landlord/Property Manager is very simple. There is something important about to happen that has a bearing on either the Landlord/Property Manager or the Resident regarding the property. The law wants to make sure that the affected other party actually got the notice about the issue pursuant to law. That is how important it is to make sure notice or communication is actually served on the other party properly/timely. Some states are very specific while some states are not at all that specific about how a notice must be served on the other party. Follow the law in your state regarding the requirements for serving/delivery notice to the Resident.

The following is general information on service or delivery of notice to a Resident:

2. ALWAYS USE WRITTEN COMMUNICATION – WHETHER NOTICE OR OTHERWISE:

Any communication to a Resident should be put in writing to avoid, "I said," "He/she said," later on. Please, help yourself out and make a personal commitment; always put every communication to a Resident in writing and do nothing verbally. If you do something verbally due to the timing needs or circumstances, then follow it up with a written communication.

How does communication differ from a notice? Communications are those items that the law may not require the Landlord/Property Manager to put in writing. A notice is a communication that materially or significantly affects the Resident's lease or occupancy where failure to properly deliver said notice does not allow the Landlord/Property Manager to proceed on the matter. My look at it is that if it is important enough to discuss, it should be in writing. When you make a practice out of not putting all communication in writing, you run the risk of misunderstanding and unintentional or intentional distortion of the facts by the Resident.

3. DELIVERY OR SERVICE OF THE NOTICE TO THE RESIDENT:

How do you get a notice or communication to a Resident and make it count? Serving or delivering a notice or communication to the Resident is a VERY simple procedure. Generally, there are only two sure ways to hand "deliver" or "serve" a notice to a Resident.

> 1. *"Hand delivery,"* means that the notice is actually placed into the hands of the Resident, a signer on the lease agreement. Making physical contact at the door, at the car, at the job, walking down the sidewalk, in the office, etc., with the lease signer is really good enough. If the person will not take the notice in hand, then you can simply drop the paperwork. They are served.

> 2. *"Alternative Hand Delivery,"* means that the notice is delivered into the hands of a person who is an occupant (their usual place of abode) and who is of suitable age and discretion.

>> a. Usual place of abode simply means that the person actually lives there, and;
>> b. Suitable age means that the person is at 14 years of age (in most jurisdictions).
>> c. Suitable discretion is a judgement call.

Let's say 14-year-old little Johnny answers the door. You have to ask some questions. How old are you? Why are you home at 1:00 in the afternoon on a school day, etc. If the notice is about little Johnny burning down the guard shack, then you know little Johnny is not of suitable discretion.

 Little Jimmy just burned down the guard shack on the property. Jason is 17 years old. He has spiked green hair, a nose ring, and weird circle thingies in his ears. He dropped out of high school to become a tattoo and body piercing want to be. Landlord goes to the premises to serve an immediate termination notice for Jason burning down the shed, and who answers the door? Right! None other than little Jimmy, the young pyromaniac. Do you serve little Jimmy, and does it count as good service? No, don't serve little Jimmy! He will likely set it on fire and burn your property down. Simply go back at another time or follow whatever other statutes/rules are available to you for service.

Suitable discretion goes to competency as well. If the person is mentally or emotionally disabled, (and arguably little Jimmy is both) and not the actual signer of the lease agreement, then go back at another time, and follow whatever other statutes are available to you. However, if little Jimmy is the signer on the lease, yes, you serve little Jimmy, if he is over 18, of course.

Let's say a Property Manager who does not know all of the occupants that reside at the property goes to serve a notice. A lovely grandmother type person comes to the door in a cooking apron with flour about her face and hands and has little kids holding on to her legs. Do you serve her? Maybe. Ask yourself the questions. Suitable age? Yes. Suitable discretion? Appears to be. Is this her usual place of abode, the place where she actually resides? Don't know? Ask her. If so, and the answer is yes, check your lease after you serve and make sure she is actually a Resident. If she is not a Resident on the lease but she just told you she does live there, then re-serve the notice on the Lessee and also serve another notice for unauthorized occupant.

If you question the legality of service at all, then do not rely on the service as being a good serve. Find another way to get the notice into the hand of a signer of the lease or legal occupant or follow your state statute or local ordinance that allows for a different method of delivery.

Be careful with this service element in general.

Often Landlords/Property Managers serve notices in all kinds of strange ways. I often have Landlords/Property Managers ask me:

    a. Can I put the notice in the mail?
    b. Can I put the notice under the door?
    c. Can I give the notice to one of their kids?
    d. Can I put the notice under their windshield wiper?

e. Can I put the notice in an envelope and put it between the door and the door jamb?

f. Can I call the Resident and tape record me reading the notice to the Resident over the phone?

g. Can I send the notice by certified mail, return receipt requested?

h. Can I go in and tape in on the toilet and the fridge?

i. Can I send the notice by UPS or FED-X?

j. Can I put the notice in their garage?

k. Can I serve the babysitter?

l. Can I email the notice?

m. Can I text the notice?

n. Etc.

The answer to all of the foregoing questions is: Only do what your State requires or allows.

Where a State is silent on how a notice must be delivered to a Resident be extra careful. For instance, in Idaho there is no specific State rule for how a Resident must be served a notice. So, in that case, know your judges. Think like a judge. A judge is going to inquire whether the way you delivered the notice is adequate to ensure the Resident got the notice. This is not an area to fudge on. A good judge will make you start over if you are sloppy. Think about you being the Resident. What would make sense for you to be served a notice that might be trying to communicate that you were about to be evicted? Satisfy what the judge wants. Do it right for the Resident. Go out of your way to see that the Resident gets the notice. This is not a time to be nonchalant. Be vigilant, even if the Resident is trying to avoid you.

Some state statutes allow for service of notice to be delivered by:

1. Hand Delivery to someone of suitable age and discretion and who is a Resident therein. Check your jurisdiction of age requirements, and/or;

2. Certified mail, return receipt requested, or;

3. Certified mail;

4. Registered mail;

5. Courier service, signed for by the Resident;

6. Send certified (or Certified mail return receipt requested) and post in a conspicuous place on the property.

7. Motion granted by the court for alternative method of service.

Remember, this is a Resident's home that you are attempting to affect in, likely, some negative way. The courts are concerned about due process. The courts want to know that there is little to no question that the Resident really got, or should have got, the notice before taking away rights to their home or contract in some way. That is

176

reasonable and fair. Too often Landlords/Property Managers take this process lightly or perform it carelessly and do not follow very simple, but proven and effective procedures. Sure, sometimes those requirements take time or seem difficult. Landlords/Property Managers sometimes get too impatient instead of doing what the law, or a judge, requires. This can get a Landlord/Property Manager into rally deep trouble, really quickly. In the case of delivery of notice the law is intended to protect the Resident from unreasonable Landlords/Property Managers and vice-versa. Fortunately, the law is simple to follow and is easily habit forming, especially if we go back to the golden rule and the simplicity of the law. Sure, usually the Resident knows they screwed up and knows what is about to happen. But again, the rule protects Residents with the simplest of procedure for one of their most precious needs, their home. Do it right – every time. There is no reason at all to go astray here. It is simple to do it right, but it may take some additional time that I realize Landlords/Property Managers do not want to lose.

If you question the legality of service at all, then do not rely on the service as being a good serve. Find another way to get the notice into the hand of a signer of the lease or legal occupant or follow your state statute or local ordinance that allows for a different method of delivery.

SERVING COURT DOCUMENTS

Delivering/serving legal process or court documents on a Resident is a bit different than just serving a notice from the Landlord/Property Manager in one way. With notices from the Landlord/Property Manager you just need someone to service those notices that is an adult who is of good character. If your state has no rules as to who can service your notices, I suggest that whoever serves your notices be at least 18 years old, of sound discretion and of a high reputation and integrity. If you ever have to call upon the person that served the notice to testify in court, such personal characteristics will be important for credibility purposes. However, serving Court documents is generally governed by court rule as to who can actually deliver such documents. The Landlord/Property Manager notices are not legal documents (legal process).

So, who can serve the legal/court documents? Generally, only a peace officer, constable or registered/licensed process server (officer of the court) can serve legal process/ legal documents/court documents. Process servers are generally licensed by the Court after passing a written competency test and have to pass an FBI background investigation.

COMMON TYPES OF NOTICES FOR RESIDENTS

Now, let's look at various types of violation(s) of the lease and the simple notices a Landlord/Property Manager can use to make the Resident aware of the ramifications of their violation(s). Understand that each State has specific statutes/rules that describe certain language and days that must be contained in your notices. Therefore, I have provided some templates that may help you draft your notices. Remember, you have to be up to date on your jurisdiction rules and what exactly it requires to be put in a notice. However, the following templates will give you some great ideas for what you need to accomplish to put a Resident on notice of what they have done to violate the lease agreement.

SECTION 8 – GOVERNMENT ASSISTED HOUSING WARNING AND DISCLAIMER

The following notices are NOT for Section 8, Public Housing or any Government Assisted Residents. Some of the language in the following notice can be used in certain public housing notices, however the cure times will be different than your State/local rules and some of the instructional language is different. If you have rented to public housing Tenants in any way you are governed by additional Federal laws and there are additional and separate notices that must be served on such Tenants. I recommend you have an attorney in your area for all of your Resident violation forms.

See the Private Sector Housing Samples:

1. RESIDENT'S FAILURE TO PAY RENT

Your state law may have statutory provisions and specific time lines that apply regarding such a violation for curative purposes. Many States use either 3 or 5 days for this notice.

The following is typical statutory language for most states regarding failure to pay rent:

A Resident may not withhold rent for any reason not authorized. If rent is unpaid when due and the Resident fails to pay rent within ____ (__) days after written notice by the Landlord/Property Manager of non-payment and the Landlord's/ Property Manager's intention to terminate the rental agreement if the rent is not paid within that period of time, the Landlord/Property Manager may terminate the rental agreement by filing an eviction action. Before the filing of an eviction action the rental agreement shall be reinstated if the Resident tenders all past due and unpaid periodic rent and a reasonable late fee set forth in a written rental agreement. After an eviction action is filed the rental agreement is reinstated only if the Resident pays all past due rent, reasonable late fees set forth in a written rental agreement, attorney fees and court costs. After a judgment has been entered in a special detainer action in favor of the Landlord/Property Manager, any reinstatement of the rental agreement is solely in the discretion of the Landlord/Property Manager.

The Landlord/Property Manager may recover all reasonable damages, resulting from non-compliance by the Resident with the rental including, but not limited to, court costs, reasonable attorney fees and all quantifiable damage caused by the Resident to the premises.

What constitutes a breach?

Very simple, the Resident did not deliver rent on or before the 1st day of the month, or whenever your lease agreement indicates it is due. You must serve the non-payment notice if you want to get the clock ticking for the eviction process.

How to handle this breach.

Serve the following notice.

Notice Form to Serve/Deliver for Failure to Timely Pay Rent.

TO: _____
     _____
     _____

FROM:_____
     _____
     _____

DATE:_____

_____(___)DAY NOTICE

_____(___) DAY NOTICE FOR NON-PAYMENT OF RENT AND INTENT TO TERMINATE RENTAL AGREEMENT

     You are advised that your rent is due and owing from the _____ day of _____, 20_____ to the _____ day of _____, 20_____ in the sum of $_____, plus applicable late charges and/or other charges. You have ____ (___) days from the date of this notice within which to bring your rent, and any applicable late charges current. Should you fail to pay this amount within____ (___) days after service of this Notice, your rental agreement whereby you hold possession of the above described property will be terminated, and an eviction action may be instituted against you. Further, even if your rights under the rental agreement are terminated, you will still be liable for the remaining payments stated in your rental agreement.

     Based on your breach, all payments must be made in certified funds or they will not be accepted.

                   By_____

                       Title:_____

❑ Hand delivered
❑ Certified mail
on the _____ day of
_____, 20____:
By:_____
Title: _____

2. BOUNCED OR "NSF" RENT CHECK

Your state law may have statutory provisions and specific time lines that apply regarding such a violation for curative purposes. Usually, States have a statutory provision time line of between 15 and 30 days for this type of notice, and it must be accomplished before the prosecutor will move forward on the bad check.

What constitutes a breach?

Again, very simple, the Resident tendered you a check. You deposited the check into the bank, and it was returned to you as non-sufficient funds. Unfortunately, you did not learn of this for a couple of weeks. By using the following form, you accomplish several goals at the same time. You serve a _____ (___) day notice for failure to pay rent. You also notice the Resident of his/her obligations and State law, and you start the preparation of the case for the County Attorney's Fraudulent Check Enforcement Task Force so they can file criminal charge against the Resident.

How to deal with the breach.

Serve the following notice.

Notice Form to Serve / Delivery for Bounced or NSF Check

TO: _____
     _____
     _____

FROM:_____
      _____
      _____

DATE:_____

_____(___)DAY NOTICE for Non-Sufficient Funds

**_____(___) DAY NOTICE FOR NON-PAYMENT OF RENT
AND INTENT TO TERMINATE RENTAL AGREEMENT**

You are advised that your rent is due and owing from the _____ day of _____, 20_____ to the _____ day of _____, 20_____ in the sum of $_____, plus applicable late charges or other charges. You have ____ (___) days from the date of this notice within which to bring your rent, and any applicable late charges current. Should you fail to pay this amount within ____ (___) days after service of this Notice, your rental agreement whereby you hold possession of the above described property will be terminated, and an eviction action may be instituted against you. Further, even if your rights under the rental agreement are terminated, you will still be liable for the remaining payments stated in your rental agreement.

Furthermore, pursuant to State Law, not only will you be evicted if you fail to pay in full within ____ (___) days, even if you are evicted for failure to pay rent, you will have _____ (___) days to make good your payment instrument with a certified funds check, or you will be subject to the remedies provided in the statute. You will then also be subject to collection proceedings and all obligations under the lease agreement.

Based on your breach, all payments must be made in certified funds only, or they will not be accepted.

By_____
Title:_____

- Hand delivered
- Certified mail

on the _____ day of _____, 20___:
By:_____
Title: _____

182

3. MATERIAL NON-COMPLIANCE OF THE LEASE AGREEMENT – (___) DAY NOTICE

Your state law may have statutory provisions and specific time lines that apply regarding such a violation for curative purposes. Many states use 10 days for these situations.

What constitutes a material breach or non-compliance of the lease agreement? Basically, any failure to adhere to any important provision or clause agreed to by the parties. In my mind, almost everything in the lease is material or you would not have it in the lease at all.

For Example:

> A. Loud noise or party
> B. Unauthorized pet
> C. Unauthorized occupant
> D. Swimming after posted pool hours
> E. Barking dog
> F. Dog at large
> G. Violation of the rules or regulations
> H. Cussing at neighbors. Getting in their faces, etc.
> I. Violating the peace and quiet enjoyment of other Residents
> J. Unauthorized parking. Using someone else's parking space.
> K. And the list can go on and on.

How to handle the breach by notice to the Resident:

You serve a _____ (___) day notice on the Resident depending on your law. The Resident then has _____ (___) days to cure or repair the non-compliance. In some cases, it will mean the Resident simply stops what he was doing, and the issue is resolved. In other situations, it may require the Resident to take an affirmative action to repair or replace something. Again, you must be time and date specific. You must also describe the situation in enough detail as to put the Resident on notice as to exactly what it is you claim was violated. If the Resident fails to cure within the _____ (___) day cure period, and the Resident has not moved, you can proceed to court for eviction.

Notice Form to Serve/Deliver for Material Non-Compliance Breach.

NOTE: This notice is only for the first violation of its type. In some states if a same or similar situation takes place during the lease or any renewal thereof, there is second _____ (___) day notice that can be served which gives the Resident an additional notice of a second similar violation where there are no further cure periods and gives the Resident _____ (___) days to vacate the property.

For the first material non-compliance use the following notice.

TO: _____
_____
_____

FROM:_____
_____
_____

DATE: _____

(___) DAY NOTICE

_____ (___) DAY NOTICE OF INTENT TO TERMINATE
RENTAL AGREEMENT FOR MATERIAL BREACH OF LEASE

You are hereby notified that you have committed a breach of your lease agreement by committing the following act(s):

_____
_____
_____
_____

You are hereby notified that if the above-referenced breach(es) is/are not remedied within _____ (___) days, your lease will terminate, and you will be required to vacate the premises within _____ (___) days after service of this notice. Understand, that if you fail to remedy the above listed breach(es) in the specified time, even if you vacate the premises instead, you will still be responsible for all rent as outlined in your lease agreement. You will also be responsible for releasing charges, cleaning charges, attorney's fees, collection costs and possibly other charges. Should you fail to remedy, resulting in your tenancy terminating, and then also fail to vacate the premises within the said _____ (___) day period, a special/forcible detainer action will be filed against you pursuant to State/Local law to obtain possession of the subject premises.

By_____

Title:_____

( ) Hand delivered
( ) Certified mail
on the _____ day of
_____, 20___:

By: _____
Title: _____

185

4. SECOND MATERIAL NON-COMPLIANCE DURING THE LEASE – SAME OR SIMILAR VIOLATION

Your state law may have statutory provisions and specific time lines that apply regarding such a violation. Many States specify that if a second same or similar violation occurs, then the Resident does not get to cure the breach but must vacate with 10 days of delivery of the notice.

If there is an additional act of material non-compliance of the same or a similar nature during the term of the lease, or any renewal thereof, after the previous remedy of non-compliance, your jurisdiction may allow the Landlord/Property Manager to institute an eviction action ten days after delivery of a written notice advising the Resident that a second non-compliance of the same or a similar nature has occurred. This is a great remedy. Check your jurisdiction or ask your Landlord/Property Manager attorney.

What constitutes such a breach?

The same or similar violation that occurred in the first breach. If it is something different or not similar to that violation of the first breach, then you serve another first material non-compliance notice as set forth above.

1. The first violation is loud music. The second violation is a barking dog. That violation is the same or similar, so you serve the same or similar notice below.

2: The first violation is loud music. The second violation is an unauthorized occupant. In this case you use the material non-compliance for second breach because the violation of unauthorized occupant is not the same of similar as loud music.

How to handle the breach

Here the Resident has no further right to cure. If the violation is the same or similar, in that case the Resident must either move or see the judge in a court date regarding the Resident's repeated material non-compliances.

TO: _____
_____
_____

FROM:_____
_____
_____

DATE: _____

_____ (___) DAY NOTICE

_____ (___) DAY NOTICE OF INTENT TO TERMINATE
RENTAL AGREEMENT DUE TO **SECOND** BREACH AND
NONCOMPLIANCE WITH RENTAL AGREEMENT

On _____, 20___, a first _____ (___) day NOTICE OF INTENT TO TERMINATE RENTAL AGREEMENT FOR MATERIAL BREACH was issued to you for the following reasons:

_____
_____
_____
_____

On _____, 20_____, a second, same or similar breach has occurred described as follows:

_____
_____
_____
_____

You are hereby notified that your tenancy has been terminated and you must vacate the premises within _____ (___) days after service of this Notice. Please come to the Manager's office prior to the expiration of the _____ (___) day period to arrange for your move-out inspection.

By_____

Title:_____

❑ Hand delivered
❑ Certified mail
on the _____ day of
_____, 20___:
By: _____
Title:_____

5. Material and Irreparable Breach

Your state law may have statutory provisions and specific time lines that apply regarding such a violation for curative purposes:

If there is a breach that is both material and irreparable and that occurs on or off the premises, including but not limited to, an illegal discharge of a weapon; homicide; prostitution; criminal street gang activity; activity regarding a criminal syndicate; the unlawful manufacturing, selling, transferring, possessing, using or storing of a controlled substance; arson; threatening or intimidating; assault; acts that have been found to constitute a nuisance, or an act that otherwise jeopardizes the health, safety and welfare of the Landlord/Property Manager, the Landlord's/Property Manager's agent or another Resident, or involving imminent or actual serious property damage, the Landlord/Property Manager shall deliver a written notice for immediate termination of the rental agreement.

What constitutes a breach?

These types of notices should only be used in the most egregious of circumstances involving a breach that is both material and irreparable. It is not for calling people names, a loud party, leaving a car parked in a red zone, failing to clean up dog droppings, or the like. It is something very serious. This notice should be used only when the violation clearly qualifies. Again, remember that the judge has to decide that the actions of the Resident are significant enough for the court to dispossess the Resident of the dwelling within 24 hours. Therefore, the allegations and the evidence that you present to the court better be convincing. You do not want to tick off the judge if the matter goes to Court. There are more trials regarding allegations for immediate termination than for any other alleged violation. The judge is bound to decide the case by a preponderance of the evidence, or that it is more likely than not that the allegation occurred. But be realistic, the court is not going to dispossess the Resident unless the court is very certain of the allegations based on the law and the evidence presented to the court are compelling. Your job is to show the court that what the Resident did was in fact MATERIAL and IRREPARABLE as set forth below.

Material: This mean the violation is important to the lease, Landlord and Tenant act, state or local law, manager, staff, or other Residents or the community in general.

Irreparable: This means that the violation is one that cannot be taken back or repaired.

How to deal with the breach. You must serve the notice first.

Notice Form to Serve/Deliver for Material and Irreparable Breach

TO: _____
_____
_____

FROM:_____
_____
_____

DATE:_____

NOTICE OF IMMEDIATE TERMINATION

Please be advised that as a result of your breach described below which was both material and irreparable, your tenancy at the above-referenced property has been terminated.

_____
_____
_____
_____

Demand is hereby made that you immediately vacate the subject property. If you fail to vacate, an eviction proceeding may proceed against you. You will be responsible for the remainder of the lease until the end of the lease or until the premises are re-rented, whichever comes first. Pursuant to this immediate termination notice, your rights to possession are terminated, but your obligations shall continue as you have breached your obligations under the lease.

_____
Management

❑ Hand delivered
❑ Certified mail
on the _____ day of
_____, 20___:

By: _____
Title:_____

6. ACCESS OF THE UNIT BY LANDLORD/PROPERTY MANAGER

Your state law may have statutory provisions and specific time lines that apply regarding such a violation for curative purposes:

Most states require the Landlord/Property Manager to give the Resident written notice for access to the property, and for limited purposes such as inspection of the property, to show the property for sale, to make agreed upon or necessary repairs, and all during reasonable times. A Landlord/Property Manager obviously cannot use such a notice to harass the Resident. Most States require a 24-, 48- or 72-hour notice, absent a legitimate emergency. An emergency is not that the Landlord/Property Manager could not get the access notice served. An Emergency usually means something like fire, flood, blood, terrible odour, ooze, serious damage to the property, etc. Perhaps a welfare check would be a good reason to access without notice, but you must have a legitimate reason for the welfare check and have a police officer or someone from social services with you if you perform a welfare check. Remember, the time of entry has to line up with the delivery time of the notice regarding the date/time of proposed entry by Landlord/Property Manager.

You hand deliver a Landlord/Property Manager access notice to Resident on July 2 at 8:00pm. What date must be the Landlord/Property Manager access notice to Resident on July 2nd at 8:00pm. What date must be the access date. If your State statute requires a 24 hour notice to access, then no earlier than July 5th. You might ask why all the way till the 5th? Assuming that the State access law is that an access notice has to be served 24 hours before entry, the soonest you could access just by day and time would be July 4th at 8:01pm. However, 8:01 pm is not a reasonable time. So, you wait until July 5th.

Can you say in the access notice that Landlord/Property Manager will enter sometime during the day on July 5th? No. Why? You have to be reasonable about the time frame. Depending on what you will be doing, you have a right to access for the time it will take to do what needs to be done. So, you want to give the Resident a time frame of your choosing, say between 10:00 AM and 1:00 PM or 4:00 PM through 6:00 PM whatever the circumstances suggest. You don't have the right to make it hard on the Resident, just like the Resident does not have the right to make access hard on you. Give a reasonable notice timeline. The better way to do it is to communicate with the Resident and see if you both can come to an agreement as to the date and time. Ask the Resident when a good time would be to drop off the access agreement. Most Residents will appreciate your efforts working with them as opposed to just deciding and laying the notice on them.

• Does the Resident have a right to be present? Absolutely.

• Does the Resident have the right to refuse or not allow access during the July 5 time for either 10:00 am and 1:00 pm or 4:00 PM through 6:00 PM? No, not really, unless there is some insurmountable situation that arises.

• Can the Landlord/Property Manager use the Landlord's/Property Manager's key to access the unit if the Resident is not home once a proper notice has been served? Yes.

• What if the Resident physically will not let you in? Then you serve the Resident with a notice for a material violation of the lease agreement and move forward accordingly.

Notice Form to Serve/Deliver Landlord's/Property Manager's
Notice to Access the Unit:

TO: _____
_____
_____

FROM:_____
_____
_____

DATE:_____

NOTICE OF LANDLORD'S/PROPERTY MANAGER'S ACCESS

    Be advised that pursuant to State Statute ABC, Section XYX, Landlord/Property Manager, or his/her/their agents, shall enter into the dwelling unit to inspect the premises on the _____ day of _____, 20_____, between _____ and _____. You have no right to unreasonably detain Landlord/Property Manager or his/her/their agent from entering the dwelling unit on the date and times listed above. If you do, you will be subject to commencement of court action.

By_____

Title:_____

❑ Hand delivered
❑ Certified mail
on the _____ day of
_____, 20___:

By:_____
    Title: _____

7. HEALTH AND SAFETY BREACH

Your state law may have statutory provisions and specific timelines that apply regarding such a violation for curative purposes. Most States have a 5-day cure period.

If there is a non compliance by the Resident materially affecting health and safety, the Landlord/Property Manager shall deliver a written notice to the Resident specifying the acts and omissions constituting the breach and that the rental agreement will terminate FIVE (5) days after receipt of this notice if the breach has not been remedied during that FIVE (5) day period. However, if the breach is remediable by repair or the payment of damages or otherwise, and the Resident adequately remedies the breach before the date specified in the notice, the rental agreement will not terminate.

What Constitutes a Health and Safety Breach?

Health and safety violations are rarely used. They should be used only when the circumstances are such that it is obvious that health and safety is at risk to the property or other Residents. If you are involved in a situation where you believe Resident's actions affect the health and safety of either the Landlord/Property Manager, Resident or other Residents, consider carefully the proof that will be necessary to prove that the actions constitute a health and/or safety violation. Again, witnesses with first-hand knowledge will be necessary at court for testimony as to the breach. Some Examples are:

A. Infestation of roaches in Resident's premises causing infestation in adjoining units.

B. Extreme amount of clutter (boxes, papers, etc.) in the Resident's premises – fire hazard.

C. Leaving garbage or other junk in or near the premises.

How to Handle the Breach?

If the Resident is involved in such a breach of the lease affecting health and safety, the Landlord/Property Manager must deliver a notice specifying the act or omission regarding the breach, and the Resident will have _____ (___) days to cure the breach. If Resident fails to cure the breach within _____ (___) days after delivery of the notice, Landlord/Property Manager can start the eviction process. Be as accurate as you can about date, time and event. Lay it out so there is no question by the Resident or by the judge as to what you are alleging in the notice to cure.

Practical Point: Proof = Evidence

The Landlord/Property Manager will have to prove to a judge that the violation occurred if Resident decides to defend against the notice. Therefore, take photos and/or video of the original violation. Then, after the _____ (___) days have expired, take photos/video again to show that the violation has not been cured during the notice period. Obtain as many credible witnesses as you can with first-hand knowledge of the violation. You must also present proof that violation has not being cured within the notice period. Remember, although the burden of proof is only a preponderance of evidence, or more likely than not, we are still talking about a Resident, and possibly their family, who are about to lose their home. A judge wants to be sure about his/her decision. So, think of the burden more in terms of clear and convincing evidence. Make the judge's job easy. Have your evidence organized and sound. If you are not prepared or do not have the quantity and quality of convincing evidence you need to win the case, the judge will remember you as a problem Landlord/Property Manager. In the judge's mind you will be labelled as a Landlord/Property Manager who is not careful and is not concerned enough about the Residents. You want the judge to remember your property as one that runs a clean operation and is on the ball. Then, when there is a close call on a difficult case, you are more likely to get the call based on your past integrity in the Court. If you get on a judge's bad side, it will take a long time to earn the court's respect back. Always be honest, respectful, and reasonable. It is like a basketball referee that constantly gets an attitude or lip from a player. Having been a basketball and baseball referee/umpire, after a player constantly give you mouth/lip, you are just looking for some minor violation to call a foul or infraction on that player so he can visit his friends on the bench. It's just human nature.

NOTE: Sometimes the health issue goes to the Resident's ability to take care of themselves. In such a case, it may be helpful and prudent to contact County Adult Protective Services so they can conduct a welfare check and provide assistance. I would hesitate calling Resident's family. Let Adult Protective Services make those calls. This is a touchy issue. It is like Justice White of the U.S. Supreme Court when he was asked how to explain pornography. He indicated that he may not be able to explain it, but he knew it when he saw it. The same will apply with a Resident who may be a danger to himself or other Residents. The fear, of course, is that the Resident may burn down the building or hurt themselves. This could go to physical or mental problems that are manifested by the Resident's behavior.

THE FORM to Serve/Delivered for Health and Safety Breach:

TO: _____
           _____
           _____

FROM:_____
           _____
           _____

DATE: _____

(___) DAY NOTICE

_____ **(___) DAY NOTICE OF INTENT TO TERMINATE**
RENTAL AGREEMENT FOR MATERIAL BREACH OF LEASE

      You are hereby notified that you have committed a breach of your lease agreement by committing the following act(s):

_____
_____
_____
_____

      You are hereby notified that if the above-referenced breach(es) is/are not remedied within _____ (___) days, your lease will terminate, and you will be required to vacate the premises within _____ (___) days after service of this notice. Understand, that if you fail to remedy the above listed breach(es) in the specified time, even if you vacate the premises instead, you will still be responsible for all rent as outlined in your lease agreement. You will also be responsible for releasing charges, cleaning charges, attorney's fees, collection costs and possibly other charges. Should you fail to remedy, resulting in your tenancy terminating, and then also fail to vacate the premises within the said _____ (___) day period, a special/forcible detainer action will be filed against you pursuant to State/Local law to obtain possession of the subject premises.

                     By_____

                             Title:_____

( ) Hand delivered
( ) Certified mail
on the _____ day of
_____, 20___:

By: _____
      Title: _____

8. 30 DAY NOTICE OF INTENT TO TERMINATE LEASE AGREEMENT

How to terminate the month-to-month residency:

The following form is the one used to notify Resident that you are terminating their month-to month lease agreement. You only use this notice if the Resident has actually completed the initial term and is now on a month-to-month lease agreement

SAMPLE 30-DAY TERMINATION NOTICE

30-DAY TERMINATION NOTICE

TO: Residents

_____

_____

_____

FROM: Landlord or Property Manager

_____

_____

_____

DATE: _____ ___ 20__.

30-DAY NOTICE

PERIODIC THIRTY (30) DAY NOTICE OF INTENT TO TERMINATE MONTH-TO-MONTH RENTAL AGREEMENT

Please be advised that your tenancy will terminate on the ___ day of _____ 20___. Please be advised that prior to your tenancy terminating, you will be required to vacate the subject premises described above and have a joint move-out walk through . If you fail to vacate the premises as demanded, a special detainer and/or forcible detainer proceeding will be initiated against you. Please contact the office to schedule a move-out walk through and inspection.

By_____

Title:_____

❑ Hand Delivered
❑ Certified Mail, Return Receipt Requested
on the _____ day of
_____, 20___, to:

By: _____
Title:_____

9. Non-Curable, Material Falsification or Misleading Information On The Application:

Your state law may have statutory provisions and specific timelines that apply regarding such a violation for curative purposes:

For a non-curable violation(s) of the Resident providing materially fraudulent or misleading information on the application, the Landlord/Property Manager must serve/deliver a notice to Resident to vacate and surrender possession of the property within _____ (___) days after service of the notice, if Landlord/Property Manager desires the ability to go to court if the Resident does not move. This is a good reason to take a thorough and complete application. It is not uncommon that a Landlord/Property Manager finds out after possession has already been given to the Resident, that the Resident lied or mislead Landlord/Property Manager on the application. Don't beat around the bush in the notice. Be specific regarding what was untrue or misleading that is material. The way you can judge material is whether you would have rented to the Resident had you known the information on the application was untrue or misleading at the time of review. Remember that you must have such a clause in your application giving you this right to terminate.

Notice Form to Serve/Deliver for NON-CURABLE False or Misleading Information on the application.

TO: _____

_____

_____

FROM:_____

_____

_____

DATE:_____

_____ (___)-**DAY NOTICE**

_____ (___) DAY NOTICE OF INTENT TO TERMINATE
RENTAL AGREEMENT FOR BREACH OF LEASE FOR RESIDENT PROVIDING
MATERIALLY FALSE OR MISLEADING INFORMATION ON THE APPLICATION

You are hereby notified that you have committed a non-curable breach of your lease agreement by providing Landlord/Property Manager with materially false or misleading information on the rental application regarding:

[ ]   Criminal History/Record
[ ]   Prior Eviction Record
[ ]   Current Criminal Activity
[ ]   Other Material Falsification/Untrue/Misleading information described as follows:

_____
_____
_____
_____

Therefore, demand is hereby made that you vacate the subject property within ____ (___) days following service of this notice.

By_____
Title:_____

- Hand delivered
- Certified mail

on the _____ day of
_____, 20___:

By: _____
Title:_____

200

10. Curable, Material Falsification or Misleading Information On The Application:

Depending on the jurisdiction, for a curable violation(s) of false or misleading information on the application, the Landlord/Property Manager may serve/deliver a notice to the Resident to vacate and surrender possession of the property within ____ (___) days after service of the notice, if Landlord/Property Manager desires the ability to go to court if the Resident does not:

A. Provide true, accurate and not misleading information to the Landlord/ Property Manager to replace the information Landlord/Property Manager believes was false, inaccurate and/or misleading. If the Resident does not comply with the curable violation notice, then the original information Resident provided becomes non-curable and the Landlord/Property Manager must then follow the non-curable notice provisions above.

B. If the Resident does provide the replacement information that is true, accurate and not misleading, then the violation may be cured if the new information, after investigation of the new information provided would allow the Resident to qualify pursuant to Landlord's/Property Manager's rental criteria.

C. If the Resident does not qualify for residency upon the new information provided based on Landlord's/Property Manager's rental criteria, then the Resident must vacate. If the Resident fails to vacate, then Landlord/Property Manager must serve Resident the Non-Curable Notice to get the eviction process going.

Don't beat around the bush in the notices. Be specific regarding what was inaccurate, untrue or misleading that is material.

The way you can judge the word material is whether you would have rented to the Resident had you known the information on the application was inaccurate, untrue or misleading at the time of application review.

Notice Form to Serve/Deliver for CURABLE False or Misleading Information

TO: _____

_____

_____

FROM: _____

_____

_____

DATE: _____

_____ (___)-DAY NOTICE

_____ (___) DAY NOTICE OF INTENT TO TERMINATE
RENTAL AGREEMENT FOR BREACH OF LEASE FOR RESIDENT PROVIDING MATERIALLY
FALSE OR MISLEADING INFORMATION ON THE APPLICATION IF RESIDENT FAILS TO
PROVIDE LANDLORD WITH ACCURATE AND TRUE APPLICATION INFORMATION

You are hereby notified that you have committed a curable breach of your lease agreement by providing Landlord/Property Manager with a materially inaccurate, false, and/or misleading information on the rental application. The information that is believed to be false inaccurate, or misleading was:

[ ]   number of occupants in the dwelling;
[ ]   number or type of pet(s) in the dwelling;
[ ]   income of the Resident;
[ ]   Resident's social security number;
[ ]   current employment information;

_____

_____

_____

You have _____ (___) calendar days to provide complete, accurate, truthful and not misleading information to Landlord/Property Manager. If you fail to comply within the _____ (___) period by delivering to Landlord/Property Manager replacement information that is accurate, complete, truthful and not misleading, then your breach shall become NON-CURABLE. If the information provided after investigation by Landlord/Property Manager is made into the truthfulness and completeness of the replacement information and meets Landlord's/Property Manager's rental criteria, no further action will be taken. If, after investigation by Landlord/Property Manager, the replacement information does not meet Landlord's/Property Manager's rental criteria, you will be given a notice to terminate the lease agreement.

By_____
Title:_____

- Hand delivered
- Certified mail

on the _____ day of
_____, 20___:

By: _____
Title:_____

202

11. UNAUTHORIZED OCCUPANT – SQUATTER, FORECLOSURE

Your state law may have statutory provisions and specific timelines that apply regarding such a violation for curative purposes:

What constitutes a breach?

1. A squatter that the cops won't help you get out of the house.
2. You purchased a trustee's deed and the old owners, or someone they let live there, is/are still there.
3. You foreclose on a property and the former owner won't leave.
4. You have no idea who is occupying the property, but they have no business in the property.

How to deal with the breach.

Serve the notice and start the process of time running for the eviction. In this case you may not even know the names of the people who are in your home without permission. In that case you will call them John Doe and Jane Doe. Every State has a type of eviction for this situation, so there is a statute that you can cite in your notice.

Notice Form to Serve/Deliver an Unauthorized Occupant Notice:

TO: _____
_____
_____

FROM:_____
_____
_____

DATE:_____

NOTICE TO VACATE

NOTICE IS GIVEN PURSUANT ABC STATUTE, SECTION XYZ - YOUR OCCUPANCY IS UNAUTHORIZED. YOU HAVE ____ (___) DAYS FROM THE DATE OF SERVICE OF THIS NOTICE TO REMOVE YOURSELF AND YOUR PERSONAL PROPERTY FROM THE PREMISES. IF YOU FAIL TO VACATE AS DEMANDED, LEGAL ACTION WILL BE TAKEN FOR POSSESSION OF THE PROPERTY, FAIR MARKET RENTAL VALUE, COURT COSTS, AND ATTORNEY FEES.

By_____

Title:_____

❑ Hand delivered
❑ Certified mail
on the _____ day of
_____, 20_____:

By: _____
Title:_____

12. MUTUAL TERMINATION AGREEMENT

Sometimes it is wise just to agree to let a Resident out of the lease to get rid of a problem. In that case, you can simply enter into a mutual termination agreement so both parties can move on without litigation. The agreement does not have to be fancy, long or expensive – just tight.

SETTLEMENT, MUTUAL TERMINATION AND RELEASE AGREEMENT

SETTLEMENT, MUTUAL TERMINATION AND RELEASE AGREEMENT

IT IS AGREED upon mutual consideration by and between _____ and its owners, managers, employees, associates, partners, members (all hereinafter referred to as "Landlord/Property Manager"), and _____, and any and all occupants (hereinafter referred to "Resident"), that the lease agreement by and between Landlord/Property Manager and Resident dated the _____ day of _____, shall terminate by mutual agreement on the ___ day of _____ 20____ at 5:00 P.M.

Resident agrees that Resident and all occupants will vacate the residence located at _____, on or before the ___ day of _____ 20____ at 5:00 P.M. and hereby gives, conveys and delivers complete possession of the premises to the Landlord/Property Manager at said date and time without any further notice requirements whatsoever.

Resident understands and agrees that failure to vacate the subject property described above as stated shall still entitle Landlord/Property Manager to physically take control of the premises or to immediately institute an eviction action to enforce this agreement for removal of Resident from the subject premises without further notice and at Landlord's/Property Manager's sole discretion. Resident further agrees that failure to vacate the subject premises by the date and time set forth above shall constitute a willful holdover and such holdover shall be in bad faith.

All parties understand that any and all claims, rights, demands, and or damages of any kind past, present and future arising out of, or that may have arisen out of the Lease Agreement listed above, are hereby released and forever waived with an agreement to hold the other harmless, with the exception of those obligations created by this Agreement for Resident to leave the premises in a clean, safe and habitable condition upon vacating on the date indicated. The security deposit shall be returned to Resident within fourteen business days from Resident vacating the property, provided the condition of the premises is delivered in a clean, safe and habitable condition.

DATED this _____ day of _____, 20____.

RESIDENT(S)   OWNER/LANDLORD/PROPERTY MANAGER:

_____   _____

_____

Principle # 11

MOVE OUT INSPECTION

You already have a move-in inspection report in your file with a move-in video tape recording of the property before you gave possession to the property. Just retrieve it for the move-out inspection. Once you have served/delivered or received a lease termination notice, you will need to serve/deliver to the Resident a MOVE-OUT INSPECTION notice providing a time for you and the Resident to walk through the unit and you will fill out the MOVE-OUT INSPECTION report to determine what the unit looks like and what is needed to bring the property back to good condition, if anything.

It is best to time this inspection for the day that the Resident has most everything out of the unit. Again, take video of the condition of the home and write everything down on the MOVE-OUT INSPECTION form so you can compare the move-out inspection form with the move-in inspection form to make it easy to see what the Resident will be responsible for. Have the Resident sign the move-out inspection report when you complete the walk through. If the Resident will not sign the move-out inspection form, then make detailed notes on the move-out inspection report form as regarding the exact reasons the Resident gave for not signing.

Now you can see why it is so important to have the move-in inspection sheet and move-in video. Remember, once you make all the repairs needed, if any, and once the unit is ready to rent again, take another video so you have evidence of the condition of the property before you rent it again.

NOTICE OF MOVE-OUT INSPECTION

TO: _____
_____
_____

FROM:_____
_____
_____

DATE:_____

NOTICE OF MOVE-OUT INSPECTION

This is Landlord's/Property Manager's formal notice that you may be present at the move-out inspection which will take place on:

Month	Day	Year	Time

By_____
Title:_____

❑ Hand delivered
❑ Certified mail
on the _____ day of
_____, 20__:

By: _____
Title:_____

208

Principle # 12

COURT DO'S AND DONT'S

Well, something went sideways. You are looking at a court date. Either the Resident did not pay and did not move out, some dispute occurred that could not be worked out, the Resident has filed some kind of claim like withholding of security deposit, the attorney general got involved, or you are trying to collect some money. Whatever the issue is, we are going to take another chronological journey through the courthouse and the court room.

1. If you have an attorney, your attorney will prepare you for court. Don't worry. Worrying will not help you. This is not brain surgery. The facts about your position will get heard. So, take a deep breath. Listen and learn from your attorney and act accordingly. If you don't have an attorney, you either need to get one, or at least you need to get familiar with court procedure and etiquette. Go visit a court room and watch a trial like the one you are going to have. Learn how things are really done in your jurisdiction. It is usually not like TV.

2. Treat Every Court Clerk With Dignity And Respect even if they are jerks to you and are not helping get your issues solved. If you don't act with grace under pressure it will only get worse. The clerks are overworked, underpaid and under-appreciated. And, let's be honest, do you think most of them really want to be behind that window stuck in front of people with problems, in front of a computer or dealing with file cabinets all day for so little pay. Furthermore, if you don't treat them well it will get to the judge's ears, and your case will not go as smoothly as it could go.

3. Dress Appropriately. Wear clean pressed dress clothes. Don't dress too fancy. Hold back on the cologne and the perfume. Dress conservatively and pleasantly. Avoid jewelry and necklaces. No fancy watches. Cover tattoos. You hair/beard should be sharp, crisp and neat. Of course, do not were a hat. These things all build credibility.

4. Be Prepared. I mean be really, really prepared. Know your case and your documents/exhibits inside and out. Know them all better than the opposition. Every document needs to be in perfect order for presentation to the judge. Have a copy ready to hand or show to the Resident/Resident's attorney and copy ready to hand or show to the judge as exhibits. Have the documents in separate stacks for easy access. Handle any paperwork or exhibits in a simple, straightforward, matter of fact way, like it is second nature to you. It also builds credibility.

5. Do Not Have Paperwork Spread All Over The Desk. The same goes for any non-paper exhibits. Look organized. Be organized. It also builds your credibility.

6. Be Yourself. Be sincere, polite, cheerful, humble, disciplined and respectful of everyone (even the opposition). Don't try to be someone else. A judge and/or jury will see the fakeness. It builds credibility.

7. When the judge walks into the room, stand up and do not sit until the judge says, "be seated."

8. When You Talk, Stand Up First. Speak clearly, calmly and confidently. Look the judge in the eyes when you speak. It builds credibility.

9. Don't Ramble. Clearly state your case. Succinctly state your positions and your arguments. Don't repeat the same things over and over. Plainly and simply present the evidence. Do not talk about things that are not specifically important or relevant to the case. The judge wants to hear the facts about the issues, not information that does not matter or information that wastes time. The judge does not want to hear you say how nasty, dishonest, terrible and mean the opposition is. The judge wants the facts in an orderly fashion so the judge can follow exactly what happened. Your job is to paint a clear picture. The judge will make the determinations about the facts from the information that you present and how you present it.

10. When The Opposition Is Testifying, Do Not Talk. Do not make faces. Do not roll your eyes. Instead, focus on the testimony. Take notes so that you can counter the lies they are spewing. You will get your chance. Don't get anxious. Relax. The judge is watching you. Be cool. Remember, the judge does not know you. If you act like a nut in court, then the judge is going to think you are a nut and that you are not credible.

11. Don't Interrupt The Judge – EVER. If you are going to hand an exhibit to the judge, ask first by saying, "May I approach Your Honor". Respect for the court is paramount.

12. When You Give Your Opening Statement, this is the time that you tell the judge everything that you are going to prove when your witnesses testify. It is THE time to let the judge know about your case and what to expect in testimony, and THE time to set in the mind of the judge how the judge should be thinking.

13. Don't Needlessly Interrupt The Opposition. Don't let the witnesses ramble on direct or cross examination. Do not let the opposition testify about anything that someone else said. That is called hearsay. Do not let the opposition testify about something for which they have no background, education, or understanding. That is call lack of foundation. Do not let the opposition testify about things that have little to do with the case just to try and make you look bad. That is called lack of relevance. Never ask the other side's witness an open-ended question. Only ask yes or no questions for which you know the answers. Cross is your time to shine. Your time to expose them. Watch some YouTube videos on how to cross examine a witness. It is an art and a science. This is where you can impress the judge, if you do it respectfully and intelligently. It is my favorite part of law.

14. After All The Evidence Has Been Presented, then you get to give your closing argument and tell the judge, "Just like I told you in the opening argument," then you go A, B, C, D, F, F etc., and lay out your case showing why the judge should rule for you, based on the facts that were presented and the law. Thank the judge for his/her the time and patience listening to all of the evidence.

BONUS PRINCIPLE

CRITICAL INFORMATION THAT EVERY OWNER, LANDLORD AND PROPERTY MANAGER MUST KNOW

PREMISES LIABILITY BASICS

What is premise liability in regard to a rental property?

Premises liability is a legal concept that typically comes into play in personal injury cases where the injury was caused by some type of unsafe or defective condition on a rental property.

Premises Liability is the legal theory that an Owner/Landlord/Property Manager can be responsible for damages arising out of an injury occurring on the property, entitling the injured party to damages. In all states, Owners/Landlords/Property Managers that rent out any property must make reasonable efforts to maintain the property in a safe condition for Residents, guests, invitees and staff. Failure to keep the property reasonably safe may result in "premises liability."

Examples of common situations that can give rise to premises liability are listed below, but said list is not all inclusive:

- ☐ Animal Bites
- ☐ Holes or Indentations in Landscaping, Grass, etc.
- ☐ Uneven Concrete or Asphalt
- ☐ Trees Growing Under Concrete
- ☐ Slippery Floors
- ☐ Unsalted Areas
- ☐ Criminal Activity on the Property
- ☐ Failure to Properly Screen Residents
- ☐ Failure to Properly Screen Staff
- ☐ Unlocked Electrical Boxes
- ☐ Unlocked Pool and Spa Gates
- ☐ Unlocked Laundry Room
- ☐ Unlocked Maintenance Room
- ☐ Unlocked Exercise Room
- ☐ Inoperable Access Gates
- ☐ Inoperable Cameras

- ☐ Unlocked or Unsecured Guest Facilities
- ☐ Inadequate Security
- ☐ Swimming Pool/Spa Injury
- ☐ Inadequate Maintenance
- ☐ Unsupervised Children on Property
- ☐ Playground
- ☐ Poor or inadequate Lighting in the Parking Lot
- ☐ Poor or inadequate Lighting Anywhere on the Property
- ☐ Unmaintained Property in General
- ☐ Latent Defects at the Property
- ☐ Vehicles
- ☐ Fake Cameras on the Property
- ☐ Holes or Indentations in the Grassy Areas.
- ☐ Chipped, Cracked, Uneven Concrete

How do the kinds of conditions listed above make the Owner/Landlord/Property Manager liable for damages?

First, the Landlord and/or Property Manager is the Owner's agents. The Landlord/ Property Manager is/are doing, or should be doing, the things for which the Owner is responsible. The Landlord/Property Manager is also responsible for their own actions and inactions. Your duty is to make the entire premises reasonably safe and habitable.

Second, most of the conditions on the list above happen due to negligence of the Owner/Landlord/Property Manager.

So, what is negligence and how can Owners/Landlords/Property Managers understand in simple terms how negligence has a bearing on them in relationship to the property?

Simply put, negligence is an examination of the following by Owner/Landlord/ Property Manager – it is about duty to others and how that duty is handled by Owner/ Landlord/Property Manager.
When looking at each item on the list above, did the Owner/Landlord/Property Manager know or should they have known about a danger or peril on the property [refer to the list] and did the Owner/Landlord/Property Manager take reasonable steps to remedy the danger of peril so that damages did not happen to someone for whom the Owner/ Landlord/Property Manager owed a duty to protect, i.e., Resident, occupant, guest, or an invitee like a vendor or a contractor?

Let's examine this idea regarding how an attorney for a plaintiff would examine it if his/her client was damaged by one the conditions on the list or something similar thereto.

This is Webster's legal definition of negligence:

"Failure to exercise the care that a reasonably prudent person would exercise in like circumstances"

That is a good start for reflection, but there is more to analyse. Negligence law has four prongs or issues to think about.

1. Duty: A duty is simply a legal obligation. In order to be sued for Negligence, the Defendant must have owed a duty to the Plaintiff. The duty of a Landlord/Property Manager is to provide a reasonably safe place to live to the Resident, Resident's occupants, Resident's guests and Resident's invitees.

2. Breach: A breach is a violation of a law or duty owed to another. The Defendant must breach his/her duty in order to be liable for negligence. If you owed a duty of care to plaintiff, did you provide that duty of care? If not, you breached. If you did not breach a duty of care, you are not liable for negligence. The way to tell if a breach occurred is to look to proximate causation and foreseeability.

3. Proximate Cause or Causation: The breach of duty must have caused harm to the Plaintiff. If you breached a duty of care, did it cause the harm the Plaintiff is claiming? If so, the causation prong of the negligence factors is met. However, it is not always a simple answer, especially when you have multiple factors that did or could have caused the plaintiff's harm.

Here is a great way to think about this prong of negligence. Under the traditional rules of legal duty in negligence cases, a plaintiff must prove that the defendant's actions or inactions were the actual cause of the plaintiff's injury. This is often referred to as "but-for" causation, meaning that, but for the defendant's actions or inactions, the plaintiff's injury would not have occurred. A plaintiff must prove that the defendant's actions or inactions were the actual cause of the plaintiff's injury. The negligent act or lack of action of the defendant was the proximate cause (and not some other reason) of the damages to the plaintiff (person filing the lawsuit).

4. FORESEEABILITY: Even if there is clear evidence of an owed duty, a breach of that duty, and causation, you cannot succeed on a negligence claim unless you can also show foreseeability and actual damages.

Not only must there be evidence that the injury would have never occurred "but for your actions or inaction," the result of the action or inaction must have been foreseeable. This means that a person of ordinary intelligence and circumspection must have reasonably foreseen that his or her act or lack of action would imperil another. The foreseeability test basically asks whether the person causing the injury should have reasonably foreseen the general consequences that would result because of his or her action or inaction. The law usually limits the scope of liability based upon the foreseeability of the type of harm and the manner of harm, but not the extent of the harm.

In a nutshell, a simple way to think about negligence is, did the Landlord/Property Manager know, or should the Landlord/Property Manager have known, about a danger or peril on the property and failed to take or make timely and reasonable remedies to correct that danger or peril?

WHAT ABOUT ACTUAL DAMAGES. The Plaintiff must suffer harm in order to sue for negligence. If the plaintiff suffers no harm, there is no actionable case. This means the plaintiff must suffer some sort of quantifiable harm. If you are hit by a car but miraculously did not sustain any injuries (physical, emotional, monetary, etc.), then you have no damages and are entitled to no recovery for anything regardless of any wrongdoing by the defendant.

Owner/Landlord/Property Manager has a tree root growing up under some concrete on a walkway at the property this is pushing up one of the concrete pads so that one concrete pad is over one-half inch higher than the abutting concrete pad. This situation has evolved over time and it has been like it is now for a couple of months. One night, a friend of a Resident that lives down the walkway from the defective concrete walks to his friend's house and trips on the defective concrete lip where the concrete has lifted. He falls and breaks multiple bones because he has brittle bone disease. He loses his income because he cannot work, loses his car, his house and his girlfriend, as a result after spending months in the hospital. How do you analyse this set of facts?

1. Did the Owner/Landlord/Property Manager have a duty of reasonable safety to the Resident's friend, who came to visit, to provide a reasonably safe property? Yes, the Owner/Landlord/ Property Manager had that duty.

2. Did the Owner/Landlord/ Property Manager breach their duty to provide a reasonably safe property? We do not know for sure, so we have to continue the analysis.

3. "But for" the actions or inactions of Owner/Landlord/ Property Manager (failing to repair a danger that either the Owner/Landlord/Property Manager knew about or should have known about) would this event have happened? First, did the Owner/ Landlord/ Property Manager know or should have known about the concrete issue. Well, the issue had been there for a couple of months. Arguably the Owner/Landlord/ Property Manager knew about the issue. Since the Owner/Landlord/ Property Manager had a duty to maintain the premises, the Owner/Landlord/ Property Manager should have known about the danger. An investigation would have ensued to determine if the Owner/Landlord/ Property Manager actually did know. But, even if the Owner/Landlord/

Property Manager did not know, a reasonable person would conclude that since it is the Owner's/Landlord's/Property manager's property, and they had a duty of reasonable safety, that they should have known about the danger.

An Owner/Landlord/ Property Manager is responsible to walk the property and look for these exact kinds of defects, and if the concrete was lifted a half inch, it could not have been missed and should not have been missed. Further, since the defect was from slow tree root growth, it would have been visible for some time. But what about the Resident, did he know about the defective concrete, did he have a duty to tell his friend. The Resident has no duty to maintain the property, so there is arguably no duty to warn his friend. An argument could be made that injury was the fault, or partly the fault of the Resident friend. However, the Resident friend does not have the same duty to warn his friend because he does not have a duty to keep the property in a safe condition as does the Owner/Landlord/ Property Manager.

4. Next, was the harm suffered foreseeable? Well, a reasonable person would conclude that a trip and fall was foreseeable, at night in this particular scenario, that a person could fall and get injured. How would the Owner/Landlord/ Property Manager ever know that the injured party had brittle bone disease and would suffer all those injuries, and have such extensive losses? It would appear that the extent of the damages would not be foreseeable. However, there is another principle that comes into play. You get your Plaintiff as they are, brittle bone disease and all. The Owner/Landlord/ Property Manager knows that invitees to the property might have all types of issues. The nature and extent of the injuries are not the kind of foreseeability the law is concerned with, only whether the trip and fall was foreseeable because of the danger existing on the property that the Owner/Landlord/Property Manager either knew about or should have known about.

5. So, because a there is a duty of reasonable safety due to the Resident and the Resident's guests and invitees, there is a "but for" causation, and there is foreseeability for the type of event that occurred (even though the extent of the damage suffered may not have been specifically foreseeable). Whatever damages can be proven as a result of the injuries suffered from failing to remedy a foreseeable event caused by Owner/ Landlord/ Property Manager, are all recoverable.

Let's look at an unforeseeable type of harm Example: A person who causes injury to another is not liable if the type of harm did not foreseeably flow from the negligent act.

If the Owner/Landlord/Property Manager fails to perform an adequate criminal background investigation on a Resident and did not find a misdemeanor conviction two (2) years ago for disorderly conduct for arguing with a neighbor to the extent that it disturbed the peace. That convicted person then stalks a female Resident in the community, kidnaps her, sexually assaults her, kills her, burns the

216

body and throws it over a bridge. The attorney for the family sues the Owner/Landlord/ Property Manager for negligence. How do you analyse this set of facts?

1. Did the Owner/Landlord/Property Manager have a duty to the dead Resident to provide a reasonably safe property? Yes, the Owner/Landlord/ Property Manager had a duty to the dead Resident to ensure an adequate background investigation was performed on the Resident that caused the harm. Any Owner/Landlord/ Property Manager that fails to meet this duty, such as by knowing of a dangerous condition or failing to know of a dangerous condition, can be held liable for injuries that result from a criminal act.

2. Did the Owner/Landlord/ Property Manager breach their duty to provide a reasonably safe property? We do not know so we have to continue the analysis.

3. "But for" the actions or inactions of Owner/Landlord/ Property Manager would this event have happened? Arguably, an intelligent answer would be that the harm would not have happened had an adequate criminal background investigation been performed and the Owner/Landlord/ Property Manager had not rented to the Resident. Should the Owner/Landlord/ Property Manager have rented to the perpetrator with such a criminal history for the protection of the property and the duty owed to the dead Resident? The rental criteria would be reviewed to determine if a person with such a criminal history would have been allowed to enter into a lease, and if it would have been negligent to allow such a person to enter a lease. If it is hard to determine, you still must continue on with the analysis.

4. Here is the real determining factor. Is it foreseeable that if the Owner/Landlord/ Property Manager rents to a person with a disorderly conduct misdemeanor conviction two years ago for arguing with a neighbor would put the Owner/Landlord/ Property Manager on notice that the Owner/Landlord/ Property Manager should have known that such a person would stalk, kidnap, rape, burn and discard the body of another Resident? The answer to that question is easier to answer. A reasonable person would find that leap too big to make. No reasonable person would think or even consider that the Owner/ Landlord/ Property Manager should have known, notwithstanding the mistake in not performing an adequate criminal background investigation of the Resident, that a resident that has a very minor misdemeanor for arguing in public with a neighbor, that such a Resident would ever engage in such a terrible and heinous crime. There is no nexus between the two situations. Therefore, there is no liability on Owner/Landlord/ Property Manager, even though damages are overwhelming. You never get to the damages because there is not foreseeability.

We could spend a lot of time on this subject, but if you understand these few pages you are in great shape and can ensure that your property is not going to become a premises liability burden. But you must remain vigilant about maintaining and operating your property.

CONCLUSION

Don't think being a successful landlord is difficult. It is not. It is just one correct step at a time. You need a good support group, including educational classes, a competent Landlord attorney, a good accountant and an understand of what to do along the landlord road. You got this. If you follow the principles in this book, you will be successful.

∽

Denny Dobbins
The Law Offices of J. D. Dobbins, PLLC
16333 Monrovia Street
Overland Park, Kansas 66221
913.346.6000

Denny Dobbins
The Law Offices of J. D. Dobbins, PLLC
4140 East Baseline Road, Suite 208
Mesa, Arizona 85206
480.241.9129